National Institute of Economic and Social Research
Policy Studies Institute
Royal Institute of International Affairs
Joint Studies in Public Policy 2

THE FUTURE OF PAY BARGAINING

National Institute of Economic and Social Research
Policy Studies Institute
Royal Institute of International Affairs

Joint Studies in Public Policy

STEERING COMMITTEE

National Institute of Economic and Social Research
Policy Studies Institute
Royal Institute of International Affairs
Joint Studies in Public Policy 2

THE FUTURE OF PAY BARGAINING

Edited by
F. T. BLACKABY

Heinemann · London

Heinemann Educational Books Ltd

LONDON EDINBURGH MELBOURNE AUCKLAND TORONTO
HONG KONG SINGAPORE KUALA LUMPUR NEW DELHI
NAIROBI JOHANNESBURG IBADAN
KINGSTON

ISBN 0 435 83921 7 cased.
ISBN 0 435 83922 5 paperback.

First published 1980

Published by Heinemann Educational Books Ltd
Filmset by Northumberland Press Ltd
Gateshead, Tyne and Wear
Printed in Great Britain by Richard Clay (The Chaucer Press) Ltd
Bungay, Suffolk

Contents

Preface

This book is the second in a series of Joint Studies in Public Policy. Three Institutes – the National Institute of Economic and Social Research, the Policy Studies Institute and the Royal Institute of International Affairs – have come together to launch this series. The Steering Committee of the series selects a policy problem; a set of papers is commissioned; they are intensively discussed over two days by a working party of about thirty people; then, together with a report of the discussion, they are published rapidly. The Nuffield Foundation has provided the initial finance for this joint venture, and we are very grateful to them.

The problem of the system of pay bargaining in Britain is one which has been with us for a long time, and it has led to a wide range of suggestions for change. The discussion has, I think, moved on from the arguments about the efficacy of temporary incomes policies to a debate about more permanent reforms. This is not, therefore, a replay of the old arguments about whether there should be an 'incomes policy' or not; indeed the term 'incomes policy' covers so many very different ideas that perhaps it should be dropped.

The papers in this book describe the existing institutions, and the changes that are taking place in them, and present the arguments about the link between these institutions and our problems of inflation and unemployment. There is a summary of the policies followed in other countries, and an array of the plans which have been put forward for the United Kingdom. The debate about these matters will go on, and I think this book is one which those engaged in the debate will find it useful to read.

Donald MacDougall
Chairman, Steering Committee

July 1980

Contributors and Participants

Contributors

R. A. Batchelor, Centre for Banking and International Finance, City University

E. Bendle, Centre for Banking and International Finance, City University

F. T. Blackaby, Deputy Director, National Institute of Economic and Social Research

Sir Henry Phelps Brown, Emeritus Professor, University of London

W. A. Brown, Deputy Director, SSRC Industrial Relations Unit, University of Warwick

R. Close, Director General, British Institute of Management

W. W. Daniel, Policy Studies Institute

A. J. H. Dean, Department of Economics and Statistics, OECD

R. J. V. Dixon, Director of Social Affairs, CBI

Professor B. Griffiths, Director, Centre for Banking and International Finance, City University

P. Lilley, W. Greenwell and Co.

Professor D. Metcalf, University of Kent

C. T. Saunders, Sussex European Research Centre, University of Sussex

M. FG. Scott, Nuffield College, Oxford

T. Sheriff, Philips Industries (formerly Research Officer, National Institute of Economic and Social Research)

K. Sisson, University of Warwick

P. Warburton, London Business School

Other Participants

C. Blyth

A. Braun

Professor D. Colander

M. Fogarty

Aubrey Jones

R. Layard

Professor A. Lerner

Sir Donald MacDougall (*Joint Chairman*)

D. Marsden

Professor J. E. Meade

J. Pinder

M. V. Posner (*Joint Chairman*)

R. Scott

G. D. N. Worswick

1 Introduction
F. T. Blackaby

The nature of the argument about pay bargaining has changed in recent years. There are fewer enthusiasts than there used to be for temporary incomes policies. Although they are frequently effective in the short term, they tend to be followed by an explosion when they are abandoned. The arguments are rather about whether there is a need for some more permanent changes in the existing UK system of pay bargaining, and about the form such changes might take. This is what this book is about.

Preliminary Questions

Before considering the possible need for changes in any system, it is a good idea to have an up-to-date picture of what that system looks like, and how it works. Brown (Chapter 6) provides such a picture, describing (amongst other things) the decline in the private sector of multi-employer industry-wide bargaining, and the consequent virtual disappearance of employers' associations' control over pay bargaining. On the other hand, he notes that the giant companies which are responsible for a large number of plants are tending to raise the level of their bargaining away from the individual plant. He argues that wage drift is much less important than it used to be, and notes the spread of job evaluation. On the union side, he discusses the spread of the office of shop steward throughout almost the whole of employment.

Daniel (Chapter 7) reports on a survey of one bargaining round in manufacturing industry. He concludes that the ability of employers to pay appeared to have little influence over the formal, periodic increase in rates of pay: financial circumstances influenced the degree of difficulty with the negotiations rather than the outcome. The major influences over the level of settlement appeared to be compensation for past increases in the cost of living, and comparability. He also concludes that trade union bargaining power was more likely to be used to protect members from an inadequate increase than to exploit fully the advantages of favourable financial circumstances.

Saunders (Chapter 9) asks the question – which groups gained and which lost in the 1970s: the study covers industries and negotiating groups. It shows that – although there were gainers and losers – the gains and losses were not very big. There were not many groups which, over nine years, either gained or lost more than 5 per cent, in real terms, compared with the average experience.

Sheriff (Chapter 10) asks what we can learn from wage equations – for example, whether they enable us to say with any degree of certainty at what level of unemployment money earnings will start to decelerate. He looks at two types of equation: the 'expectations-augmented Phillips curve', which implies that the rise in money earnings depends on the degree of unemployment and on price expectations; and the 'target real wage hypothesis', which implies that trade unions, in their bargaining, aim at a certain rate of increase in (post-tax) real earnings. He concludes that neither of the equations which embody these views has shown a good forecasting performance in recent years, and follows Artis in questioning whether underlying economic forces are in fact more important than social and political factors in determining the wage rate. Warburton, in comment, declares his belief that there is an active aggregate labour market in the UK, in which both demand and supply factors matter, but in which the adjustment mechanism is inefficient.

In thinking about what might be done in Britain, it is useful to know about the present state of affairs in other industrial countries. Dean (Chapter 8) describes the arrangements in seven other industrial countries. In his comment he praises in particular the arrangements in Austria; he discusses the advantages and disadvantages of centralisation, and of a forum; and he considers how far relative success is the consequence of some degree of social consensus, and what factors are important in bringing such a consensus about.

Should There be Reform: if so, What Reform?

Scott (Chapter 2) asks the question whether, with the existing system of free collective bargaining, it is possible to combine tolerable rates of price increase with tolerable levels of unemployment. He gives a number of reasons for thinking that the natural level of unemployment – defined as that level of unemployment at which inflation might stop accelerating – is high in the UK, and concludes 'unless the wage-fixing system can be reformed, it looks as if we shall get the worst of both worlds: both high unemployment and high inflation.' Batchelor, Bendle and Griffiths (Chapter 3) present an alternative view, which is also critical of trade union monopoly power, but which argues that it only influences the structure of relative wages within a total rate of inflation constrained by monetary growth.

Lilley, in comment on these two papers, considers that there is no reason to suppose that the natural rate of unemployment is at present any higher than the actual rate; he also considers that union monopoly power is rather more deleterious than Batchelor, Bendle and Griffiths suggest. Metcalf argues that the level of unemployment which measures a given shortage of labour has risen considerably over the last decade; however, he agrees with Scott that 'it would be better to find a way of controlling inflation which does not require yet further increases in unemployment'.

Blackaby (Chapter 4) arrays some of the current proposals for changes in the pay bargaining system, and identifies seven different elements, or types of proposal. There are the proposals which emerge from the idea of a 'Social Contract' or 'concerted action' – proposals which give rise to suggestions for an annual forum of some sort. There are proposals for synchronisation of pay settlements; and specific proposals for the public sector. Some proposals are variations on the constitutional structures we have had in past incomes policies – of a norm, with some institution considering the justification for exceptions. There is a group of proposals which can be treated rather separately, of tax-based or market-based incomes policies. A further group might be labelled 'institutionally radical', in that the changes proposed go well beyond anything previously tried. Finally, there are the proposals whose purpose is either to weaken the power of trade unions or to strengthen the powers of employers.

In comment on these proposals, Dixon suggests reform in three main areas: the reform of pay structures, including the compression of the annual bargaining round; the encouragement of attitudinal change, including the idea of a national economic forum; and proposals to rectify the balance of power between employers and employees. Close endorses the idea of an economic forum, and also of a relativities board, or procedure; like Dixon, he rejects the idea of a 'norm', or any formal incomes policy. Sisson considers that there is major scope for reform in public sector pay, along the lines of Basnett's proposals (page 76), and with public sector pay decisions coming at the end of the wage round; he also argues for greater coordination among employers, suggesting that trade unions are essentially reactive bodies. Phelps Brown reviews and comments on the various suggestions in the light of recent experience – for example, the great bargaining power individual trade unions have shown, and the fact that trade unions are becoming more like business unions. He also comments 'There is this to be said at the last about the radical plans, that it is hard to see what can be done that is practical at the present time by edging forward with existing institutions.'

The discussion – reported in Chapter 5 – wrestled with a number of questions: whether the level of unemployment which measured a given degree of labour shortage had risen, and if so how much; the evidence for and against an effect from unemployment on the rate of increase in money earnings; rational expectations as applied to the labour market; and the question whether any policy should be concerned with the money wage or the real wage.

In the examination of other countries' experience, the conference noted the importance – in West Germany for example – of centralised negotiations, and of strong employers' associations negotiating with strong trade unions. In discussing what was wrong in Britain, there was some difference between those who described the problem simply as that of monopoly, and those who pictured the situation rather as one of fragmented labour monopolies, leading to competitive bargaining.

The range of views on what should be done was wide – again, with some wanting to raise the level of bargaining and others wishing to lower it. The questions considered included the problem of pay settlements in the non-market public sector; the synchronisation of wage settlements; the idea of a forum, and what it should do; the problems of a norm, and of the exceptions to it; the issue of sanctions; and the proposal for a Market Anti-Inflation Plan.

The papers, together with a report of the discussion, went to the printer four weeks after the end of the conference. Contributors courteously agreed to shortened versions of their papers. The rapidity of publication is due in great measure to Mrs K. Jones, Secretary of the National Institute, who did the bulk of the editing, and to Mrs A. Wright for her assiduous typing of successive drafts.

2 The Need for Radical Reform
M. FG. Scott

The Question at Issue

What reasons are there for believing that, with the existing system of free collective bargaining, it is not possible to combine tolerable rates of price increase with tolerable levels of unemployment, at least in the next ten or twenty years?

Before addressing this question its terms must be clarified. The 'existing system' is that which has evolved over the past century or so. It may include incomes policies of the kinds we have had since the Second World War, none of which has lasted more than a very few years. It is still evolving, and one must allow for likely changes other than those which could be described as a radical reform. 'Tolerable rates of price increase' excludes indefinitely accelerating inflation. No society has yet been able to tolerate that. It is arguable whether a fairly steady rate of inflation of, say, 10, 20, 50 or even 100 per cent per annum would be tolerable. Widespread indexation, which is often resorted to in countries experiencing such high rates of inflation, probably helps to make it more tolerable. Even in such cases the inflation rate can rise to rates such that indexation lags behind or becomes increasingly unreliable. Hence there is some inflation rate which even the best indexed system cannot tolerate. However, that is not a very helpful conclusion, since one hopes that actual inflation will never reach such dizzy heights. At lower levels, it seems clear that quite rapid rates of inflation *can* be tolerated for a good many years, although their disruptive effects on the social fabric should not be underestimated.

It is evident that the levels of inflation or unemployment which people will tolerate depend on their recent experience and on what the alternatives appear to be. Let us consider unemployment. As Brittan [1] vividly put it: 'In the 1950s and early 1960s the Treasury behaved like a simple Pavlovian dog responding to two main stimuli: one is a run on the reserves and the other is 500,000 unemployed.

On the whole (although not invariably), it was officials who panicked on the first stimulus, and ministers on the second.' Ministers, no doubt correctly, took the view that voters would not tolerate 500,000 unemployed (about $2\frac{1}{4}$ per cent of employees) and, on average, unemployment (defined so as to exclude those temporarily stopped, school leavers and students seeking work during vacations) from 1950 to 1966 was only 359,000, or 1.6 per cent of employees, and the quarterly average exceeded 500,000 in only five out of the 68 quarters.

What would generally be regarded as tolerable now? Laslett [21] produced some evidence to suggest that frictional unemployment had risen by about 1 per cent (of the number of employees) since the full employment era of 1950–66. There were several reasons for this, such as increased registration for unemployment benefit by part-time workers and a higher ratio of benefits when unemployed to income after tax when employed. The latter has been estimated by Nickell [15] to have increased unemployment from 1964–5 to 1973 by only about 0.2 per cent of employees. If one adds 1 per cent to the average of 1.6 per cent for 1950–66, one gets 2.6 per cent as a 'tolerable' level of unemployment now. The increase compared with the full employment era would then be either 'statistical' or 'voluntary', and would not represent a waste of manpower, given the level of unemployment benefits which had been decided upon. Of course, it might be possible to reduce this level further by various measures to improve the working of the labour market, including the provision of more part-time work and better housing policies with more rented accommodation becoming available. While such changes are both possible and desirable, and important as well, I shall ignore them in what follows since they do not affect the essentials of the argument.

However, while 2.6 per cent might represent a reasonable target which, if hit, would cause general satisfaction, it must be recognised that much higher rates could be (and, in fact are being) tolerated. From 1976 to 1979 registered unemployment, defined as above, averaged 5.5 per cent, and the seasonally adjusted quarterly average never fell below 5.1 per cent. Far from this leading to a revolution, it (plus, of course, the other accompanying events) led to the election of a Conservative government pledged to pursue a policy of reducing inflation by policies which were likely to increase unemployment still further, at least temporarily – and unemployment has indeed increased.

What, then, is the electorate's view of a 'tolerable level of unemployment'? As with inflation, so with unemployment: the fact that high levels are being tolerated does not, unfortunately, mean that their ill effects on work habits, resistance to change, the level of material well-being and the social fabric are thereby lessened or avoided. As recent history shows, what is 'tolerable' depends on the alternatives. If inflation is sufficiently rapid the electorate may be prepared, it seems, to tolerate policies leading to 5 per cent or more unemployment if it believes that this is necessary to counter inflation. If inflation were to reach 400 per cent per annum, the electorate might well support a government pledged to deflation despite the existence of 20 per cent unemployment.

Commonsense suggests that if *that* were indeed the situation to which the present system was leading us, it would undoubtedly be one with *both* intolerable and damaging levels of inflation *and* intolerable and damaging levels of unemployment, even though, in another sense, both were being tolerated. In order to clarify the argument and make it more precise, this relation between the inflation and unemployment rates which people are prepared to tolerate must be recognised.

We must also recognise that we do not know how much unemployment is needed to stop inflation accelerating. This level has been called the 'natural level of unemployment'. Reasons for believing that unemployment does affect the rate of inflation, and the possible size of the natural level of unemployment, are discussed below. The concept is of key importance for the argument of this paper. Here we need to assume only that there is *some* level of unemployment which would be sufficiently high to stop inflation accelerating, and that there is considerable uncertainty about its magnitude. There are those who would not even accept that, and we consider their position at the end of this section.

For the others, we now bring together the two considerations mentioned in the last two paragraphs in Chart 2.1. It is assumed, for illustrative purposes, that the most likely case is that 6 per cent unemployment would stop inflation accelerating. It is also assumed that the electorate will only tolerate an average level of unemployment as high as this if the alternative is quite rapid inflation, so that, on average, there has to be about 20 per cent inflation on average for people to tolerate 6 per cent unemployment on average. This assumed most likely case is at M (the mode) in Chart 2.1. Every point in the diagram is a possible equilibrium in the sense that it represents an average level of unemployment which stops inflation accelerating (that is, it is a natural level) and is coupled with the average inflation rate which is necessary to make people tolerate that level of unemployment. Every point has a probability attached to it, since we do not know the true relationships, but (it is assumed) only the

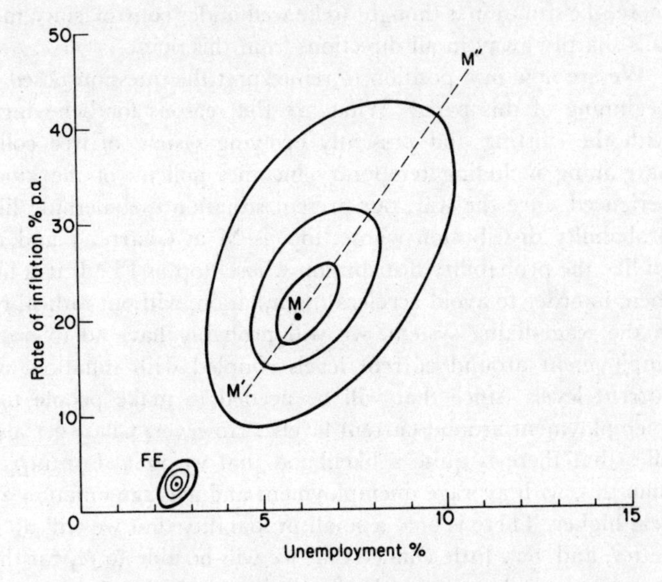

Chart 2.1 Unemployment and inflation

probabilities. These probabilities are to be measured in a plane vertical to the diagram, and the contours show the relevant heights, or probabilities. So M is at the top of the 'hill', being the most probable situation. The ridge line M′M″ shows that, if the natural level of unemployment is higher (lower) than at M, then the rate of inflation likely to accompany it will also be higher (lower). The descent from M towards M″ is, however, less steep than from M to M′. This is because it seems quite likely (for reasons discussed below) that the natural level of unemployment is a good deal higher than at M, while the chances that it is appreciably lower than at M diminish rapidly. Hence the probabilities are skewed in the way shown, and there seems to be quite some likelihood that we shall end up in a Latin American situation with both very high unemployment and very high inflation.

At FE in Chart 2.1 a contrasting situation is illustrated. This is something like the position which appeared to exist in the 1950s and early 1960s. The most likely natural level of unemployment is put at 2½ per cent, and a low level of inflation, 3 per cent per annum, is all that is necessary to make people willing to accept that. Furthermore, the situation is thought to be well under control, since the 'hill' falls sharply away in all directions from this point.

We are now in a position to reinterpret the question posed at the beginning of this paper. What are the reasons for believing that, with the existing and presently evolving system of free collective bargaining including temporary incomes policies of the kinds experienced since the war, our present situation is something like the probability distribution whose 'top' is M in Chart 2.1 and not at all like the probability distribution whose 'top' is FE? If it *is* like M, then, in order to avoid accelerating inflation, without radical reform of the wage-fixing system, we will probably have to tolerate unemployment around current levels coupled with inflation around current levels (since that will be needed to make people tolerate unemployment around current levels). However, Chart 2.1 also implies that there is quite a likelihood that we may do much worse than this, with average unemployment and average inflation a good deal higher. There is only a small probability that we will do much better, and very little chance that we will be able to repeat the low average unemployment and inflation levels which existed from 1950 to 1966. For that to occur, that is, for FE in Chart 2.1 to become our situation, we need a radical reform of the wage-fixing system. The reasons for all this are set out in what follows.

To conclude this section, we must take account of the view that unemployment makes no difference to inflation. Those who believe this, despite the counter-arguments advanced below, may yet accept that governments, including UK governments under both Conservative and Labour administrations, have behaved as though they believed that higher unemployment *does* tend to reduce inflation. Unless this is so, it is difficult to explain why unemployment has been allowed to rise so much in the last decade. Persistence in this belief will mean that faster inflation will lead to higher unemployment. The question then is whether the existing system of free collective bargaining will lead to the continuation of current rates of inflation or, perhaps, still faster rates since, if it does, governments will probably allow unemployment to remain at current levels or, perhaps, climb still higher. Much of what follows is as relevant to this question as to the question posed in the preceding paragraph.

The Natural Level of Unemployment

The natural level of unemployment is that level which would suffice to stop inflation accelerating. The idea is familiar to some, but perhaps not to all. In what follows, we first explain it by reference to the Phillips curve. Next, we review some evidence for the existence of such a curve for the United Kingdom since, if the curve does not exist, the case for believing in a natural level of unemployment is much weakened. Finally, we consider some evidence on the natural level itself.

The Phillips curve postulates a relationship between the level of unemployment and the rate of wage increases. The lower is the former, *ceteris paribus*, the higher will be the latter. There are various ways in which one could justify the assumption of such a relationship, depending on whether one is thinking of a system in which wages are fixed by atomistic bargaining between individual employers and individual workers or one in which collective bargaining is the rule. In the former case it is fairly obvious that the employer's position is strengthened, and the employee's weakened, by the existence of more unemployed workers. Where the latter is the case, it also seems reasonable to suppose that workers will be more cautious in pressing wage demands, and readier to accept smaller increases in pay in relation to the rates of increase in prices which they expect, the higher is unemployment. It is true that, even when unemployment is as high as at present – around 6 per cent – the overwhelming majority of workers are employed – 94 per cent. Hence, it might seem, they have little to worry about so long as they bargain collectively. Nevertheless, there will always be particular groups of workers whose position is weakened by higher unemployment. They may be non-unionised, will generally be unskilled and often especially young. In so far as workers compare their own situation with that of others, the more the weaker groups suffer from unemployment, the less likely is it that the stronger groups will feel it necessary to improve their position, and they may also become more worried about their own security. Furthermore, at least some employers will find it easier to recruit workers at existing wage rates, and so will be less inclined to accede to wage demands. Higher unemployment is generally accompanied by lower profits, and this is an additional reason why employed workers may feel more insecure – their employer may be forced to close down, or to shed large parts of his labour force, if wages rise so as to squeeze his profits too far. This seems likely to be a fairly powerful factor limiting the increases in wages which workers will feel it safe to secure, at least so far as the private sector is concerned. However, it is important to distinguish this motive for caution (the fear of squeezing profits too far) from the other (the fear induced by the existence of high unemployment). In the past the two have generally gone together, but the need to keep them conceptually distinct will become clear in what follows.

There is a strong link between wage costs and prices, since wages (used, for short, to include all incomes from employment) constitute such a large fraction of total costs. If we assume that the share of all non-wage costs and profits in prices is a constant fraction, then prices will move in direct proportion to changes in wage costs per unit of output. Assuming, for example, that labour productivity and wage rates are growing steadily at 2 per cent per annum, then wage costs per unit of output will be constant and, given our assumption about other costs, prices will also be constant. Finally, let us assume that unemployment is 6 per cent and that, at this level of unemployment, workers on average are content to accept a 2 per cent per annum rate of wage increase, which is also a *real* increase of 2 per cent per annum since prices are stable.

The position is then as at E_1 in Chart 2.2, and is an equilibrium situation which could persist indefinitely. Suppose, however, that the government decides to lower unemployment from 6 to 3 per cent by expansionary monetary and fiscal measures. Then the Phillips curve predicts that this will encourage workers to press for bigger wage increases and will weaken employers' resistance to wage demands. In Chart 2.2, it is assumed that this results in wage rates increasing at 6 per cent instead of 2 per cent per annum which, given our

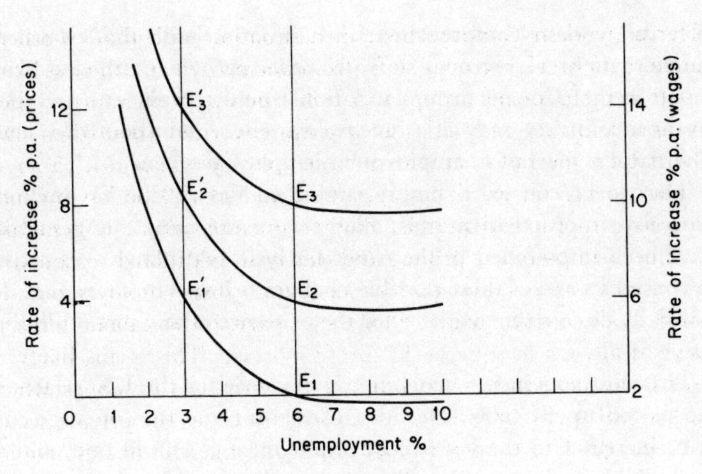

Chart 2.2 Phillips curves

other assumptions, means that prices will increase at 4 per cent per annum instead of 0 per cent per annum. The economy has thus moved from E_1 to E'_1.

However, E'_1 is no longer an equilibrium situation which can persist indefinitely. When unemployment falls to 3 per cent, workers and employers agree on wage increases which are 4 per cent per annum faster. They do so with a past history (in this example) of stable prices, so that each employer or body of workers thinks that the extra 4 per cent is a *real* increase. Their expectations are not fulfilled, since prices rise 4 per cent faster. Once this is realised, it seems reasonable to assume that workers will want, and employers be prepared to give, nominal wage increases which are 10 per cent per annum instead of 6 per cent per annum – that is a *further* 4 per cent per annum. This will then take the economy to E'_2, and, by a similar process of reasoning, it cannot rest there but will go on to E'_3, and so on with inflation indefinitely accelerating.

The only way to stop this acceleration, on these assumptions, is to allow unemployment to rise once more to 6 per cent. At that level workers are prepared to accept real wage increases of 2 per cent a year, which is all that they can in fact get on these assumptions. If, for example, unemployment were allowed to increase to 6 per cent after the economy had reached E'_3, inflation would subside from an annual rate of 12 per cent to 8 per cent (and wage increases from 14 per cent to 10 per cent). Inflation would remain at 8 per cent a year indefinitely, so long as unemployment remained at 6 per cent. The natural level of unemployment is then 6 per cent.

This is, of course, a highly simplified description of any real economy. In practice one must allow for a great many changes which have been impounded in the *ceteris paribus* clause above. We return to consider some of these possible changes below. First, however, let us briefly discuss the evidence for the existence of any sort of Phillips curve at all.

The most convincing econometric evidence for the UK relates to the period up to 1966. The idea of relating the rate of wage and price increases to the level of unemployment is an old one, and as Rothschild [20] has pointed out, several economists had done so before Phillips. Phillips's own study [19] covered the period 1861–1957. His data, modified in some respects, was subjected to a further detailed analysis by Lipsey [12], who tested for the relation between wage-rate changes, on the one hand, and three other main variables: the level of unemployment, the change in the level of unemployment, and the rate of price increases. Broadly speaking, he found that all three were significant in explaining wage-rate changes, with the importance of price changes increasing in the later years of the period and the responsiveness of wage rates to the level of unemployment declining. There have been several other econometric studies covering the postwar years which also concluded that the level of unemployment and the rate of changes of prices were both important explanations for the rate of wage-rate changes (in the UK and other countries, notably the US).

After 1966, unemployment and inflation both increased together, which seemed to contradict the Phillips curve. Furthermore, attempts to predict wage-rate increases on the basis of past relationships embodying the Phillips curve broke down. However, it was still possible to rescue the Phillips curve by allowing for expectations in a way that the earlier studies failed to do. Once one recognised that expectations of faster inflation would shift the curve outwards, as in Chart 2.2, it was easy to see why unemployment and inflation could increase together. Econometric studies for the UK, the US and other countries, claimed to demonstrate that this is what happened.

Furthermore, the growing importance of price increases as a factor explaining wage-rate increases in Lipsey's 1960 study, based on Phillips's data, was also explicable in these terms. The firm expectation of long-term price stability had been eroded, and workers' and employers' expectations had become more volatile. Since expectations cannot easily be identified, and since attempts were made from time to time to control wages and prices, the result was to make any econometric testing of the Phillips curve much more difficult, but it was a perfectly defensible view that the curve was still there, even though it was now much harder to detect.

We discuss below some alternative interpretations of Phillips's data which reject the notion that the level of unemployment exerts a powerful influence on the rate of wage increases, and so, on inflation. Before doing so, let us push the argument of those who believe in a natural level of unemployment through to its conclusion. What do past studies suggest that natural level to be?

A preliminary point is that, for there to be a natural level, there must be no money illusion. That is, workers and employers must not be fooled in the long run by the absolute size of money wage or price increases, but must adjust their bargains in *full* proportion to the going rate of inflation, at least after some time. It does seem plausible that this is so, and there is little doubt that the 'norm' for wage increases has grown considerably in the last fifteen years along with inflation. Most of the major econometric forecasting models of the UK economy now assume that in this sense there is no illusion (see Brown, Enoch and Mortimer-Lee [5]).

If there is no money illusion, and if the Phillips curve exists, and if, in the long run, prices must rise as fast as wage costs per unit of output (as seems plausible, since profits cannot be squeezed indefinitely, nor can the share of taxes, nor can the terms of trade be expected to improve indefinitely), then accelerating inflation can only be avoided by keeping unemployment at the level at which wage rates would rise as fast as labour productivity when inflation is zero. This is the natural level of unemployment. In Chart 2.2 productivity grows at 2 per cent per annum, so, when prices rise 0 per cent per annum, wage rates can rise at 2 per cent per annum in the long run, and 6 per cent unemployment is required to restrain them to that rate of increase. We can superimpose on that any constant rate of inflation we like, but that makes no difference to the

Table 2.1 Unemployment rate required for wage increases to equal the rate of growth of labour productivity

Study	Period	Growth of productivity (% p.a.)	Unemployment required (%)
Brown	1886–90	1.5	5 or 6
	1895–6		3 or 4
	1905–6		4 or 5
	1911–12		3 or 3.5
	1935–8		14 or 15
Phillips	1861–1913	2.1	2.3
Lipsey	1923–39	2.1	1.8
	1948–57		
Klein and Ball	1948–58	2.1	2.1
Dicks-Mireaux and Dow	1950–6	2.5	2.0

Sources: Brown, A. J., *The Great Inflation, 1939–51*, London, Oxford University Press, 1955: the estimates were obtained apparently by reading off from the scatter-diagram, relating wage-rate changes to unemployment levels, the levels of unemployment corresponding to wage-rate increases of 1.5 per cent a year on the straight lines joining successive points in the cyclical upswings for the years shown (see text). The other estimates were derived, from the studies listed, by Bodkin, R. G., Bond, E. P., Reutger, G. L. and Robinson, T. R., *Price Stability and High Employment: The Options for Canadian Economic Policy*, Economic Council of Canada, Special Study No. 5 (Table 3.20, p. 70), Ottawa, The Queen's Printer, 1967. Presumably it is assumed that the other explanatory variables (such as rates of change of prices or unemployment) takes zero values. The studies are: Phillips, A. W., 'The relationship between unemployment and the rate of change of money wage rates in the UK 1861–1957', *Economica*, November 1958; Lipsey, R. G., 'The relationship between unemployment and the rate of change of money wage rates in the UK 1862–1957: a further analysis', *Economica*, February 1960; Klein, L. R. and Ball, R.J., 'Some econometrics of the determination of the absolute level of wages and prices', *Economic Journal*, September 1959; Dicks-Mireaux, L.A. and Dow, J. R. C., 'The determinants of wage inflation in the United Kingdom, 1946–1956', *Journal of the Royal Statistical Society*, Series A (General), Part 2, 1959.

figure of 6 per cent unemployment. Hence, to find the natural level of unemployment, all we need to do is to find from estimates of the Phillips curve what level of unemployment is consistent with wage rates growing as fast as productivity when inflation is (expected to be) zero. Some estimates for the UK are summarised in Table 2.1.

The first set of figures, from Brown [4], are not strictly comparable with the remainder. The former are derived by considering only the upswings of various cycles. Had the same analyses been performed on the downswings, the critical levels of unemployment would have been lower. Brown himself suggests subtracting 1 or 2 percentage points from the figures in the table to obtain estimates which correspond to some steady average level of unemployment. His figures for pre-1914 then range from, say, 1.5 to 4.5 per cent, and an unweighted average of the four estimates, with Brown's adjustment, is 2.7 per cent. This is only a little above the figure of 2.3 per cent for much the same period based on Phillips's data, and the difference could be due to the faster rate of growth of productivity assumed.

Brown's estimate for the 1930s upswing, which he puts at 10 to 12 per cent after adjustment for the difference between upswings and downswings, is of quite a different order of magnitude to the pre-1914 figures (or the post-1945 ones). He attributes most of the increase to the greater level of structural unemployment in the 1930s. The very heavy levels of unemployment to be found in the depressed areas would not have done much to weaken the bargaining power of labour in the more prosperous parts of the country. However, he thought that some part of the increase in what he termed the 'critical' level of unemployment was due to the increased bargaining power of organised labour ([4], pp. 94–5).

The estimates in Table 2.1 from the studies covering the immediate post-Second World War years are rather lower than the pre-1914 figures, but not significantly so, and one of them assumes a still faster rate of growth of productivity. Two other postwar studies should be mentioned. Paish [16] estimated the margin of spare capacity in the economy, and its associated level of unemployment, which was 'consistent with long-term price equilibrium'. He put the capacity margin at 5 to 7 per cent and the associated unemployment at 2 to 2½ per cent. Laidler [11], reporting on a study of the natural level of unemployment stated that 'preliminary results of work in progress at Manchester University suggest that it is perhaps a little less than 2 per cent in Britain, although such an estimate is necessarily subject to a wide margin of error'.

If we can brush aside the 1930s figures as referring to a period with unusually heavy structural unemployment (but can we?), the above evidence suggests that the natural level of unemployment in the UK is really quite low. Even if we add on 1 per cent to the post-Second World War figures to allow for changes in registration habits, a higher ratio of unemployment benefits to post-tax income from employment and similar factors, the natural level now would appear to be only about 3 per cent.

Table 2.2 Increases in earnings and prices and the level of unemployment

	Average earnings (1)	Tax and prices (2)	Real net earnings (3)	Unemployment level (4)
	(percentage increase over previous year)			(%)
1976 Year				5·3
1977 Q1	10.7	18.4	−6.5	5·5
Year				5·7
1978 Q1	10.1	4·5	5·4	5·9
Year				5·7
1979 Q1	13·9	6.4	7.0	5.6
Year				5·4
1980 Q1	19.6	16.9	2.3	5·7

(1) New series, average earnings for the whole economy.
(2) CSO tax and prices index.
(3) Index numbers of column (1) divided by those for column (2).
(4) Average of monthly unemployed seasonally adjusted, excluding school leavers and students, as percentage of mid-year number of employees.
Source: CSO, *Economic Trends*.

It is, however, very difficult to reconcile a figure as low as that with the events of the last four years, 1976–9, for which the essential statistics are given in Table 2.2. The main point is that, although unemployment has been well above 5 per cent throughout this period, the rate of increase of money wages has been accelerating, and real earnings after tax have been growing at a rate which cannot be sustained in the long run with current rates of growth of productivity. During these four years average real earnings after tax have grown at about 2 per cent per annum. Before 1973, this would have been sustainable, but in the UK, as in many other countries, productivity has been growing much more slowly since 1973: only 0.5 per cent a year compared with 2.5 per cent in 1950–73 (NIESR [14]). With such slow growth, real post-tax earnings increases of 2 per cent a year can only be met by squeezing the share of profits, or of the government, or by allowing the balance of payments to deteriorate. The current share of profits is already so low that investment is falling, and this must tend to reduce productivity growth. There are limits to the cuts which can be made in government expenditure, and the balance of payments is in deficit and must be improved for a sustainable position to be reached. The years 1976–9 were ones in which exploration for and output of oil and natural gas statistically added close to 1 per cent per annum on to the rate of growth of gross domestic product, and so even the very low rate of productivity increase registered over this period has been greatly exaggerated (by reference to its sustainable level) by the once-for-all gains from North Sea oil and gas. Hence, if more than 5 per cent unemployment is required to prevent real post-tax earnings growing faster than 2 per cent per annum, much more than 5 per cent unemployment may be needed to prevent real post-tax earnings growing faster than what appears to be the present sustainable rate of productivity growth.

Average earnings did not rise smoothly during 1976–9, whether in money terms or real terms. A deceleration was followed by an acceleration which makes it difficult to interpret the underlying trend. In the previous paragraph we concentrated attention on the average over the four years 1976–9 when unemployment was consistently high, but that may not give the true picture. It could be argued that the recent acceleration to 20 per cent is still part of the rebound from the severe restraint in 1975–6, and will subside of itself if unemployment remains close to 6 per cent. Even so, it does seem clear that the natural level is well above 3 per cent (if only because of the slow down in productivity growth). In the next section we give reasons for thinking that it could be well above even 6 per cent.

Criticisms of the Phillips Curve

Phillips's study, and those which preceded and succeeded it, demonstrated convincingly that the rate of increase of wage rates in the UK behaved cyclically. When the economy expanded faster and unemployment fell, wage rates grew faster. When the economy grew more slowly, and unemployment rose, wage rates grew more slowly. What was less clear, and what was much disputed, was the correct interpretation to put on these facts. Thus Kaldor [10], argued that it was swings in prosperity, and, in particular, rising or falling profits, which caused the fluctuations in the rate of growth of wage rates, and not changes in the level of unemployment.

Lipsey and Steuer [13] subjected this view to statistical tests which showed, they claimed, that while profit levels were a better explanation of wage rate changes than unemployment in the interwar years in the UK the reverse was true for the years before 1914 or after 1945. Some other studies for the US ([2]; [3]) showed that profits were related to the rate of increase in wages, but pointed out that this relationship could be explained by a joint relationship with some other factor e.g. price increases or (in cross-section studies) concentration ratios or degree of unionisation.

Phelps Brown [17] attributed the cyclical behaviour of wage-rate increases to changes in expectations and pointed out that regional Phillips curves were lacking, and that 'In the United Kingdom, average wage-earnings in the regions of persistently higher-than-average unemployment have risen since 1960 by more, if anything, than the national average.' He therefore questioned whether the balance of supply and demand for labour was the controlling factor, and suggested that expectations about the rate of change of prices and wages were much more important – and that this explained the changes in behaviour which had occurred since the Second World War. Before then, bargains in each industry were conducted on the expectations of general price stability, and took the cyclical form noted by Phillips. After the war, it was realised that all prices and wages could rise together, without endangering prosperity, and so the pace of advance quickened, but still remained cyclical to some extent. From 1969 onwards, however, the caution of older men, whose memories stretched back to the 1930s, gave way to the militancy of younger men whose experience was only of a long period of prosperity. There was a wage explosion, perhaps triggered by the events in Paris in 1968, and we are now in a world in which prices and wages can be expected to rise much faster and by amounts which bear no relation to changes in productivity.

At first sight it might appear that Phelps Brown's insistence upon the importance of expectations is quite consistent with the view of the Phillips curve and natural level of unemployment given above. There is, all the same, a profound difference between them. Both agree that expectations are important in determining the rate of wage-rate increases, but, whereas the Phillips curve adherents believe that the level of unemployment also has an important effect, the others deny this, certainly so far as the postwar years, and *a fortiori* the more recent years, are concerned. Thus Phelps Brown identifies himself with Harrod's view [8] 'that money wage increases have largely become an institutional phenomenon depending on bargaining processes which are not much influenced by current economic conditions and unemployment' although he concedes that expectations of inflation 'could be broken up by a sufficiently great and sustained depression' (Phelps Brown [17], p. 243).

One can distinguish two strands in this anti-Phillips curve line of thought. First, there is the view taken by those (like Kaldor) who stress the importance of profits and prosperity as compared with unemployment. Secondly, there is the view taken by those (like Godley [6]) who believe 'that the rate of wage inflation will be changed, quite simply, whenever there is widespread pressure to change it. The going rate has only a weak inertia that may readily be shoved from one position to another.' Accordingly, this second view stresses the importance of non-economic factors.

On the first of these views, a deflationary monetary and fiscal policy can be expected to reduce the rate of wage increases and inflation since it reduces profits and prosperity. Bargainers willl not ignore the threat of bankruptcy. There seems to be some evidence for this view in recent events, where the threat of shut-down has led to the acceptance of relatively small wage increases in some cases, but it carries with it a serious implication: it may not be possible to reconcile reasonable price stability even with a high level of unemployment. The reason is that, when bankruptcy threatens a good many firms (and is sufficient to hold wages in check), investment will be low. Furthermore, such investment as there is will tend to be biased in the direction of labour saving rather than labour using (see Scott with Laslett [21], Chapter 5). Consequently, the demand for labour will probably fall and unemployment will grow, and there will be no limit to this process. Any reflation of the economy to raise profits and encourage investment sufficiently to make demand for labour grow as fast as supply will risk touching off an inflationary spiral. The events of the later 1930s, when wage rates and prices rose as the economy expanded despite unemployment well in excess of 10 per cent, show that this could indeed happen. Hence reasonable price stability, on this view, would be compatible only with *growing* unemployment.

Even if one believes in the Phillips curve, one has to admit that, in past studies, *part* of the correlation between wage-rate changes and the *level* of unemployment may have been due to the sort of factors just mentioned. Hence, even if the level of unemployment does exert an independent effect on wage-rate increases, the size of that effect may have been exaggerated in these studies. Unemployment may then have to rise a good deal higher than a straightforward application of the Phillips curve would suggest before it reaches the 'natural level'. One has to envisage a situation in which, perhaps, 10, 15 or even 20 per cent of the labour force is unemployed, but the firms in the economy are sufficiently profitable to be investing at a rate which makes the demand for the labour of the remaining 90, 85, or 80 per cent grow as fast as the supply. In this (prosperous) part of the economy, workers are not deterred from pressing wage demands by the imminent threat of bankruptcy (for, if they were, the firms would not be investing enough). The restraint on wage increases is provided by the high level of unemployment, and by that alone, and, for that to be sufficient, unemployment may have to be very high.

The second anti-Phillips view is that the 'going rate' is pushed about by social and political factors, unrelated to the economic situation. Here again, a believer in the Phillips curve who recognises the force of this argument (for which the wage explosion in 1968–70 is evidence), has to admit that, depending on the strength of these factors, the 'natural level' of unemployment might fluctuate considerably, and might turn out to be a good deal higher than econometric studies of the pre-1966 period would suggest. There may be social or political factors which have led to an increase in militancy which, independently of price expectations, has pushed out the Phillips curve, and which may explain why unemployment in excess of 5 per cent since 1976 has failed so far to bring inflation down. Some possible factors are the following: the diminishing numbers and influence of workers and union leaders with memories of the hard interwar years (Phelps Brown [17], [18]); the increasing size of public sector employment in which the threat of bankruptcy is non-existent or seems more remote; increasing unionisation, especially of white-collar workers who now represent a much larger fraction of the total labour force (this factor may be peculiar to the UK, and its absence in the US partly accounts for the decline in unionisation there); changes in class attitudes and a decline of 'deference' (Goldthorpe [7]).

All we have sought to demonstrate in this section is that there is much uncertainty about the natural level of unemployment, and that, on the whole, the doubts suggest that it may be a good deal higher than 5 or 6 per cent. It is this uncertain situation which is portrayed in Chart 2.1 at M, and which creates the case for reform of the wage-fixing system, for it means that monetary and fiscal policies alone are very unlikely to be able to reduce unemployment permanently below 5 per cent, and perhaps not even below 10 per cent or even more. We will then be unable to achieve tolerable levels of unemployment through monetary and fiscal policies. Nor is this all: it seems unlikely that we will be able to bring down inflation very much either, because high levels of unemployment will be tolerated only if the alternative appears to be high rates of inflation, and, for that to appear so, inflation will have to be at least moderately high. In short, unless the wage-fixing system can be reformed, it looks as if we shall get the worst of both worlds: both high unemployment and high inflation. If anyone finds that implausible, let him remember what has happened over the past ten to fifteen years. Is that not just what has happened?

Are There No Other Easier Solutions?

No one should harbour the illusion that reforming the wage-fixing system is going to be easy. It is not for me to discuss the difficulties here, but they clearly are immense. Since my task is to make out the case for reform, however, I do need to show that there are no other easier solutions to the dilemma with which we are confronted. In the preceding sections it has been argued that monetary and fiscal policies alone are unlikely to prevent either high unemployment or high inflation. In this section I review the most obvious other possible policies. Since space is limited, what follows is merely a list with a summary of the main points against each one.

Old-fashioned incomes policies

The incomes policies we have had since the Second World War have been many and various, but none of them has lasted for more than a couple of years or so and their effects on inflation have been questionable. They seem to have slowed it down for a time, but to have then been followed by a period of 'catch up' which has undone their initial effects. In order to be operable they have had to be simple – for example, a wage freeze, or a flat-rate or uniform percentage increase for all. Such simple formulae, however, cannot cope with a complex changing situation, and so exceptions have had to be admitted. There is a limit to the number of these which any reviewing body can handle and, furthermore, once the suspicion grows that the exceptions are being used as a way round the norm which the more powerful bargaining groups can exploit, the whole system can fall into disrepute and degenerate into free collective bargaining. It has proved unrealistic to expect individual bargaining groups to hold back for any length of time (once the immediate crisis seems past) when they are unsure whether other groups will hold back as well. Union leaders do not feel that it is their job to impose wage restraint on their members, and may find themselves replaced by more militant leaders who promise to do more. Nor will employers normally think it worthwhile to endure serious strikes in the interests of wage and price stability. They prefer good industrial relations and uninterrupted production.

Import restrictions combined with reflation

It has been argued (notably by the Cambridge Economic Policy Group in their *Economic Policy Reviews* for 1975–9, but import restrictions have also received the powerful support of the TUC) that the main obstacle to an expansionary monetary and fiscal policy is the resultant worsening in the balance of payments. If this led to a rapid depreciation of the exchange rate it would seriously aggravate inflation. If, however, restrictions on imports of manufactures were imposed the CEPG argue that inflation could actually be easier to reduce. Their view is that wage demands aim at achieving a certain target real increase in wages. If sufficient real resources can be provided for wage earners, these targets can be hit, and inflation can then be brought down. If not, inflation will remain high or accelerate. Reflationary policies expand production and productivity and provide the extra resources. It might seem, then, that reflation is all we need, but the CEPG view is that it must be combined with import restrictions because the alternative would have to be depreciation of the exchange rate. The latter would reduce the resources available to satisfy wage demands, as compared with import restrictions, for two main reasons. First, more resources would accrue as profits in export industries and, secondly, our terms of trade would worsen.

The CEPG argument must be rejected. It ignores the main reason why governments both here and abroad have been afraid to reflate their economies, namely, that this would speed up inflation through its effects in strengthening the demand for labour, increasing profits and generating expectations of rising prices and wages. The target wage theory, on which the argument rests, is inadequate, since it cannot explain why we have not had explosive inflation long ago – it is too much of a coincidence to suppose that the targets just happen to have been set at the right levels. Something else must have restrained wages, and that must surely have been the level of demand for labour and fears of bankruptcy.

As well as this fundamental objection, it seems likely that import restrictions would require just as great an increase in profits as exchange-rate depreciation, the only difference being that all the increase would be concentrated in industries producing import substitutes. Furthermore, there would be a loss of real output due to inefficiency, and the pressure for wage demands would be increased as the monopolistic positions of unions in particular industries (e.g. motor vehicles) were strengthened. Finally, retaliation by foreign countries against our exports could easily offset any gain we might otherwise have obtained through improvements in the terms of trade. Import restrictions, far from providing an easier escape route, are likely to make matters worse.

Direct measures to increase employment and reduce unemployment

A wide variety of measures may be considered under this head: increased employment in the public sector; employment subsidies for the private sector, including cuts in what are effectively taxes on employment such as national insurance contributions; keeping young people on longer at school, or providing them with temporary employment of various kinds; inducing or compelling older workers to retire sooner; and shortening hours of work by, for example, reducing the standard working week, eliminating overtime or having longer holidays. Many of these measures, or similar ones, have been advocated by the Trades Union Congress [22]. Some of them can be defended on the grounds that they would be desirable even if there was no *general* problem of inflation and unemployment. But as solutions to the problems considered in this paper I regard them as inadequate, for the following reasons.

Firstly, and most importantly, the problem we are facing is not a lack of measures which will increase employment. We do not need fancy schemes for that – general cuts in taxation would do, and do it more efficiently. The problem arises precisely because it is feared that the effect of such measures would be inflationary. If unemployment is reduced, and the demand for labour strengthened, then wage demands will increase, and expectations of inflation will be strengthened. If that is admitted, then particular measures which increase employment in particular directions have to be offset by general measures which reduce it everywhere else, and no net gain in employment has been achieved. Secondly, some of the measures do not even reduce unemployment in any genuine sense, but merely conceal it, thus adding to the already considerable level of concealed unemployment and over-manning. Thirdly, if workers resist real wage cuts, which would encourage employment and reduce inflation, why will they accept work-sharing schemes which reduce real wage rates for them and probably do not even reduce inflation?

Growth of small firms and self-employment

This is not so much a set of measures which the government might take, as a natural outcome of a period of prolonged heavy unemployment. If the doctor's treatment will not work, perhaps the patient can cure himself? The cure might proceed in the opposite direction to that taken by a country whose traditional sector is gradually shrinking and providing labour for an expanding modern sector. If that is called a developing country, Britain could become an undeveloping country. Wages in the more heavily unionised public sector, and those paid by large firms, would remain well above those in non-unionised small firms and in self-employment but employment by the latter would grow. Wages and prices in this unorganised sector would respond more flexibly to monetary and fiscal measures, and this would eventually enable inflation in the economy to become controllable without the necessity for very high levels of unemployment.

I would not want to say that this could not be a solution, but it seems unlikely that it would be reached at all quickly, and it would involve a heavy cost. Large firms benefit from considerable economies of scale, and provide most of our exports. If they are to shrink, we must forgo a lot of real income and find some other ways of earning or saving foreign exchange. Presumably tourism, agriculture and handicrafts would all flourish, and English language teachers and British *au pair* girls would be much in demand. It is a possible solution, but perhaps not a particularly attractive one. Furthermore, its achievement could be frustrated if small firms and the self-employed could somehow be successfully organised to bargain collectively for their 'rights'. That would be difficult, but one should not underestimate the British genius for collective organisation.

Growth of producer cooperatives

Again, this might to some extent take place spontaneously, but it could also be promoted by legislation. Jay [9] has suggested that workers should be given control over the enterprises in which they work, which would then have to sink or swim in the market environment. He envisages a withering away of national trade unions, and believes that inflation would subside and employment would be high. The Liberal Party has favoured increased profit sharing by workers, which is a step in the same direction.

The cooperative solution is a radical one which could evoke considerable resistance. It is by no means clear that it really qualifies as an easier solution than reform of the wage-fixing system. However, let us consider it on its merits. Would national trade unions really wither away? What would there be to stop the mine workers forming (or rather, maintaining) a national union which would push up coal prices and wages much as at present? True, the members of a cooperative would not want some of their number to become unemployed, but is that essentially different from the employees of an existing firm who bargain collectively? They could, as now, prefer higher wages to expanding employment opportunities, and there are theoretical grounds for supposing that a workers' cooperative would do so to a greater extent than if employment were controlled by a private employer. It is hard to see how industrial relations within a large cooperative would differ much from industrial relations in any giant firm, so that either big firms must shrink or else the reform achieves little for this important sector of the economy. Craft unions could still represent interests cutting across those of other workers, and could exploit their bargaining positions to improve wage differentials, or could engage in demarcation disputes and resist new methods of work as at present. In short, it is far from clear that even a radical reform along these lines would achieve its objectives.

Conclusion

No government likes restricting demand and seeing unemployment grow. Equally, no government likes expanding demand and seeing inflation accelerate. Democratic governments reflect public opinion in both cases, and public opinion is right to regard both high unemployment and high inflation as damaging and dangerous. Governments have shown by their actions that they believe that, when inflation is rapid, it is dangerous to expand demand, and so they have been prepared to let unemployment grow. We have thus, since 1966, experienced the unpleasant combination of accelerating inflation and rising unemployment. Thus far, neither monetary and fiscal policies nor incomes policies have succeeded in preventing this. Reasons have been given for doubting whether they can succeed in restoring low inflation and low unemployment, at least in the foreseeable future.

Worse still, we may not yet have reached the end of the road, since wages and prices may to some extent have been held in check by a squeeze on profits and threat of widespread bankruptcy which, if it is maintained, will reduce investment still further. The result will be that demand for labour will continue to fall and unemployment will continue to grow. For a sustainable situation to be reached, with enough investment to prevent unemployment from growing, profits and investment have to be higher than at present. Wages and prices will then be held in check only by unemployment, and that may require a considerably higher level of unemployment than at present. Before a democratically elected government is prepared to tolerate that, the alternative will have to appear to be a still higher rate of inflation, and that may require an actual rate of inflation faster than the present one. Hence, with present arrangements, and only monetary and fiscal policies available to deal with the situation, we may end up with more unemployment and more inflation than at present.

Perhaps this is unncecessarily gloomy, but, even if we remain as at present, the level of unemployment and rate of inflation are both uncomfortably high and their long-term effects, economic, social and political, must cause concern. We have briefly considered some possible remedies for this state of affairs, but they have all been found wanting.

The conclusion reached is, then, that there is a great need to reform the wage-fixing system. Some way needs to be found to make it possible to reconcile a low level of unemployment, sufficient profits and prosperity for investment to expand the demand for labour as fast as supply, and a low rate of inflation. We have not been able to do this with the present system, and the results are plain to see.

References

[1] Brittan, S., *The Treasury under the Tories 1951–1964*, Penguin Books, 1964.

[2] Bodkin, R. G., *The Wage-Price-Productivity Nexus*, Philadelphia, University of Pennsylvania Press, 1966.

[3] Bowen, W. G., *Wage Behaviour in the Postwar Period: An Empirical Analysis*, Princeton, Princeton University Press, 1960.

[4] Brown, A. J., *The Great Inflation, 1939–1951*, London, Oxford University Press, 1955.

[5] Brown, R. N., Enoch, C. A. and Mortimer-Lee, P. D., *The Interrelationships Between Cost and Prices in the United Kingdom*, Bank of England, Discussion Paper No. 8, 1980.

[6] Godley, W. A., 'Inflation in the United Kingdom' in L. B. Krause and W. S. Salant, *Worldwide Inflation*, Washington, DC, Brookings, 1977.

[7] Goldthorpe, J. H., 'The current inflation: towards a sociological account' in F. Hirsch and J. H. Goldthorpe, eds., *The Political Economy of Inflation*, London, Martin Robertson, 1978.

[8] Harrod, Sir Roy, *Towards a New Economic Policy*, Manchester University Press, 1967.

[9] Jay, P., *A General Hypothesis of Employment, Inflation and Politics*, London, Institute of Economic Affairs, Occasional Paper 46, 1976.

[10] Kaldor, N., 'Economic growth and the problem of inflation – Part II', *Economica*, November 1959.

[11] Laidler, D. E. W., 'The end of "demand management": how to reduce unemployment in the 1970s' in M. Friedman and D. E. W. Laidler,

Unemployment versus Inflation? : An Evaluation of the Phillips Curve (with a British Commentary), London, Institute of Economic Affairs, Occasional Paper 44, 1975.

[12] Lipsey, R. G., 'The relationship between unemployment and the rate of change of money wage rates in the U.K. 1862–1957: a further analysis', *Economica*, February 1960.

[13] Lipsey, R. G. and Steuer, M. D., 'The relation between profits and wage rates', *Economica*, May 1961.

[14] NIESR, *National Institute Economic Review*, November 1979.

[15] Nickell, S. J., 'The effect of unemployment and related benefits on the duration of unemployment', *Economic Journal*, March 1979.

[16] Paish, F. W., *Studies in an Inflationary Economy*, London, Macmillan, 1962.

[17] Phelps Brown, E. H., 'The analysis of wage movements under full employment', *Scottish Journal of Political Economy*, vol. 18, 1971.

[18] Phelps Brown, E. H., 'A non-monetarist view of the pay explosion', *Three Banks Review* No. 105, 1975.

[19] Phillips, A. W., 'The relationship between unemployment and the rate of change of money wage rates in the UK 1861–1957', *Economica*, November 1958.

[20] Rothschild, K. W., 'The Phillips curve and all that', *Scottish Journal of Political Economy*, November 1971.

[21] Scott, M. F., with Laslett, R. A., *Can We Get Back to Full Employment?*. London, Macmillan, 1978.

[22] Trades Union Congress, *Trades Union Congress Economic Review 1980*, London, 1980.

3 Inflation, Unemployment and Reform

R. A. Batchelor, E. Bendle and B. Griffiths

There is widespread agreement that the smooth operation of the labour market can make a great contribution to economic welfare. There is also widespread agreement that present wage bargaining practices in the United Kingdom are not conducive to the maximisation of social welfare. Economists of different doctrinal persuasions differ, however, over the exact route by which alternative wage bargaining systems confer social benefits or costs. This means that the precise case for reform of the wage bargaining system can be based on at least two rival diagnoses of the British disease. It also means that disagreements arise over the precise direction in which reform of the wage bargaining system should proceed.

One popular, neo-Keynesian, view is that the wage determination system determines the overall rate of inflation obtaining at any given rate of unemployment. Reform of the system is seen as necessary because of the persistently high rate of inflation experienced in the UK over the past decade. Reform is seen as working by improving the terms of the trade-off between inflation and unemployment, by using administered pay ceilings as substitutes for increased unemployment in achieving some target reduction in the rate of inflation.

The alternative, monetarist, view is that the wage determination system can influence only the structure of relative wages within a total rate of inflation constrained by monetary growth. Reform of the system is urgently needed because of the coincidence of two factors. The first is the growth of public sector employment and of union power in the private sector. The second is the rapid pace at which the comparative cost advantages of traditional manufacturing industries are being eroded. Reform of the system of wage bargaining is seen as a means of promoting the necessary reallocation of labour away from industries, occupations and regions where demand is low and towards industries, occupations and regions where demand is high. The essential element in such a reform is the freeing of labour markets from monopolistic elements, both on the part of employers – especially the state – and employees.

For reasons elaborated below, we reject the neo-Keynesian argument. Both in its analysis and in its advocacy of administered wage arrangements it presupposes irrational and unselfish attitudes on the part of firms and unions. We maintain the second view, that it is the behaviour of relative wages which is crucial. In the third section below we identify the nature and extent of the costs to society of the perpetuation of monopolistic elements in the labour market, using a simple model of rational company and union behaviour. In the final section, we consider what progress can be made towards achieving, if not perfect competition, at least effective competition in labour markets. Our suggested criteria for the evaluation of reforms are: first, that market-based solutions should be preferred to administered solutions, and, second, that the framework should assume rational and self-interested behaviour on the part of all parties to the bargain.

Wage Determination Systems

We start by defining terms. In each labour market a more or less unionised labour force must strike a bargain with a more or less monopolistic employer, subject perhaps to constraints imposed by the government. A particular configuration of these demand, supply, and regulatory factors defines a particular system of wage determination. The UK supports a wide variety of such systems.

Unionisation

The classification of industries according to their trade union density – for which 1974 figures are given in Table 6.1, page 132, shows that the highly unionised group consists largely of workers in public sector industries and services, and in traditional branches of engineering. The less unionised group consists of a range of private sector manufacturing industries, construction, and agriculture and fisheries.

Privately provided services, including distribution and financial services, are the least unionised sectors.

The extent of unionisation is not a completely reliable guide to their bargaining power. For one thing, unions in the UK are still predominantly occupational rather than industrial in character. A single union may be involved in negotiations with several industries. Conversely a single employer may have to negotiate with a large number of unions. The extent to which employees in a particular industry are concentrated into a small number of unions would therefore provide a more meaningful measure of bargaining strength. A further problem is that unions differ considerably in their strength of purpose. One measure of this would perhaps be the frequency or duration of strikes, though the most powerful unions may well achieve their objectives through the exercise of a strike threat, rather than an actual strike.

Concentration

The monopoly power enjoyed by firms in each industry determines the flexibility with which they can meet union demands. The most highly monopolised industries are those run by the state itself. Not only have these industries very few competitors to put pressure on profit margins, they are also a short step away from the printing press. The fact that such industries cannot credibly advance the argument that no cash is available to meet union demands makes them a potent source of distortions in relative pay.

Concentration and unionisation are strongly correlated. The problem of union power in wage bargaining, and in attracting and organising members, is the obverse of the capacity of monopolised industry to generate the excess profits or excess cash which form the object of dispute. One result of this correlation of union power with concentration is that the organisational level at which the wage bargain is struck within the industry is considerably higher in high-unionised, concentrated sectors. The settlements in the highly unionised sectors are predominantly national. Among the less unionised industries there are far fewer bargains of this nature and a significant number are settled without benefit of any collective agreement.

The regulatory framework

The government has been involved in regulating the wage determination system on two levels. First, it has been involved either directly or indirectly as a partner to the wage bargain. Second, it has provided a framework of legislation which affects the power of trade unions and commercial monopolies.

The government may become a party to the bargain in three ways. In the narrowest sense, it is involved as employer in the negotiation of public sector pay. More broadly it has sought through a succession of incomes policies to impose its own desired outcomes on private sector bargains. The history of these schemes is summarised in Table 3.1. The policy has in most cases consisted of the setting of

Table 3.1 The experience of generalised incomes policy

Period of policy	Norm for wage increases	Wage inflation		
		Preceding 6 months	During policy	Succeeding 6 months
1948–50	0.0	3.0	2.2	10.7
1956	None	7.7	3.4	6.7
1961–2	0.0	5.4	2.7	
1962–3	2.5		3.9	
1963–4	3.5		4.1	4.9
1965–6	3.5	3.9	5.0	
1966–7	0.0		4.1	
1968–9	3.5		5.8	
1970	4.5		8.9	13.6
1972–3	0.0	21.0	2.9	
1973	5.5		13.7	
1973–4	7.0		18.5	
1974–5	21.0		25.0	28.3
1975–6	12.0	32.7	18.6	
1976–7	4.5		4.3	
1977–8	10.0		19.0	
1978–9	5.0		12.0	20.3

Source: Chronology is from B. Griffiths, *Inflation: the Price of Prosperity*, London, Weidenfeld and Nicolson, 1976, Table 12, updated from *National Institute Economic Review*, various issues. Wage inflation estimates are from *Economic Trends* and relate to basic weekly wage rates.

either a norm for wage increases or a ceiling to such increases, uniformly across all bargaining groups. The policy has normally provided for arbitration in the case of anomalies in relative pay arising out of the timing of the imposition of the wage freeze. These policies have worked in so far as wage inflation and expectations of inflation were invariably reduced in the short term. The most striking feature of all these policies, however, is that they invariably break down, and in the long run have no effect on the pace of inflation (Henry and Ormerod [3]).

In periods when there is no formal incomes policy, government legislation still impinges on the actions of unions and firms. In particular, over the past decade attempts have been made to limit the power of unions to operate a closed shop and to exercise the strike weapon as an early recourse in pay disputes. These provisions of the 1971 Industrial Relations Act were, however, largely repealed in 1974. Conversely, the scope of investigation of the Office of Fair Trading and the Monopolies Commission has been progressively widened, and the costs of firing workers substantially raised by redundancy payments requirements and the provision of a tribunal to deal with complaints of unfair dismissal.

Proposed reforms to the regulatory framework of the wage bargaining system can take the system in one of two directions. Either we can seek to redesign the administrative and consultative procedures of incomes policy in an attempt to make it permanent; or we can seek to strengthen the competition legislation and make the treatment of union monopoly symmetrical to that of industry monopoly. The choice between these paths is dependent on whether the wage determination system is seen as exerting a sinister influence over macroeconomic stabilisation, or whether it is seen as raising primarily microeconomic problems over the efficient allocation of labour among industries.

Wages and Macroeconomic Stabilisation

Views on how the determination of nominal wages impinges on the level of real activity in the economy have changed radically over the past decade. These changes reflect the declining status of the Phillips curve, the negative relationship between money wage inflation and unemployment which characterised the British economy in the period 1870–1960. This was first regarded as a binding constraint on the mix of inflation and unemployment which could be achieved under a given labour-market structure. In the face of mounting empirical evidence in the 1960s and 1970s that the relationship had become, if anything, positive rather than negative the constraint was re-evaluated as a temporary phenomenon, the result of adaptive inflation expectations. It was subsequently discarded altogether, as the monetary basis of inflation was conceded and as the notion of rational expectations gained acceptance.

This revolution in the description of how the economy functions has led to a reappraisal of the various prescriptions for reform of the wage determination system. Briefly, imposed wage norms and synchronised settlements, which appeared helpful under the original Phillips curve constraint, are unnecessary and even damaging to macroeconomic stability under rational expectations.

The Phillips curve constraint

According to the negatively sloping non-linear relationship between the rate of nominal wage inflation and unemployment found by Phillips [8], wage stability was consistent with an unemployment rate of 5 per cent and a 5 per cent wage inflation with an unemployment rate of 1.5 per cent. Lipsey [5] rationalised this relationship in terms of the disequilibrium dynamics of a labour market in which the demand for labour was a negative function of the money wage, and the supply a positive function of the money wage.

This set-up is capable of generating Phillips observed relationship if two further assumptions are granted. First, excess demand for, or excess supply of, labour must be assumed to give rise to inflation or deflation in money wage rates in proportion to the size of the imbalance. Second, voluntary unemployment – that is, unemployment occuring because workers are not willing to take jobs where some vacancies exist – must be assumed unrecorded. The first assumption creates a causal chain running from the level of unemployment to the rate of change of wages. The second, rather awkward, assumption is necessary to make sense of the observed relationship at times when there is excess demand for labour and wage inflation is consequently positive.

Starting at any point on the Phillips curve, for example where the unemployment rate is 1 per cent and inflation about 9 per cent, market forces will push the economy to the equilibrium point where wages are stable but unemployment has risen to around 5 per cent. This point may not be socially optimal. However, macroeconomic policy can only shift the market equilibrium along the Phillips curve by artificially raising the demand for labour and so rekindling inflationary pressures. The complementary role envisaged for less orthodox policies is to shortcircuit the responses of wages to disequilibrium between labour demand and supply. For example, by imposing a wage norm below 9 per cent it might be possible to move off the Phillips curve and reduce inflation with no cost in terms of raising unemployment above its initial value of 1 per cent.

The natural rate constraint

The above interpretation of the Phillips curve was rapidly discredited by events and more careful theoretical analysis. Throughout the 1960s and 1970s, the Phillips relationship appeared to shift about in a disconcerting manner. From 1961 to 1967 the relationship held up well. In 1968–9 wage inflation started to run at rates much higher than would previously have been implied by the modest rates of unemployment then experienced. By 1970–4, a new, negatively sloped relationship seemed to have been established with inflation consistently running 10–15 per cent per annum faster at any given rate of unemployment than predicted by the original Phillips curve; and in 1975–9 the relation appears to have shifted even further to the right.

The initial response to this evidence of a shifting trade-off between inflation and unemployment was, understandably, a shift in the focus of policy away from traditional demand management devices designed to move the labour market along a given Phillips curve, and towards incomes policies which held some promise of reversing the upward drift of the curve by imposing wage ceilings. Two developments soon led to a questioning of the intellectual basis for such policies towards wage determination.

The first was the recognition that the new higher rates of inflation had a monetary origin. In spite of the almost continuous manipulation of wage inflation throughout the 1960s and 1970s the positive association between monetary growth and subsequent wage and price inflation has now been established.

The second development was the reinterpretation of the original

Phillips curve. The key step was the recognition that the demand for and supply of labour depended not – as in the Phillips and Lipsey accounts – on money wage rates but on expected real wage rates. In this interpretation the Phillips curve does not reflect a causal link from unemployment to wage inflation, but constitutes a representation of the simultaneous effects of inflation expectations errors on unemployment and wages. These arise because firms and workers, faced with a rise in nominal demand as a result of, say, monetary expansion by the government, tend to be optimistic about how much of the increased purchasing power represents a real increase in demand for their own products and services, as against the amount which will eventually feed through into a general price rise. Thus a monetary expansion will lead to an underestimate of the eventual rate of inflation and an overestimate of how much output should be produced. Money wages will be raised to attract labour to produce this output, and to workers this increase will represent an expected real increase. For as long as inflation is underestimated, labour utilisation will be higher than normal. Conversely if inflation is overestimated labour utilisation will be low.

The original Phillips curve is explained by Friedman [2] as the manifestation of this negative relationship between unemployment and inflation expectations errors in an era when inflation expectations were always roughly zero, and each nominal wage change was interpreted as a real wage change. It is tempting to adduce a similar explanation for the awkward shift of the Phillips curve in the 1970s. The observations for 1971–4 could be produced by the same labour market as the observations for 1961–7 if we assumed inflation expectations rose from zero to 10–15 per cent between the two periods. Similarly the observations for 1975–9 could be deflected towards the original relationship if expectations of 15–20 per cent per annum were prevalent. If this explanation were convincing there would be some case for persisting in the use of centrally imposed wage norms as a means of correcting these expectations errors.

There are three compelling objections to the use of general wage norms as a means of transmitting information to the labour market. First, less cumbersome alternatives exist. The most obvious course is to exploit the relationship between monetary growth and subsequent price inflation by announcing and adhering to monetary targets. Rational expectations in the light of this information will eliminate most errors. Second, expectations errors do not wholly explain the behaviour of wages and unemployment in the 1970s. Batchelor and Sheriff [1] have used direct evidence on inflation expectations to show that, from 1971 onwards, the rate of unemployment consistent with fully anticipated inflation did shift outwards by almost 2 per cent. Third, there is good reason to suppose that, in its various aspects, the system of wage determination has an important bearing on this 'natural' rate of unemployment. The appropriate criterion for choosing a wage determination system is, thus, not whether it will enable a target rate of inflation to be attained, nor even whether it will break inflation expectations. The issue is whether it imposes a greater or lesser cost on society in terms of unemployment. To this issue we now turn.

Microeconomic Efficiency

To comprehend the effects of the wage determination system on unemployment, we need to move away from the analysis of aggregates towards the analysis of individual markets.

Unions, monopolies and structural change

As a baseline, we consider first the equilibrium of the two-sector model in Chart 3.1. In this model sector I is monopolistic. It faces a downward sloping demand function for its product, and hence confronts its labour force with a demand schedule D_O which is a downward sloping function of the wage in sector I relative to the wage in sector II. Given a supply function of labour S_I, equilibrium employment is N_O and the relative real wage W_O. We assume that this equilibrium is consistent with utility maximisation on the part of a union which has joint relative real wage and employment objectives. The union indifference curve U_O passing through the equilibrium point is thus tangential to the demand function D_O.

Sector II is perfectly competitive, and hence non-unionised, and the demand for labour at the equilibrium relative wage W_O is infinitely elastic, but the supply of labour is constrained to be the difference between the full-employment level of employment F and the supply S_1 of labour to sector I. Given the equilibrium of sector I, the supply of labour to this sector II is thus $F - N_O$. Now suppose there is a fall in the demand for the product of sector I, to

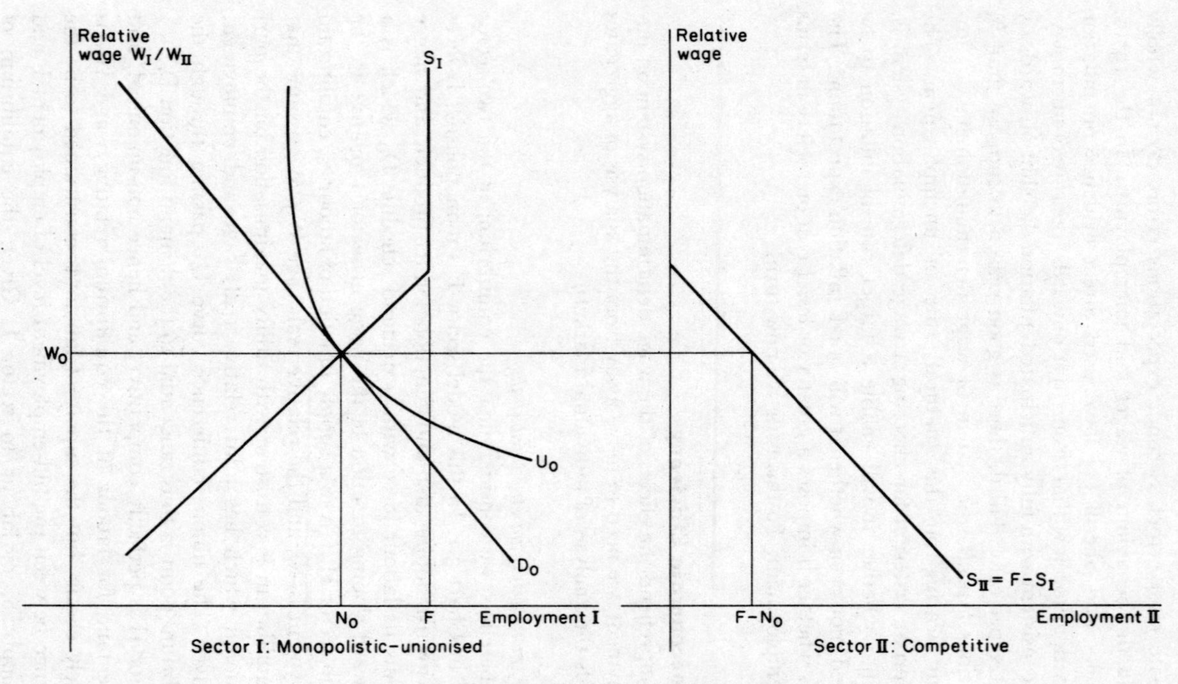

Chart 3.1 Two-sector model: initial equilibrium

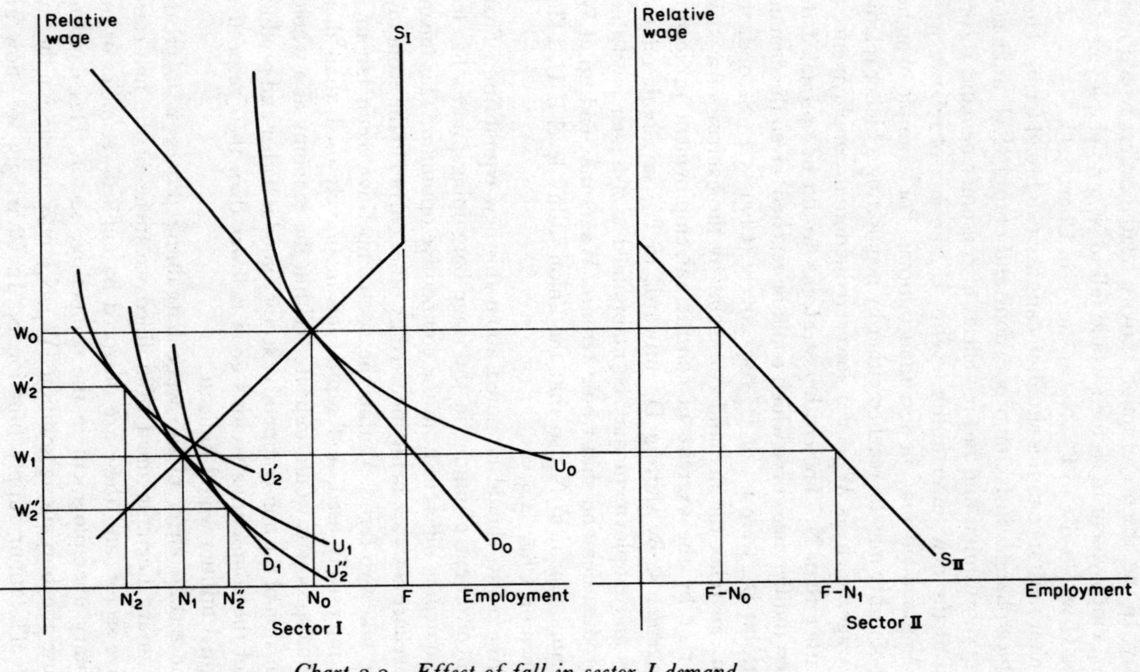

Chart 3.2 Effect of fall in sector I demand

D_1 say. In the absence of union activity relative wages would move to W_1, employment in sector I would fall to N_1, and employment in sector II would rise to $F - N_1$, as shown in Chart 3.2.

Union resistance to this situation can take two broad forms. These produce changes in factor proportions and output levels analogous to the substitution and income effects of consumer demand theory. First, at the new lower utility level of U_1 the mix of relative wage and employment may be less than optimal. For example a higher level of utility may be reached either by negotiating a higher relative real wage, such as W_2, or a lower reduction in employment, to N_2'' rather than N_1. These other strategies would be optimal if the highest indifference curve which could be reached, given the demand constraint D_1, were U_2' or U_2'' respectively (Chart 3.2). Second, the union can relax the demand constraint by the exercise of a strike threat or by the exercise of contractual employment protection arrangements. By shifting D_1 outwards to D_3, say, both relative wages and employment may be maintained at a higher level than the product demand shift would require. Wages may end up at W_4 and employment at N_3, so that the union utility level is U_3. This is shown on Chart 3.3.

Three points should be noted about this new equilibrium. First, the involvement of unions in the wage bargaining process has led to an outcome different from the competitive optimum. This means that welfare costs are being incurred by other parties in the economy. These take two forms. Within the non-competitive sector labour is more intensively used, and capital less intensively used, than their marginal products would indicate. Within the economy as a whole, production of the non-competitive sector's good is higher and production of the competitive sector's good is lower than their respective marginal utilities would indicate.

The second effect of the wage bargaining process is to create involuntary unemployment or unfilled vacancies in the non-competitive sector, and these are mirrored by unfilled vacancies or involuntary unemployment in the competitive sector. This happens because the bargaining solution (W_4, N_3) may not lie on the individual's labour supply function S_1. In Chart 3.3 we show an equilibrium where in moving from W_1, N_1 the employer has been more willing to concede higher wages than higher employment. At the new wage W_4, $N_4 - N_3$ workers would be prepared to work but

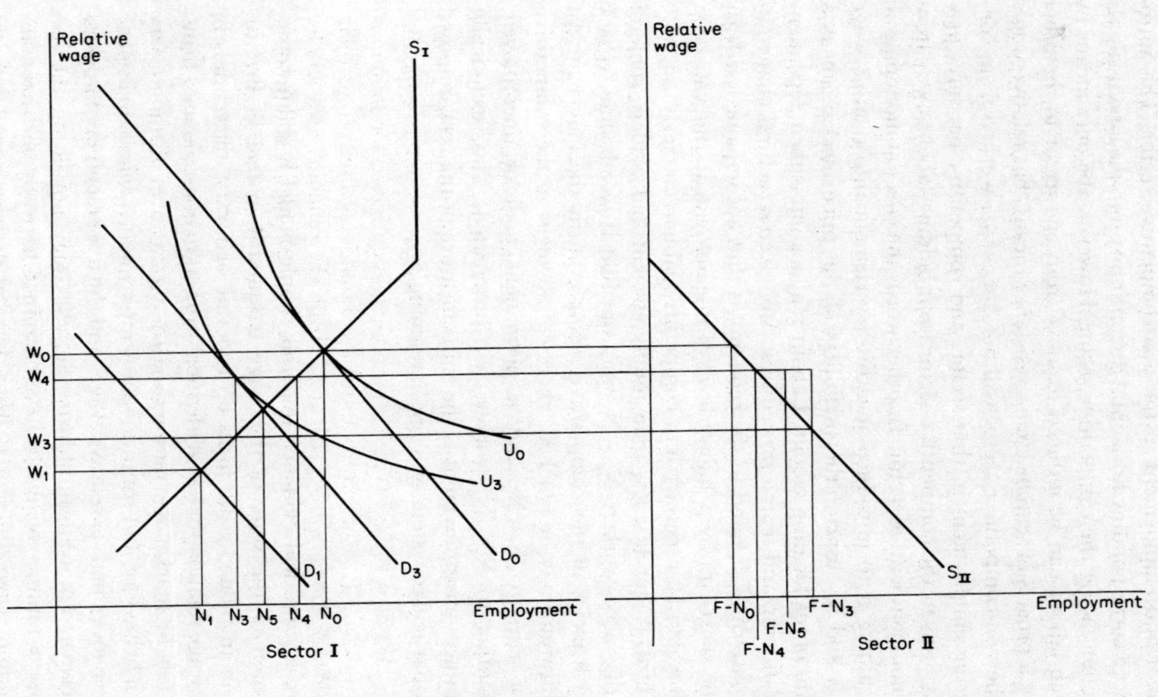

Chart 3.3 Effect of unions on labour utilisation

cannot find employment in the non-competitive sector. This introduces a corresponding horizontal discontinuity into the labour supply function facing the competitive sector. However, the only means by which labour can be induced to move from one sector to the other is by a process of search. Union resistance means that relative wages in the non-competitive sector will not discourage workers from considering employment in that sector, and competitive pressures prohibit firms in the competitive sector from bidding labour away from the non-competitive sector. In other words the effect of monopolistic bargaining is to introduce an arbitrary element into relative wage levels and so suspend the usefulness of the price mechanism as a means of reallocating labour. Labour reallocation is then dependent on rationing and search procedures. Any given structural change in the pattern of demand in the economy is thus accompanied at least in the short run by a higher level of unemployment and vacancies than would be necessary in a competitive labour market.

Third, if search is less than totally efficient and costless, some of the displaced workers $N_4 - N_3$ may not find it worthwhile to seek out vacancies in the competitive sector even in the long run. An equilibrium may be reached where employment in the competitive sector rises to $F - N_5$ and a permanent pool of unemployed, amounting to $N_4 - N_5$ workers will be created. This, technically voluntary, unemployment is the third measure of the costs imposed by a particular system of wage bargaining.

Empirical evidence

There is empirical evidence that this simple model is a fair representation of the state of the wage bargaining system in Britain. Unions in monopolistic firms do generate arbitrary differentials in their wage relation to that of identical workers in non-unionised firms. The labour market is characterised by a great deal of unnecessary search behaviour and transitional unemployment. Unions do impede the free movement of relative wages and the free responses of workers in seeking to move from industry to industry.

First, a number of studies have examined the scale of the union–non-union wage differential from detailed cross-sectional data on individual workers. The three major studies in the area, by Layard, Metcalf, Nickell [4], by Mulvey [6], and by Mulvey and Foster [7].

are unanimous in finding an average differential of 25 per cent for individuals subject to collective agreements.

Second, from a model of responses of industry labour flows to price and non-price incentives, Pissarides [9] concludes that '... relative wages have been more rigid than relative vacancy and unemployment levels, so "job availability" has been an important factor by which labour was encouraged to move to expanding sectors. Although the latter did succeed in inducing some movement, the results of this paper support the view that where used, relative wages have been very effective in inducing labour movement.' In other words if relative wages were allowed full rein, structural changes in British industry could in practice be accommodated with much less transitional and search-discouraged unemployment.

The role of the unions in this process may be gauged by examining the effect of movements of relative earnings on employment in the non-unionised and unionised sectors. Over the period 1965–79, in the industries which have relatively low trade union density, there is a strong positive relationship, which suggests that a 1 per cent change in relative earnings will accelerate or decelerate the relative growth of employment (that is, relative to employment growth in general) by about 1.7 per cent. However, the relationship in the strongly unionised industries tells a different story. First of all, earnings have tended to rise faster than average in these industries, in spite of the fact that employment growth has been consistently lower. Moreover, although there is still a positive response of employment to relative earnings growth, the relationship is much less strong. A 1 per cent fall in relative earnings inflation will, for example, be associated with a reduction in employment in the unionised industries of only 0.3 per cent.

The Direction of Reform

From these theoretical and empirical considerations we draw two morals for the design of a regulatory framework for wage bargaining. First, no direct controls over the outcomes of wage bargains throughout the economy can change the long-run rate of inflation. Indeed, we argue below that such policies are often redundant and always autodestructive. Second, the problem of wage regulation should be viewed as one aspect of competition policy. The implementation of this policy in the private sector involves the elimination of monopoly in product and labour markets, or, when this is impossible, the establishment of symmetrical bargaining power on both sides of the labour market. In the public sector, the same principles should be applied. Activities should be subject when possible to a market test, and, when this is impractical, the power of the employing organisation to generate cash from taxation, price rises or borrowing must be constrained by rigid, centrally imposed ceilings.

The futility of incomes policy

The long-run rate of inflation is governed by the rate of monetary growth relative to productivity growth. Generalised incomes policies can, however, influence short-run wage movements, and short-run real activity, in two ways.

First, by promulgating a wage norm, expectations about inflation can be concentrated around its actual value during the life of the policy. This ensures that no short-term hiring or firing decisions will be made on the basis of mistaken beliefs about the change in real demand underlying the observed changes in nominal demand. Incomes policies can thus be used to promote rational expectations or at least break irrational expectations.

Second, by locking workers into contracts for the duration of the policy the government could conceivably use macroeconomic instruments to achieve a real expansion or contraction. A money stock increase in excess of the wage norm would, for example, encourage firms to increase production and profits, and hire more labour – driving unemployment below its natural rate. In this case, incomes policy is used not to make expectations rational but to prevent workers acting on their expectations by negotiating higher wages. A similar locking-in effect could be achieved without a wage norm if all major unions could be persuaded to synchronise annual wage settlements.

Neither of these rationales for incomes policy is convincing. In the former case the policy would inevitably collapse unless monetary growth was consistent with the wage norm. But in such circumstances the norm would be redundant since prospective inflation could be readily assessed by reference to the current rate of monetary growth.

In the latter case the progressive real income loss suffered by workers would not be tolerated.

Moreover, any short-run macroeconomic benefits of a generalised incomes policy are bought at the price of freezing wage differentials across industries irrespective of the differing demand and supply conditions they may face. Suppose in Chart 3.3 that demand for Sector I output rose from D_1 to D_0. The presence of any incomes policy prevents the necessary rise in relative wages from W_1 to W_0 since money wages in both sectors I and II are constrained by the wage norm. Excess demand for labour in expanding sectors will build up during the life of any such policy, imposing costs similar to those imposed by monopoly power itself. The accumulation of such disequilibria will also, however, give rise to increasing opposition from both unions and management to the incomes policy.

In short, in an economy pursuing responsible monetary policies a generalised incomes policy is unnecessary, while in an economy pursuing an inconsistent monetary policy or subject to structural change a generalised incomes policy is intrinsically self-destructive. In all cases the failure of the policy is the result of rational, self-interested, behaviour on the part of unions and employers. These fundamental traits of economic man cannot be ignored in the design of regulatory frameworks for wage bargaining.

Competition, co-determination and cash limits

The relevant test for whether a particular wage determination system is producing desirable results is a market test. The presence of monopoly on either side of wage negotiations produces distortions in relative prices, a sub-optimal capital–labour mix, and a degree of structural unemployment. Reforms to the regulatory framework should aim to eliminate these monopoly elements. Since the government acts both as an employer and a regulator, and since the most acute problems of control arise in the public sector, it is helpful to treat the reform of private sector and public sector wage determination separately.

Efficiency in private sector wage determination can be promoted by two types of reform. One involves legislating against the exercise of monopoly power. The monopoly power of companies in product markets is already diminished by the actions of the Monopolies Commission, the Office of Fair Trading, and a body of consumer protection legislation. It has also come under continuous pressure from foreign competition as tariff barriers have been reduced over the past two decades. The problem of union monopoly power is more serious. No legislation protects the company or the consumer against union action, and it seems essential that some attempt be made to remedy this asymmetry in the treatment of one side of the wage bargain.

There exists an alternative to coercion as a means of inducing a competitive outcome from the wage determination process. The alternative is to make clear to employees in each industry that they have a community of interest with their employers. Proposals for increased industrial democracy represent a weak form of such a programme. A much stronger and more market-orientated idea is to provide a direct financial incentive to cooperation by making a substantial part of each employee's wage equity in the employing company. Experience with cooperative enterprise in the UK has not been encouraging, often because the cooperative was formed as a last ditch attempt to save a bankrupt firm. However, experience in Scandinavia, Germany and Spain, suggests that in professionally managed enterprises such a system could be viable.

In the public sector market discipline is even more difficult to effect. Much public sector pay is indeed determined on the basis of comparability exercises which take no account of the state of demand and supply in the relevant labour markets. Some semblance of a competitive outcome can, however, be imposed on the public sector in two ways. First, if a product or service can be marketed without prejudice to social objectives, it should be marketed. The privatisation of much of the public sector would diminish the distortions and disruptions caused by public sector pay disputes. Second, the negotiating body on the employer's side should be distanced from the Exchequer by the imposition of rigid limits on cash subsidies and pricing policy. Public sector unions are large, and they wield considerable power. But the obverse of their size is that they can easily be made aware of the unemployment consequences of excessive wage settlements in a way which more fragmented private sector unions cannot. As with co-determination in the private sector, the most the authorities can hope to achieve by reforming the wage bargaining system is the internalisation of what were previously external effects of the exercise of union monopoly power.

References

[1] Batchelor, R. A. and Sheriff, T. D., 'Unemployment and unanticipated inflation in postwar Britain', *Economica*, May 1980.

[2] Friedman, M., 'Unemployment versus inflation: an evaluation of the Phillips curve', Nobel address published as Occasional Paper 44, *Institute of Economic Affairs*, London, 1975.

[3] Henry, S. G. B. and Ormerod, P. A., 'Incomes policy and wage inflation: empirical evidence for the UK 1961–77', *National Institute Economic Review*, August 1978.

[4] Layard, R., Metcalf, D. and Nickell, S., 'The effect of collective bargaining on relative and absolute wages', *British Journal of Industrial Relations*, November 1978.

[5] Lipsey, R. G., 'The relation between unemployment and the rate of change of money wage rates in the United Kingdom 1862–1956: a further analysis', *Economica*, February 1960.

[6] Mulvey, C., 'Collective agreements and relative earnings in UK manufacturing in 1973', *Economica*, November 1976.

[7] Mulvey, C. and Foster, J. I., 'Occupational earnings in the UK and the effects of collective agreements', *Manchester School*, September 1976.

[8] Phillips, A. W., 'The relation between unemployment and the rate of change of money wage rates in the United Kingdom 1861–1957', *Economica*, November, 1958.

[9] Pissarides, C., 'The role of relative wages and excess demand in the sectoral flow of labour', *Review of Economic Studies*, October 1978.

Comments on Chapters 2 and 3
I *D. Metcalf*

What role do unions play in the process of inflation? Why is unemployment now four times as high as it was in the twenty years following the Second World War? These are the two central issues raised by these two papers. They are considered first. A discussion of the implications for the reform of collective bargaining follows.

Union Power and Equilibrium Unemployment

Unions clearly influence the structure of relative pay. If the earnings of workers with the same education, experience, father's occupation, region and industry are compared, those who are covered by collective bargaining have substantially higher hourly earnings than uncovered workers. And this mark-up in pay associated with union coverage rose from 18 per cent in the 1960s to 28 per cent in the 1970s (Layard, Metcalf and Nickell [8]). Simultaneously the annual rate of earnings inflation more than doubled from 7 per cent in the 1960s to 16 per cent in the 1970s. It is important to analyse the connection between the increased mark-up – partly a reflection of militancy – and the increased inflation.

A monetarist would look no further than the doubling of the annual rate of growth in the money supply from 6 per cent a year in the 1960s to 12 per cent in the 1970s as the cause of the higher wage inflation and would probably argue that the bigger wedge between union and non-union pay reflects only a change in the structure of pay and is irrelevant in explaining inflation. But the monetarist is in a fix. There is no reason why, in the monetary view, unemployment should double or why the share of profits in national income should fall so substantially.

In contrast, the cost push view is more broadly consistent with the data. The average wage tends to rise because of the higher union mark-up. This both raises inflation and, because of higher unit labour costs, boosts unemployment. The growth in the money supply comes about, in part, as the monetary authorities partially validate the higher wages. (Hicks [6]). This process was common to many European countries (Sachs [10]).

The most revealing piece of evidence concerns the share of profits in national income. A number of distinguished monetarists suggested (Economic Radicals [3]) that the acid test for cost-push inflation is to examine the split of national income between pay and profits. So the fall in the share of profits in net domestic income from 13 per cent in the 1960s to 8 per cent in the 1970s is solid evidence of union militancy and cost-push inflation.

Unemployment has quadrupled in a little over a decade but this has not yet been satisfactorily explained. The most sophisticated discussion of the equilibrium rate is by Nickell [9] who sets up a model (for males) with an inflow from employment to unemployment rate and an outflow from unemployment rate. In equilibrium, after controlling for cyclical (demand) factors, inflows equal outflows.

The inflow rate has changed very little in the last two decades but the outflow rate (defined as outflow per month/unemployment) has fallen sharply from 0.71 in 1962 to 0.25 in 1978. Unemployment has risen not because more men become unemployed but because duration lengthens. It is the outflow rate which must be explained.

Cyclical influences are controlled for by the vacancy: employment ratio, the CBI index of the proportion of companies limited by lack of orders, and by a measure of errors in expected rates of wage and price inflation. This latter measure allows for the fact that suppliers of labour and goods may misperceive the distributions of pay and prices facing them which will cause employment to (temporarily) depart from its equilibrium level.

The results show that the equilibrium rate of male unemployment rose from around 2.4 per cent in 1967 (when actual male unemployment was 3.0 per cent, to 5.2 per cent in 1977 (actual male unemployment 7.0 per cent). Changes in the age-composition of the workforce and changes in the extent of vacancy–unemployment mismatching across areas, industries and regions were not responsible. Employment protection legislation and lax enforcement of the work-test (but not a higher unemployment benefit: wage ratio) both played some part in the rise. But the most important single factor is that the outflow rate had a downward trend of 2.4 per cent per quarter, which is mirrored closely by the collapse of our production industries sector.

The Case for Reform

The case for reform of collective bargaining rests on the two facts which emerged above. First, unions play a central role in the process of inflation. Second, equilibrium unemployment is already high by historical postwar standards. So it would be better to find a way of controlling inflation which does not require yet further increases in unemployment. Before discussing this let us scrutinise the case for incomes policy on equity grounds.

Two sets of problems have emerged in the current pay bargaining system. First, there is the familiar prisoners' dilemma concerning nominal wages. All groups would prefer lower inflation. But no one group will, unilaterally, lower its settlement rate unless it is positive all others will do likewise. The second issue is real wages. Labour's share in national income has risen substantially and this has been associated with lower employment both internally and via lower exports and higher imports.

Horizontal equity can certainly give some guidance to wage policy (Layard [7]). If two occupations require similar basic abilities, pay relativities are correct if there is no more pressure of individuals wishing to enter one occupation than the other. This is indeed precisely what would happen if bargaining was truly free (i.e. atomistic). But unions, on occasion monopsonies, and the extensive public sector all ensure that bargaining is not atomistic. An incomes policy could certainly help achieve horizontal equity in public sector pay settlements yet institutions charged with fixing public sector pay either have horizontal equity explicitly excluded in their terms of reference or give scant attention to job queues when coming to their findings.

It is clearly impossible to have an objective test of vertical equity. Agreement on fair wage differentials between occupations requiring different basic abilities is out of the question. Nevertheless the majority of the pay policies of the 1970s had a notional redistributive role because they contained a flat rate component like £6, or £1 + 4 per cent, a week. Such policies were singularly unsuccessful. The dispersion of pay hardly changed in the 1970s and, in particular, pay policy was breached more comprehensively by the relatively high paid than the relatively low paid. Indeed, the 1975–7 evidence suggests it was *only* the lowest decile of the pay distribution which abided by the policy. Redistribution is not a good reason for advocating reform of collective bargaining. Such attempts at equity are better left to social security and the tax system. But an incomes policy which raised employment for a given rate of inflation would certainly have redistributive implications. In any year 70 per cent of weeks of unemployment are accounted for by 3 per cent of the workforce (Disney [2]). So any reform which reduced the risk of unemployment would have a favourable effect on distribution.

Reform of collective bargaining would permit higher employment for a given rate of inflation. In the short run it is generally agreed that if price rises are too high a lower growth of monetary demand is necessary to reduce inflation (Artis and Miller [1], p. 60). If money wage increases and unit labour costs are rising rapidly lower monetary demand will reduce employment either directly or indirectly through a squeeze on profits and therefore (labour-using) investment. If a pay policy reduces the growth of nominal wages, employment is more likely to be maintained.

In the long run the economy is constantly subject to shocks, like oil price rises or bumper world harvests, which require real consumption to fall or rise. It is easier to make the necessary adjustments if some agreement exists on pay or if the government is prepared to take some responsibility for the level of pay settlements. By contrast, the current wage bargaining systems responds to unfavourable shocks by decreasing employment either directly or via a profits squeeze rather than by decelerating real wages. Monetarist economists should not be against reforms which permit us to remain at the equilibrium unemployment rate while reducing inflation because such reforms are analogous to the case made out for indexation by Friedman [4].

Sachs [10] has shown how after the oil crisis of 1973–4 the downward resistance of real wages in Europe and Japan accounts for the persistence of the unemployment in those areas. By contrast, real wages adjusted speedily in the US and employment held up. The higher labour share in manufacturing in the 1970s was an important source of the relative slowdown in the growth of manufacturing output.

This link is particularly important in an open economy like Britain. Nominal wages, W, must be related to the prices of goods and services produced by workers. In the recent literature the *product wage* has been emphasised (W/P_v where P_v is the deflator for value added at factor cost). But in an open economy, where P_x is the price of exports, the export-product wage, W/P_x, is relevant. If W rises and firms respond by raising P_x then they become uncompetitive. If they respond by holding P_x constant they suffer a profits squeeze. The importance of the export–product/wage ratio can be shown by breaking it down into its constituent parts (this formulation was suggested to me by Nickell):

$$W/P_x = W/P_{v\,(UK)} \cdot P_{v(UK)}/P_x$$

The first term on the right hand side is the familiar product wage which influences aggregate supply. The second term allows for shifts in the demand curve. Both those who see wage inflation as the dominant problem and those who believe the balance of payments is the key to economic performance should surely be in favour of reform of collective bargaining which reduces W/P_x compared with what it otherwise would be.

Collective bargaining does need to be transformed. Reform should concentrate on the macroeconomic question of how to keep near – rather than above – the equilibrium rate of unemployment in the face of (short-run) reductions in monetary demand and (long-run) shocks. A successful pay policy represents a favourable supply shift (or shock) which reduces the price at which firms are prepared to supply a given output. So for a given growth in nominal income it would make possible a simultaneous reduction in inflation and increase in real output and employment. The authorities can then decelerate the rate of monetary growth without causing higher unemployment (Gordon [5]).

Batchelor *et al.* in Chapter 3 persistently present microeconomic reform of, for example, industrial relations and monopoly legislation as an alternative to the reform of collective bargaining. I believe they are complementary and I concur with most of their micro suggestions. But what kind of collective bargaining reform is required in order to combat inflation and shocks without reducing employment?

The evidence in favour of the following propositions is strong: (a) firms, unions and individuals are motivated by selfish behaviour; and

(b) redistribution is best achieved through fiscal and social security policy rather than wage policy. This suggests that reform should not attempt to get voluntary agreement and cooperation. It would be nice if we could get it but, alas, the world is not like that. Phelps Brown emphasises how our unions have changed from being part of the labour movement to US style business unions. So the realistic policy is to leave parties free to strike their own bargains but to modify their behaviour by taxation of excessive wage increases or by the permit plan. In such systems there is no reason for conflict between unions and governments, and employment can be sustained in the face of contraction in the rate of monetary growth to achieve lower inflation.

References

[1] Artis, M. J. and Miller, M. H., 'Inflation, real wages and the terms of trade', in J. K. Bowers, ed., *Inflation, Development and Integration: Essays in Honour of A. J. Brown*, Leeds University Press, 1979.

[2] Disney, R., 'Recurrent spells and the concentration of unemployment in Great Britain', *Economic Journal*, March 1979.

[3] Economic Radicals. Letter to the Prime Minister, 1974.

[4] Friedman, M., 'Using escalators to fight inflation', *Fortune*, July 1974.

[5] Gordon, R., 'Comments and discussion on L. Seidman, Tax based incomes policies', *Brookings Papers on Economic Activity*, No. 2, 1978.

[6] Hicks, J., 'The economic foundations of wage policy', *Economic Journal*, September 1955.

[7] Layard, R., 'Wage policy and the redistribution of income', Colston Lecture 1979, Centre for Labour Economics, Discussion Paper 47, LSE, March 1979.

[8] Layard, R., Metcalf, D. and Nickell, S., 'The effect of collective bargaining on relative and absolute wages', *British Journal of Industrial Relations*, November 1978.

[9] Nickell, S., 'What has happened to equilibrium unemployment in Britain?' Revised version of AUTE Paper, May 1980.

[10] Sachs, J., 'Wages, profits and macroeconomic adjustment: a comparative study', *Brookings Papers on Economic Activity*, No. 2, 1979.

II *P. Lilley*

A brief discussion paper must inevitably concentrate on points of disagreement rather than agreement – even though this discussant agrees with the fundamental arguments of both papers. In particular I concur with the central conclusion that the reason for seeking a reform of the British pay bargaining system is not because it causes inflation but because it causes unemployment to be unnecessarily high.

Unfortunately both papers assume that it is purely in raising the *natural* (or equilibrium) rate of unemployment that the wage bargaining system is damaging. Neither makes any reference to disequilibrium or transitional unemployment. Yet it is surely arguable that aspects of our system of collective bargaining tend also to exacerbate unemployment (a) by hindering the adjustment to shocks and (b) by itself inducing additional shocks from time to time. In other words: (a) under our wage fixing framework, the speed at which workers are priced back into work after the wages structure has got out of line with money demand is slower than need be; (b) the wage bargaining process can cause the wage structure to get out of line with monetary demand more frequently than need be. Another disappointment common to both papers (though probably attributable to their terms of reference) is that one (Chapter 3) tells us little and the other (Chapter 2) nothing about the precise features of the wage bargaining system they hold responsible for the high natural rate of unemployment. Consequently their proposals are either imprecise (extending anti-monopoly legislation to trades unions) or non-existent. This is particularly unfortunate as Chapter 4 fails to unearth anything of the general type these two authors would like except the present government's very limited proposals to reform union power and the CBI's proposed strike insurance scheme.

Chapter 2

Scott has a neat and original model to demonstrate the need for reform. The model is politico-economic rather than purely economic. It can be summarised as a series of propositions – with each of which I would take issue.

Proposition 1: the electorate believe that inflation can be curbed by allowing unemployment to increase. Similarly the electorate believes unemployment can be reduced by allowing inflation to speed up.

I am not certain that the electorate acknowledges any trade-off between unemployment and inflation. In this they are wiser than those economists who still believe in the Phillips curve. Unemployment can logically only be kept below the natural level by *unanticipated* inflation. It is paradoxical to suppose an electorate could consciously choose unanticipated inflation in order to keep unemployment down. Electors are in the same position as a man with hiccups who needs a surprise slap to cure him: if he asked someone to slap him it would not be a surprise. In my experience electors blame government for both inflation and unemployment and perceive no trade-off between the two.

Proposition 2: the higher the rate of inflation the more unemployment the electorate will tolerate.

This might be true if the electorate perceived such a trade-off. Even if that is not the case the substance of the proposition could be justified by the following reasoning. Government popularity is inversely related to both inflation and unemployment. So the government can minimise its unpopularity in the short term by reducing unemployment at the expense of a delayed increase in inflation. If there is no long-term trade-off between inflation and unemployment any government which seeks short-term popularity by manipulating the short-term trade-off will reduce its popularity in the longer term – and *vice versa.*

Proposition 3: the level of unemployment needed to stop inflation accelerating is called the natural rate.

I have paraphrased slightly the words of the paper. They surely reflect a common misunderstanding of the natural rate concept? A better definition of the natural rate is the rate which emerges when monetary inflation is fully anticipated.

Also, it is sad to see any economist perpetuate the myth that 'unemployment stops inflation'. Unemployment may be the usually unavoidable temporary consequence of policies of stopping inflation but it is not the cure itself. The reason inflation stops is the obverse of why it starts, that is monetary growth stops. Monetary restraint may or may not feed through to prices via a changed level of unemployment depending on whether the change in monetary policy is anticipated or not. To say 'unemployment cures inflation' is like saying hunger pangs cure obesity. Hunger pangs may accompany a diet (until the stomach has adjusted) but diet is the cause of slimness. However, for the purposes of Scott's model my preferred definition of the natural rate will do as well as his.

Proposition 4: inflation must reach a level at which the natural rate can be politically tolerated for inflation to be stabilised.

Proposition 5: the natural rate of unemployment is likely to be much higher than the rate of unemployment we have experienced so far.

Given the correct definition of the natural rate two conclusions follow. First, if we have ever had a period when the actual level of inflation was in line with that anticipated in wage bargains, the natural rate of unemployment would then have emerged as the measured rate. Second, if the actual level of inflation has ever fallen short of the anticipated level the rate of unemployment would have risen above the natural rate.

Since it is pretty certain that actual and anticipated rates of inflation duck and weave about each other it is pretty certain that the actual level of unemployment has bobbed above and below the natural rate. Indeed the best guesstimate of the natural rate must be the average level of unemployment recorded over a couple of business cycles. Such guesstimates certainly indicate that the natural rate has been rising. It may well continue to do so. But there is no reason to suppose that the natural rate of unemployment at present is any higher than the actual rate. The transitional rate of unemployment experienced while inflation is being curbed may be substantially higher than the natural rate.

Proposition 6: if the natural rate is higher than the level of unemployment yet experienced it follows from the previous propositions that the level of inflation necessary to make it politically tolerable will be higher than anything yet experienced.

In other words, inflation must reach an unprecedented rate before people will tolerate the level of unemployment compatible with preventing inflation accelerating even further. Scott's model suggests that the politico-economic system will be stable, (that is the government could get re-elected on unchanged policies) only at levels of inflation and unemployment which many people think would make any government unelectable! In effect Scott accepts that his stable state is unstable since he goes on to argue that something must be done to reduce the natural rate of unemployment.

Proposition 7: the natural rate is so high because of the operation of the wage bargaining system.

Unfortunately no hint is given as to what aspects of the wage-bargaining system raise the natural rate.

Proposition 8: Since all policies aimed at reducing the natural rate by direct action (incomes policies, import controls plus reflation, direct employment subsidies reliance on growth of competitive market sector, and encouragement of co-operatives) are flawed, radical reform of the wage-bargaining system is needed.

I wholeheartedly agree with this conclusion. Yet the process of argument by elimination is surely unsatisfactory. After all Benn argues rather similarly that 'everything else has been tried and failed so we must try socialism'. It surely ought to be necessary to argue more positively that a pet solution will work rather than to leave it as a residual.

Chapter 3

The Batchelor, Bendle, Griffiths paper (henceforward known as 'the BBG paper) treats the phrase 'the wage bargaining system' as a euphemism for the licensing of union monopoly power. Their thesis, like Scott's, can be reduced to a set of propositions.

Proposition 1: union monopoly power does not cause inflation:

Proposition 2: the primary impact of union monopoly power is on relative wages.

I suspect that union monopoly power has more serious consequences. First it often shields a reduction in productivity (by overmanning, demarcation rules etc). Union wages may or may not be out of line with the reduced marginal productivity of union members.

Second, union immunities discourage fixed investment since investors stand to lose the economic rent of any fixed investment to the labour force. (Investors cannot even protect themselves by entering a binding contract with the union.) Reduced investment also results in lower labour productivity.

Third, union monopoly renders the labour market less stable since in many sectors there is no clear optimal trade-off between wages and job-security. The trade-off is often between the relative wage and the political sustainability of that relative wage. The latter is immeasurable. Consequently unions will normally work on the basis of established rules of thumb about their position in the pecking order until some adventurous official causes a change. This can spark off a chain of disturbances which may result in a large section of the labour force seeking wages incompatible with the prevailing structure of demand.

Fourth, conversely it follows that if the more monopolistic unions do set wages on the basis of established rules wages may be insensitive to changes in relative productivity.

Proposition 3: competitively determined relative wages are crucial to the efficient allocation of labour.

Proposition 4: however, monopolistically determined relative wages give false signals and so suspend the usefulness of the price mechanism as a means of allocating labour.

Surely it is not the monopoly price 'signal' which does the damage, but the restriction on entry necessary to uphold the monopoly. The monopoly price truthfully reflects what is happening. It surely cannot be argued that monopolistic prices are less efficient than competitive prices at shifting resources from declining to growing industries. Of course monopoly prices result from a suboptimal allocation of resources. But monopoly prices will if anything be excessively efficient in reallocating resources between expanding and declining sectors. For example if coal miners are paid a wage above the market clearing rate that will make it all the easier to attract labour should the coal board decide to expand.

A monopolistic wage gives an all too true signal of cost to the employer. This may well result in reallocation of some labour away from that sector. Indeed union resistance to declining relative wages in declining industries would expedite reallocation. The contrast between union monopoly wages and wages in the competitive sector also signals to new employers the possibility of undercutting the temporary unionised monopoly.

Throughout the analysis BBG talk of labour allocation as if it consisted of workers seeking jobs: it also consists of employers seeking workers. They also talk of rationing and search procedures as if they represented market imperfections which are the consequence of union power. This is the deleterious consequence of taking the perfect economy model as a normative standard to judge the real world. Searching and rationing are mostly the inevitable and desirable consequences of the enormous variety of different jobs and the uniqueness of each employee.

Proposition 5: empirical evidence confirms that changes in relative wages are less effective in allocating labour in the highly unionised sectors than in the less unionised sectors.

I am more suspicious of the empirical evidence than I am of the underlying theory. The direction of causality is always ambiguous in market data. This is the regrettable consequence of the market's most desirable feature – the mutual responsiveness of everything to everything else. The relationship between relative earnings and relative employment in the non-unionised sector does not necessarily support BBG's contention that people are recruited in response to small relative price changes. It might mean that in declining competitive industries employers shed jobs or go out of business if they cannot pay the competitive wage. Likewise the relationship in the highly unionised sector could reflect the resistance of unions to job losses even if this means foregoing some of their earnings advantage. The responsiveness of recruitment to union wage policies need not come into it.

Proposition 6: consequently the government should enforce monopoly legislation against the exercise of union power.

Unfortunately it is not made clear what types of union behaviour would be prohibited. The analogy drawn between firms and unions suggests that unions would be prohibited from fixing industry-wide wage levels, but would be permitted to negotiate agreements plant by plant or firm by firm. This change is possibly desirable in principle but of little relevance in practice. The major component of pay is already determined by plant or firm bargaining in nearly all industries which are not monopolised. In the the monopolised industries – essentially the public sector industries – the situation would not be altered by restricting bargaining to a single employer since there is only one. In any case in the public sector union power derives largely from the monopolistic organisation of the employer (and access to the exchequer) rather than from union immunities.

Monopoly power is by definition dependent on restricting entry. Except where unions (and similar bodies) do control entry – e.g. through craft apprenticeships, the Dock Labour Board, stock exchange examinations – unions cannot permanently raise wages above the marginal productivity of labour. Nearly a quarter of UK output is exported. Probably an equal proportion is subject to import competition. So in at least half the economy the labour force – whether unionised or not – is competing directly with foreign labour. In such circumstances unions have negligible power over the market. The harm that unions can cause outside the public sector is therefore mainly (as mentioned earlier) in reducing the marginal productivity of union members (through restrictive practices and discouraging investment), through impeding adjustment to 'shocks' to the structure of relative wages and, occasionally, in initiating such shocks.

That is a rather more limited indictment of union power than is implied in both papers discussed above. Given that most economists would consider this limited indictment to verge towards understatement of the harm done by unions it is not clear why so few advocate dismantling union privileges or even outlawing unions entirely. Presumably a sense of 'bourgeois guilt' motivates many economists to withhold criticism from institutions which are identified with the manual working class.

However, there is a rather better reason for resisting the conclusion that unions are of no value to their members. In fact unions serve a very valuable role for their members. The union role is analogous to that played by the estate agent for someone selling his house. The estate agent uses his knowledge of the market to seek the best price compatible with sale in a desired period. Similarly the union seeks to obtain the highest wage compatible with the continuing prosperity of the firm. We should look for proposals to enhance this positive aspect of union bargaining whilst mitigating the harmful effects unions may also cause.

4 An Array of Proposals
*F. T. Blackaby**

The discussion of 'incomes policies' has long been vitiated by the assumption that 'incomes policy' is a single thing, whereas in fact there is a wide array of very different proposals for changes in the pay bargaining system. This chapter presents a survey of these proposals. It concerns itself primarily – but not entirely – with proposals for government action, since economic policy is a government responsibility. The classification of these various proposals cannot be wholly tidy; there are a great many elements which turn up in different combinations in the various plans. The discussion which follows distinguishes seven such elements.

There are proposals which emerge from the idea of a 'Social Contract' or 'concerted action'; 'traditional' proposals for a norm, with exceptions; proposals for the synchronisation of pay settlements (or compression of the bargaining round); and for changes particularly in the public sector. There are proposals to alter the balance of bargaining power – either to weaken the power of trade unions or to strengthen the power of employers. There is a group of tax-based or market-based incomes policies. Finally, there is a set of policies which might be labelled more radical, implying changes which go well beyond those which have previously been tried.

Objectives

Virtually all proposals start from the assumption that there is some connection between the pay bargaining system and inflation. Some state the objective simply as that of reducing the rate at which prices rise by reducing the rate at which money earnings rise, and others

* The section on tax-based incomes policies in particular makes extensive use of the work of M. P. Fogarty [12] and also of a number of publications by D. Colander [6] and [7].

as that of reducing the unemployment cost of an anti-inflationary policy. The difference is not material.

The actual price objective which proposers had in mind has changed in recent decades. Twenty years ago it did not seem quixotic to have stable prices as an objective; indeed one of the early texts in this area came out in favour of falling prices [9]. Current statements of the objective in this country tend to be less ambitious – for example that the rise in prices should be brought down below 5 per cent in three years [23].

Some of those who put forward proposals have other objectives as well as the anti-inflationary one. Many consider that the present system is excessively disputatious, so that one of the objectives is to produce a system in which pay questions are settled with less resort to industrial action. A number of authors suggest that as inflation accelerates, so it is likely that there will be more disputes, since it becomes increasingly dangerous to be left behind; if this is so, then any policy which is successful in bringing down the rate at which prices are rising will also tend to reduce the number of disputes. There is a third possible objective. Whereas most proposals are simply concerned to get the size of the average money earnings increase down, some are in favour of a change to a system which, in their judgement, would produce relativities which were 'fairer' than those which we have at the moment. Thus Aubrey Jones declares himself 'concerned ... with the inevitability of a degree of inequality, a degree different from the one we have, and with the need therefore to make that degree intelligible to reason, so that society can cohere better together' [15]. Wootton makes the same point [24]. The proposals of those who simply want to bring down the average number, and leave relativities as they are, will obviously differ from the proposals of those who have the additional objective of altering the relativities which the present system produces.

The 'Social Contract': the Forum

Introduction

The 'Social Contract' approach is essentially European (Chapter 8); the institutional structure in the United States is not appropriate for policies of this type. The object could be said to be that of 'internalising' the trade union movement, so that it accepted responsibility for the macroeconomic consequences of its bargaining actions in exchange for some say in the general conduct of economic policy. This policy approach is more likely to be successful if pay negotiations are relatively centralised. This has the advantage that the public interest becomes visible. In negotiations covering only a single branch of industry, it is always possible for the negotiators to preserve the illusion that the result of their negotiations affects only the workers in enterprises within the branch concerned. In central negotiations, general economic considerations can hardly be kept out.

If a government prefers to encourage a system where the bargaining in each small unit is conducted only with reference to the prosperity of that unit, and without reference to the state of the economy or to settlements reached elsewhere, then obviously there is not much scope for any kind of Social Contract approach. However, it is not easy to imagine the disappearance of national agreements in the public sector; and there appears to be some tendency for large private companies to raise the level of bargaining and to move away from a reliance on single-establishment arrangements (Chapter 6).

A Social Contract approach is one which cannot easily be run simultaneously with policies whose purpose is to limit trade union power. In such circumstances, trade union cooperation is unlikely to be forthcoming: thus when Mr Heath was looking for a Social Contract in 1972, one of the conditions which the trade union negotiators advanced was that the Industrial Relations Act should in effect be suspended.

One of the objections to an approach of this kind is that power is being taken away from democratically elected assemblies and is being given to interest groups; thus the CBI proposal in this field deliberately suggests some Parliamentary link. However, Social Contract discussions can be seen rather as attempts to impose constraints on the powers which interest groups outside Parliament at present hold; if any liberties are infringed, they are not so much the liberties of Parliament as the liberties of employers and trade unions.

Current proposals

The idea of 'concerted action' has been implicit in a good deal of government policy towards incomes since the war, although the term 'Social Contract' was not much used before 1974. In 1964 the Secretary of State for Economic Affairs, George Brown, persuaded the TUC and employers' associations to sign a joint statement of intent on productivity, prices and incomes. In 1972 Mr Heath spent a long negotiating summer in an attempt to establish a Social Contract with the TUC, but failed. The period when the term 'Social Contract' was explicitly used was 1974–9, when the negotiations were exclusively between the government and the TUC in an *ad hoc* kind of way.

Towards the end of the Labour government's period in office suggestions began to come forward for a more formal approach. The CBI, both in June 1977 and in February 1979, proposed a national economic forum with links into Parliament [8]. A national forum was also included in the pamphlet put forward for discussion by twelve members of the TUC General Council [1]. The same idea was included in the joint statement by the TUC and the government published in February 1979 [23]. The idea of 'some kind of forum' was also mooted in a Conservative Central Office document published in October 1977 [18]. It is something of a rarity to find the same policy proposal turning up in a CBI document, a joint TUC and Labour government document and a Conservative Party document.

All these publications agree that the suggested forum should discuss the economy and the economic prospects; presumably, if such an exercise were to be meaningful, it would have to include alternative forecasts of the consequences for prices, output and employment which would follow from various assumptions about the rate of increase in money earnings. However, from then on the proposals differ: some of them are very nervous of a 'norm' emerging, while others consider that this would be the main purpose of such a forum. The TUC–Labour government document avers that there is no precise arithmetical relationship between price rises of 5 per cent, a growth rate of 3 per cent and a particular level of pay settlements. (It might be argued that it is quite possible to say, with some degree of precision, that such an outcome would require a rise in money earnings of 8 per cent, unless import prices were moving substantially out of line, or unless it were desired either to increase or reduce profit-margins.) Both this document and the CBI document are opposed to the emergence of a norm or going rate. On the other hand, *A Better Way* and the proposals of Aubrey Jones and Wootton, for example, consider that the discussion of the economy must end up with a norm. The Conservative Party document is ambiguous, pointing to the dangers involved, but admitting that 'the government must come to *some* conclusions about the likely scope for pay increases if excess public expenditure or large-scale unemployment is to be avoided; and this estimate cannot be concealed from the representatives of the employers and unions whom it is consulting' [18].

If, in any new procedure, trade unions are invited to commit themselves in some way to wage restraint, they are likely to want something in exchange for that commitment. It can indeed be argued that if trade unions collectively accept lower increases in money earnings, this does not (in the medium term) imply any reduction in the rise in real earnings, but rather the contrary; there has been no real sacrifice and consequently no compensation is needed. None the less, the trade unions would feel that they were being asked to give up a freedom which they now possess. It is certainly possible for tax reductions to be offered in exchange for effective undertakings on wage restraint, so that a deceleration in the rise in money earnings does not necessarily mean a fall in the real post-tax wage. There are a number of proposals which suggest some degree of profit-sharing, or alternatively an extension of industrial democracy. The most radical suggestion here is that of Jay, suggesting a change in company law which gives ownership and ultimate control of enterprises to the people employed by them. This, in his view, is the only way of eliminating the existing alienation of the workforce from the objectives of the firms which employ them [13].

The Norm, with Exceptions

This has been the basic form of most British attempts at institutional change in the postwar period; many current proposals involve setting a norm and many involve some process of expressing judgement on exceptions to that norm. The problems to which these proposals give rise have been fairly fully explored.

The problem of setting the norm itself is more political than economic. Obviously it ought to be a figure such that, after the usual leakage, the rate of inflation would be brought down: the question for the government is to decide how ambitious it should try to be. In the early incomes policies, when the rate of inflation was much lower than it is now, the norm was set at a figure designed to bring about price stability. In the 1970s the price target became less ambitious, and the problem was to find a number which would stick.

It has been argued, for example, that the Labour government's last norm at the end of 1978 – of 5 per cent – was too ambitious, and that a figure of, say, 8 per cent might have been more successful; there is of course no way of establishing whether this is true or not. The norm has normally been a percentage; but in 1975 it was a lump sum for everyone, and on other occasions there has been a lump sum component.

There is a certain sense in which a norm is inevitably implicit in any anti-inflationary policy. If the government says that excessive pay settlements will lead to large-scale unemployment, then it is under some obligation to answer a questioner who asks what the rise in average earnings would have to be if increases in unemployment were to be avoided. The government cannot avoid taking a view about wage and salary increases in the tax-dependent public services; it also has the problem of wage increases in those nationalised industries which are powerful monopolies, notably gas and electricity. In the absence of government intervention, either on earnings or on prices, those industries are in a position to concede relatively large wage and salary awards, and increase prices to meet them.

The disadvantages of a norm are, first, that it tends to become a minimum for everyone; secondly, it inhibits the adjustment processes which should give relatively large increases to those whose skills are scarce, and which should attract labour from less profitable to more profitable firms and industries. A warning was given about the first of these disadvantages as long ago as 1958, in the *First Report* of the Council on Prices, Productivity and Incomes [9]. Experience since then has suggested that this is a valid objection; it was for this reason that in a number of the stages of the 1964–9 Labour government's incomes policy there was a nil norm. One of the current proposals suggests that the norm should be set significantly below the average rate of increase in money earnings which the government hopes to achieve.

It is not easy to establish whether in fact successive incomes policies did interfere substantially with the desirable processes of labour redistribution. The alternative to an incomes policy is not a world in which relativities are simply determined by demand for and supply of labour; under free collective bargaining the big increases do not necessarily go to occupations or industries which are short of labour, but rather to those groups which, for one reason or another, are in a powerful bargaining position. Under the 1964–9 incomes policy, the reallocation of labour was one of the permissible exceptions – 'where it is essential in the national interest to secure (or prevent) a change in the distribution of manpower, and a pay increase would be both necessary and effective for this purpose'. This particular criterion, although it was available to the National Board for Prices and Incomes, was in fact hardly ever used. The NBPI tended to take the view that, if there were insufficient workers with a particular skill required for a particular job, a short-term increase in pay was not the best way of increasing the numbers available; the problem was better dealt with by improving long-term prospects or by an extension of training.

One attempt to meet the problem of flexibility was to have a norm which did not apply to every individual pay increase, but which was: 'the maximum amount by which the average pay per head of the group may be increased in a twelve month period'. Once the total sum had been established it could be distributed as the negotiators decided – favouring one group rather than another if the negotiators so wished.

Exceptions

Whereas short-term policies, or highly informal and loose policies, can avoid considering the problem of exceptions, policies which are intended to last for some time cannot avoid this issue. This is true not only for statutory policies, but also for voluntary policies which depend for their effect on influencing public opinion through the judgements of bodies similar to the NBPI. The main criteria for exceptional pay increases which have been put forward in past incomes policies were low pay, the reallocation of labour and productivity.

For low pay the criterion was phrased as follows – 'where there was general recognition that existing wage or salary levels are too low to maintain a reasonable standard of living' [11]. However, the general experience of incomes policies was that it was difficult to shift the relative position of the low paid. There is no evidence that during periods of incomes policy the dispersion of gross weekly earnings, for either manual or non-manual workers, was significantly altered. It can be argued that incomes policies should not be used for this objective. If in the government's view the relative position of the low paid should be improved, then fiscal means should be employed.

The scarcity of labour, it has been noted, was a criterion which was not extensively used in 1964–9. However, there are those who argue that, if there are to be criteria for exceptions, then this is the only one that matters. (The issue turns up, even in the absence of any incomes policy, in the exercise of comparability judgements for pay in the tax-dependent public sector.) It is a criterion which can be used more easily for some jobs and occupations than for others. When a local authority finds that it has a waiting-list of people who want to come and work 'on the bins' but is unable to fill vacancies for carpenters, then it can reasonably conclude that its relativities are wrong. Such judgements are much more difficult for the professions: school leavers or university graduates deciding on a particular profession do not do so on the basis of a comprehensive comparison of probable lifetime earnings which would arise from the various possibilities open to them, and the relative position of a particular profession could probably worsen for a number of years before a falling-off in the quality of applicants indicated that something was wrong. There is the further point that it is not easy to turn relative numbers of job applicants into a quantitative judgement about the size of the income gap which should exist between two professions or occupations.

The criterion of productivity has been one which has in the past led to a great many problems. It was recognised from early on that any general stability of prices would be a combination of falling prices for the products of industries where productivity could rise rapidly, and rising prices for the products of industries where the productivity potential was much less. Clearly it was inappropriate that the whole of the benefits of increases in productivity, in industries where it was rising rapidly, should accrue to the employees. This is one of the inflationary dangers of 'atomised' free collective bargaining: that high wage increases work through from high productivity to low productivity industries – since the gap between the pay of, say, a computer operator in an oil company and a computer operator in British Rail cannot be allowed to widen indefinitely. The initial principle, in the early incomes policies, was that employees had to make a direct contribution by accepting more exacting work or by a major change in working practices, and that some of the benefits should accrue to the community in the form of lower prices. Productivity agreements proved in fact to be one of the major loopholes in the 1964–9 incomes policy; particularly towards the end of the period, the NBPI recommendations – for example, that productivity gains should come before the additional payment – were extensively ignored. Because of this experience, the productivity clauses in the Conservative government's Stage III policy had written into them the requirement that payment should follow and not precede the productivity gains.

Wootton suggests that exceptional treatment would be justified: first, on grounds of equity – that workers were receiving lower pay than others engaged in similar work, or were earning less than they would be entitled to if their work was valued in accordance with some accepted procedure; secondly, on grounds of economic necessity – that it was necessary to attract further recruits by the prospect of higher wages. Claims based on traditional linkages or on *a priori* assumptions that the claimants are entitled to retain their previous relative positions would not be admissible [24].

A relativities board

Any suggested policy which embodies, or implies, a norm with exceptions needs a relativities board of some kind for considering the exceptions. Those who have discussed the functions of such a board agree on two propositions. The first is that it should not be bound by excessively tight rules constraining its decisions. A prime example of the folly of such an arrangement was the experience of the Pay Board when it was trying to find some way of paying the miners more in the winter of 1973–4; it went through a whole exercise to see whether miners' bath-time could be used, within the rules which it had been given, to produce more money. Certainly a relativities board should have some general criteria, but it should be allowed some elasticity in their use – and it should also probably be prepared to make some compromises with bargaining power. It is too much to expect that one can move from a world in which bargaining power is very important, to a world in which it is not important at all, in one jump.

Secondly, a number of commentators suggest that there should not be a large number of different bodies, each engaged in trying to establish the appropriate relativity for a particular group; such bodies usually become identified with the interests of that group.

This particularly concerns the regulation of pay in the public sector.

There are other questions about the function of such a board. Should the same board deal with both prices and incomes? Aubrey Jones argued that it should, because of the desirability of tracing the chain effect of a pay increase on prices and of a price or profit increase on pay [14].

On sanctions it is, first of all, generally agreed that it would be very difficult for any length of time to operate any policy in this field if the trade unions were strongly opposed to it – though their tacit acquiescence might be sufficient. This implies a strong bias towards voluntary arrangements. The difficulty here is that the only voluntary policies in the past which have proved powerful – and that only in the short term – have been those which have been very simple: a single figure for everyone with no exceptions. Voluntary policies with extensive provisions for exceptions have had little effect. The main example here is the period from mid-1974 to mid-1975 when, in spite of a generally agreed Social Contract, the rise in earnings reached 30 per cent.

The statutory policies which have been efficacious have also been simple ones: the most effective ones have been the short-term freezes. Further, although these policies have technically included sanctions, these sanctions have not been invoked. No trade union or individual worker has been penalised for transgressing an incomes policy norm. Technically, in the period of the Price Commission under the Conservative government, if a company conceded wage increases above the agreed norm, the whole of the wage increase was to be disallowed by the Price Commission. There is no recorded case in which this did, in fact, happen.

The extant proposals are divided on the question of sanctions. Powerful sanctions are implied by some of the tax-based incomes policies – those which would tax away the whole of any 'excess' increase in income. The Meade proposal suggests the following sanctions against those who go on strike in opposition to an arbitral award of the kind which he outlines: any supplementary benefits paid would have subsequently to be refunded; tax refunds could be postponed; the striker could be treated as having terminated his contract of employment, and could lose his accumulated right to redundancy payments; certain legal immunities could be removed.

Synchronisation

The proposal that pay settlements should be synchronised, is, conceptually, a straightforward proposal. It turns up in a number of schemes. For some (for example, that of Lydall) it is an essential prerequisite. In most tax-based schemes it would make for much simpler administration. Basnett has suggested a greater degree of synchronisation in public sector settlements [2]. In the TUC–Labour government document of February 1979 it gets only a passing mention – 'in certain areas there may be advantages in synchronisation of pay bargaining, although we doubt whether it would be practicable to introduce this overnight generally' [23].

The CBI document [8] sets out the arguments for 'compression of the bargaining round' most fully. These are:

(a) The economic effects of a general level of pay increases would be much clearer. With settlements dispersed as at present it is hard for people to see the connections between pay, prices and jobs.
(b) A shorter round would enable bargaining to take place against a more consistent economic background. There would be less incentive for groups to exceed the going rate because circumstances had changed. Most important, there would be less pressure to leapfrog.
(c) Compression might encourage bargaining to be more responsive to changes in government fiscal policies and the views of a central forum. This would especially be so if dominant groups of the market sector began the round. Smaller groups would be less able to bid up the general level of settlements.
(d) Industrial stoppages over pay would be compressed into a shorter, foreseeable period. This would reduce the present year-round disruption.

The document envisages a gradual change, first to a five-month period from 1 November to 1 April, and later to a three-month period beginning on 1 January. It sets out a bargaining calendar:

May/June	Economic forum takes evidence following the budget and experience of the previous pay round.
July/August	Publication of annual economic review. Possible Green Paper. Parliamentary debate.

September/October	The CBI, TUC and Party conferences consider the review.
November/December	Main bargaining period begins, with first settlements operating from 1 November. Government decides cash limits for public sector, and outlines links between pay developments and the next budget.
February	Budget representations by CBI, TUC and others, as at present.
March	Tax-dependent public services bargain. April settlement date to coincide with start of financial year.
April	Budget, taking full account of pay developments.
May	Work on next annual review begins.

This proposal is probably not compatible with the proposal of those who want to return to a world of atomised bargaining, where individual units do well or badly according to the profitability of the individual plant or firm. The more synchronised the pay bargaining period, the greater the likelihood of a 'going rate' emerging.

Secondly, it is probably a proposal which goes along more with Social Contract ideas than with the ideas of those who put stress on weakening trade union power. A concentrated period of bargaining and settlements would probably strengthen, rather than weaken, trade union power. If a large number of negotiations are in progress at the same time, and if they break down at more or less the same time and strikes are called, then the effect of those overlapping strikes would be to reinforce each other. If there is to some extent a co-operative approach between employers and trade unions to the problems of the economy, then synchronised bargaining could have a moderating effect, as the CBI argument suggests. If, on the other hand, there is something approaching a power struggle between the trade unions and the government, in those circumstances synchronised pay bargaining could have the opposite consequence.

The Public Sector

The government, whether or not it intervenes in any way in pay fixing in the rest of the economy, inevitably has a responsibility for pay in the public sector: a number of proposals for changes have been put forward. A distinction is commonly made between the nationalised industries and the tax-dependent public sector; the CBI, for example, argued that nationalised industries should be treated as part of the market sector (although the fact that some nationalised industries are virtual monopolies presents certain problems). For the tax-dependent public sector, some arguments have been put forward for a greater degree of decentralisation and local negotiation, with individual local authorities and regional health boards fixing their own wage and salary scales. Other proposals tend in the opposite direction, to bring about a greater degree of 'equal pay for equal work' throughout the public sector. The following are some of the proposals put forward by the CBI [8], by Basnett [2], and by Aubrey Jones [14]:

(a) The unions in local government, the Health Service, and the industrial and non-industrial civil service should work more closely together, in a TUC Public Services Committee (Basnett [2]).
(b) There should be moves towards synchronisation of principal settlement dates: 'most ... manual agreements are operative from late Autumn ... but most white-collar operative dates are between April and July' (Basnett [2]).
(c) Settlements in the tax-dependent public sector should come at the end of the wages round, and consequently should follow the pattern which had been set by the market sector (CBI [8]).
(d) The various review bodies which exist in the public sector should be amalgamated, or at least brought together under some kind of general umbrella. As it is, they inevitably become advocates for the particular group with which they are concerned. If a more general relativities board of some kind were established, then these various public sector review bodies should be brought within the ambit of that board (Jones [14]; Basnett [2]). There were some differences of opinion about the function of this amalgamated review body. Some considered that it should simply provide information, and then the parties concerned should bargain about the actual awards. Others considered that the review body should make recommendations, but that they should not necessarily be binding. A third view was that it was highly desirable that negotiating parties should increasingly

be prepared to argue their case before some body, whose arbitral judgement on the matter was then accepted.

Changes in Bargaining Power

The proposals which are being enacted at the time of writing enable employers, if they wish, to take action against individuals engaged in certain forms of secondary picketing. They also limit the payment of supplementary benefit to strikers' families, by deeming that strikers will have received a certain weekly sum from their unions. The effect of any new measures of this kind is unpredictable; however, in the past employers have shown a certain reluctance to initiate legal action in industrial relations matters; and supplementary benefits have in the past provided a fairly small proportion of strikers' incomes.

There are various proposals for stronger measures of this kind – for instance, that action against secondary picketing should lie against the unions rather than individuals, or that unions should be required to hold a strike ballot if a certain percentage of those concerned request it. There is perhaps some risk that measures of this kind might lead to more unofficial action; whereas in the late 1960s the government's concern was to develop a system in which trade unions had a greater degree of control over the behaviour of their members, the proposals at present extant might seem likely, if anything, to lead to the opposite result.

On the employers' side, one main proposal was that of the CBI for a strike insurance fund – a proposal which at the time of writing is in abeyance. The commonsense assessment of such a proposal is that it would have some effect in reducing the size of wage bargains, though the suggestion has been made that such a scheme might for a time increase the number of strikes, because it would take time for the parties to adjust to the new balance of power [5].

One other suggestion for strengthening employers' bargaining power is that large companies should do more to coordinate their pay bargaining stance; this suggestion is discussed elsewhere in this book (page 146). Coordinated action by employers, of course, is likely to lead to coordinated action on the part of trade unions as well; this, therefore, is a proposal which would probably lead to more centralisation rather than less.

Tax-based Incomes Policies

The proponents of tax-based incomes policies in general accept that the unemployment cost of conventional anti-inflationary policies may be excessive. They argue for tax-based incomes policies (rather than methods involving persuasion or control) on a number of grounds: that policies of persuasion and policies of control have both been unsuccessful; that tax-based policies would not involve large new bureaucracies; that tax-based policies are much more flexible than policies of control, and minimise government intervention in determining relativities. (Some advocates of tax-based policies, for example Wootton, do not advance this last argument, since their policies would be used to enforce the norm, and since they are not in favour of preserving existing relativities.) Some advocates have developed the analogy with environmental pollution – where economists generally accept the idea of effluent taxes to 'internalise the externality' of pollution. The average wage settlement behaviour in the economy imposes a cost on society of either inflation or high unemployment; a tax will force firms and unions to take more notice of the external consequences of their internal decisions. This particular family of proposals is one which might in certain circumstances appeal to a government which stresses the market-distorting effects of other incomes policy approaches, since the existing institutional methods by which wage settlements are reached do not have to be altered.

There are a number of variations in the possible design of these suggested anti-inflation incentives; however, some – although theoretically possible – have dropped by the wayside on grounds of impracticability. For example, the anti-inflation incentives could be directed against excessive increases in output prices; however, this particular approach has not been seriously developed because of the problems of measuring output prices. The main suggestions are for tax deterrents on increases in the wage and salary bill which are too high, and some have suggested, either as an addition or a substitute, that there should be tax subsidies on increases in the wage and salary bill which are low. The suggestion that it is the wage and salary bill which should be the price on which the scheme operates has been criticised, and total value added has been suggested as an alternative. The tax could be levied on the firm, or (if wages and salaries are the input price chosen) it could be levied in some way on the employees.

There is perhaps an initial distinction to be made between those who would treat the tax as a penal tax, in which any wage or salary increase above a certain percentage is taxed away, and those who are rather concerned to exert a mild deterrent pressure on the structure of wage increases, leaving a fairly considerable spread in the increases given by different firms or industries. The first proposal is essentially a sanction for the enforcement of the norm, and this proposal belongs conceptually with those discussed in that section. The important distinctive feature of the proposals discussed in the section which follows is that variations in the wage and salary increases granted are not in any way considered culpable – indeed the purpose of the proposal is to allow variations to continue, without anyone sitting in judgement upon them.

The following exposition sets out first of all the proposal which has perhaps received most attention – a tax on the wage and salary bill per head of a firm if the figure rises above a certain percentage, with the tax to be paid by the firm. It then considers some of the variants which have been put forward.

Tax on the wage and salary bill

A typical proposal runs as follows: 'Suppose, for example, that the target of 6 per cent were set for overall pay increases in the initial year of a tax-based incomes policy programme. A firm might be confronted with a basic corporate income tax rate of 48 per cent on its profits if its average pay increase came within the 6 per cent target, but it might face a higher tax rate on profits if pay rose more than 6 per cent. An illustrative schedule might call for a 52 per cent tax rate if the firm's pay increase were 7 per cent, 56 per cent if pay rose 8 per cent, and so forth. As a result, the firm would find that large pay increases had become more costly. In a non-union situation, the firm would grant a lower wage increase to protect its profitability or market value; in a collective bargaining situation, the firm would resist demands for large wage increases more vigorously.' [20]

The main question to be addressed to a proposal of this kind is whether it would work. It is not possible, in the nature of things, to prove that something which has not been tried before will work. There is the danger that firms will accept the profit penalty, and will simply raise their prices further to prevent their total profits from being eroded; however, the failure of the company sector in general to preserve its profit-margin in recent years in this country suggests that this might not be an easy thing to do. If the proposal were introduced against trade union opposition, then it might lead their negotiators to push harder than they would otherwise have done. The only country where a policy of this kind has been tried is Hungary, where it appears to have had some success [12]. However, how far this experience is relevant to countries where trade union behaviour is rather different is open to question.

Is the proposal administratively feasible? The fullest discussion of this point has been in the US [10]. The discussion shows that the proposal is much less simple than it sounds. There is the problem of measuring the wage and salary bill: what should be done about entitlement to pensions and the large range of non-wage benefits which exist – medical reimbursement plans, low-rate loans, expense accounts, cheap food in the cafeteria, and so on. Then the wage bill has to be divided by some number which represents labour input. The simple measure is just the number of employees, or possibly the number of employee hours. There are ways in which firms could get round the imposed limit, by contracting out to independent consultancies some of the work done by high-paid staff, or by changing to part-time workers. So the suggestion has been made that labour input should be measured by a quality-adjusted series of some kind. Workers would then be allocated to classes, and the norm would be a weighted average of the percentage increases in hourly compensation to various classes. Firms might then be tempted to promote an individual into a higher class while leaving his pay unchanged.

Then there is the problem of the economic unit which would be potentially liable for the profit penalty. 'The unit for tax accounting purposes is a legal entity which, in our complex economy, often bears little relationship to the unit that enters into wage bargains with its employees.' [21] Many conglomerates which make a consolidated return consist of a number of different firms operating in a number of different industries. The penalty on the profits of any one of these firms would depend in part on the wage bargaining of all the other firms included in the consolidated return; labour and management would have no way of making sensible wage decisions in one place unless they knew what the decisions were to be elsewhere. Presumably, the unit of calculation would have to be relevant to the wage-setting process; that in turn would mean that Inland Revenue and the conglomerate firm would have to agree on a large number of separate profit figures. Great problems would arise with inter-year wage bill comparisons from new firms, mergers, sales of facilities, and so on. Given that any increase in the tax on profits has to have a legal basis and could be challenged in the courts, provision for all these assorted problems would have to be made in the legislation.

The conclusion of two officials in the US Department of the Treasury who considered these problems was that 'a tax-based incomes policy would entail significant administrative problems for the Internal Revenue Service and compliance problems for businesses. These problems could be reduced to a manageable size if the tax-based incomes policy were applied only to business taxpayers, if it were limited to wages, if the hurdle approach were adopted, and if it did not apply to small companies. The administrative and compliance problems, however, would still be significant.' [10]

Variations

One proposal is that the tax should not be on the wage and salary bill but on total value added. The main purpose of this proposal is to penalise excessive increases in profits as well as excessive increases in wages and salaries. Its proponents argue that it is no more difficult to implement than a tax on the wage and salary bill, and yet it applies equally to all forms of income. In order to encourage efficiency, all investment could be subtracted, in the year in which it is made, before arriving at value added. Ideally, value added should be divided by the number which represents not only the increase in labour input but also the increase in capital input; there are problems in measuring the latter – a firm's amount of depreciation has been suggested, or the flow value of financial capital [7]. The value added proposal is relatively new, and the problems associated with it have not as yet been fully explored.

A second variation is that the tax should be on employees, rather than on profits. This case has been strongly argued by Fogarty [12]. He does not suggest (as Wootton does) that the tax should be on each *individual*'s excess of income above the norm. He sees great problems here in adjusting permissible increases to take account of all the complications of individuals' promotion, re-grading, and career development, and considers that a flat rate of tax per head or a uniform percentage tax should be enough to make employees as a whole accept that these awards bring no profit. It should be noted that Fogarty has in mind a penalty which is high enough to take all the profit out of exceeding the norm.

Fogarty sees a number of difficulties in levying the tax on profits rather than on incomes from employment. It would be seen by trade unions as a weapon intensifying the class struggle – as an intervention on the employers' side to strengthen their determination to keep profits up and wages down; whereas success in the attempts to defeat inflation requires a certain degree of consensus. He considers it quite possible that in certain circumstances the penalty would be generally passed on into prices; alternatively he fears that it might cut dangerously into the funds available for investment. On the other hand, a pay penalty would make the process of pursuing excessive pay claims much more clearly self-defeating than the profit penalty, and would be less likely to divert the debate on national incomes policy into a class struggle over maintaining employers' profits.

There would be considerable additional problems in administering a pay penalty. These are not extensively discussed in the article by the two US Treasury officials [17], because they were under the impression that 'no one had suggested applying a stick approach to workers'. It would be very difficult to decide whether a penalty should or should not be paid until the end of the accounting year. Immense problems would arise from labour turnover. In the typical manufacturing plant, by the end of the year one third of the labour force which had been employed there at the beginning of the year would have left. Would they be able to retain their excess earnings, while those who stayed with the firm would have to pay a penalty?

Another variant, either as an addition to the tax penalty or in substitution for it, is the subsidy or award where wage increases are below a certain norm. This includes the concept of real wage insurance, which was in fact proposed by the Carter administration to Congress. Here it is usually envisaged that the payment, or tax deduction, should accrue to the employees themselves. To be effective in restraining wage bargaining, it would be highly desirable that such rewards should appear immediately: Okun therefore suggested that firms or workers be invited to 'take the pledge' to restrain wages and prices at the beginning of the tax year, and so sign up in advance [20]. There would be obvious problems if, at the end of the year, it appeared that the pledge had been broken: the problems of recouping the money from individual workers would be formidable. There is also the great difficulty which arises when the bargaining unit is not co-terminous with the unit for determining the subsidy; no worker or group of workers would know whether the deal they made would actually trigger the subsidy or award until negotiations are completed with the other bargaining units in the same firm.

Each of these variations can claim certain advantages over the proposal that firms should bear some excess tax on their profits if the increase in the wage and salary bill per head exceeds a certain number. However, it does appear that in most cases the variations add considerably to the administrative difficulty of a proposal which already has considerable administrative complications.

The 'Market Anti-Inflation Plan'

The 'Market Anti-Inflation Plan' devised by Professors Lerner and Colander [16] has a certain similarity to tax-cum-subsidy schemes. It claims the advantage that it is concerned with value added, and so covers profits as well as incomes from employment; and the problem of setting a tax or subsidy rate does not arise – the solution is left to the market. The scheme is as follows. The Federal Reserve (or some other government agency) gives each firm an amount of 'MAP Credit' (MCr) equal to its current 'net sales' (gross dollar sales minus purchases from other firms) adjusted for cost changes from increases or decreases in its employment of labour and capital and for the average national increase in productivity. This makes the total MCr just equal to the increase in total net output of goods and services in the country.

Each firm's adjusted MCr entitles it to have net sales of that amount. If it wants more net sales it must buy a corresponding quantity of additional MCr. This can come only from the sale of MCr by firms with net sales less than their MCr who would have spare MCr to sell. The price of MCr is reached by free trading on the market, just like the price of IBM shares, reaching the level where supply equals demand – where sellers offer just as much as the buyers want to buy – just as in any other free market.

Supply equal to demand means that the total of increases in net sales (by the buyers of MCr) will be equal to the total of decreases in net sales (by the sellers of MCr). Total net sales is thus kept increasing at the same rate as the net output of goods and services in the economy and there can be no inflation. Meanwhile every firm is perfectly free to set prices and wages at the levels it finds worthwhile as long as it buys or sells enough MCr to keep its MCr equal to its net sales. There are no bureaucratic interferences with any prices or wages – only some minor additions to the duties of the income tax and social security offices.

More Radical Proposals

The proposals discussed here vary considerably in their nature; they have this in common – that they would generally require substantial changes either from the existing situation, or from what has been tried in the past. That, of course, is not an argument for leaving them out of consideration; radical changes may be needed.

The Meade proposals

Meade's proposals [19] are based on a macroeconomic strategy according to which fiscal policies should be designed to maintain a steady 5 per cent a year growth in the total money demand for labour, and there should be a suitable reform of arrangements for fixing rates of pay such that against this background full employment is maintained.

The criteria which Meade suggests should be used to fix rates of pay are as follows: first, against the background of financial policies to ensure a steady annual rate of growth in the money demand for labour as a whole and of a battery of fiscal and other policies for the redistribution of income and wealth, the basic criterion for fixing rates of pay should be to maintain employment by restraining wage costs where there is a threat of unemployment and raising rates where it is necessary to maintain or expand a needed labour force. Second, comparability studies may be needed to aid judgements whether particular rates of pay are appropriate to maintain future recruitment at an adequate level; but comparability should always be based on the attractiveness of various jobs, revealed as far as possible by individual choices between jobs. Third, as far as low pay is concerned, there is a case for special state intervention in exceptional cases of exploited workers; and it is particularly important to avoid measures which are aimed at protecting high-paid workers from the competition of other less well paid workers. Fourth, there should be no impediment to individual productivity deals between workers and employers, but this should not involve any general regulations which tie increases of wages to increases in productivity. It is appropriate that existing workers in any set of jobs which is adversely affected by new technologies should enjoy protection in their pay; but it is inappropriate that such protection should be extended to new entrants.

In Meade's view there are strong objections to a comprehensive centralised incomes policy. This involves either one of two possible types of arrangement. Either there is some simple norm: this makes it impossible to relate particular wage rates to particular conditions of supply and demand. Alternatively, the system would require extended bureaucratic intervention to settle the appropriate rate for each sector of the economy. Neither of these seems satisfactory.

Meade's own proposal is one of 'not-quite-compulsory arbitration'. In the case of an unsettled dispute, either party could take the issue to the permanently established national arbitration court. This arbitral body would have the statutory duty to follow the criteria already outlined. If industrial action was taken in opposition to the terms of such an award, the party concerned would be penalised in certain ways – discussed below. This system of arbitration would operate only if one of the parties wished it to operate (though Meade suggests the government might also have the power to take any major unsettled dispute to the tribunal); and, secondly, a refusal to accept the award would not be illegal – it would merely incur penalties. Meade toys with the ingenious suggestion that after an appeal to the court, there should be 30 days free for further negotiation; at the end of that period the court would be restricted to making its award either in favour of the last offer made by the employers or in favour of the last claim presented by the employees.

On sanctions Meade states initially that a system which embodies sanctions for not accepting an arbitration award would only be possible if there were widespread support for the new arrangements. So far as employers are concerned it would be possible simply to make it unlawful for the employer to employ anyone except on terms of the award. The problem of sanctions against recusant workers and trade unionists is obviously more difficult. Meade suggests that supplementary benefit to those on strike in opposition to an arbitral award would have later to be repaid; tax refunds should be repaid; that any worker who went on strike against an award should be treated as having terminated his contract of employment – and this would have some consequences for his accumulated right to redundancy payments. There could also be some lifting of legal immunities when industrial action was taken in opposition to the arbitral award.

Phelps Brown's proposals

Phelps Brown declared himself surprised by the degree of innovation embodied in his proposals [3]. One might initially suppose that a 'workable policy' would be one that made a cautious advance from ground already explored. He found that the requirement of workability led him inexorably to a set of radical suggestions which require a change in public opinion normally only brought about by a war or similar cataclysm. He therefore suggests that a board should be set up by the government to initiate discussion of the proposals, to collect criticisms and suggestions, and so to engage the discussants in shaping the proposals.

The proposal is for a form of industrial self-government. This requires a consortium of representatives of existing negotiating bodies, each of which would send one representative to an assembly. The negotiating bodies to be incorporated in the consortium are all firms having 5000 or more employees; the nationalised industries; public administration, central and local, and wages councils covering not less than 10,000 employees. The assembly would elect five employers' and five employees' representatives to the council annually. The council would consist of the ten elected members, together with five permanent and full-time members appointed by the government.

The council would prepare incomes policy guidelines from time to time; they could, for instance, draw up rules suggesting that a settlement must not raise unit labour costs except in certain specified circumstances. They would report to the assembly; receive evidence from the government; appoint staff to direct its work; and investigate and report on cases referred to it by the staff in which it appeared that a member of the negotiating body was proposing price or wage changes inconsistent with the rules the council had devised. There would be an obligation on members of the negotiating bodies to provide early information to the staff of the council about prospective changes in prices, wages or salaries.

Phelps Brown, writing in 1972, envisaged the use of the Industrial Relations Court as a way of preventing employers from implementing changes which the council found to be inconsistent with their rules.

Wilfred Brown's proposals

These proposals [4], which require a considerable degree of synchronisation of wage negotiations, are built round a proposal for a National Council for the Regulation of Differentials (NCRD). Each year the government, after appropriate discussions with the TUC and CBI, will propose the percentage average increase in wages and salaries which should be permitted a year later. Once this figure had been approved by Parliament, it would be remitted to the NCRD. This would be a body of about 300 representatives of trade unions; they would have the responsibility of dividing up the total sum between employment groups, and would have a year in which to reach agreement. If they could not reach agreement, then all wages and salaries would be frozen until they did.

Each employment institution would have at its disposal a further increase of (say) 1 per cent of its wage bill; this would be at the disposal of a council of employees, who would be authorised to produce a differentiated distribution if they obtained a unanimous vote of the council.

A special court would be established to hear appeals: the basis of the appeal would be that the calculated average wage of the total employees was below that of the average wage of the employment group category to which the appellant's employing institution belonged.

Wootton's proposal

Wootton proposes [24] a tax-based incomes policy, which is however closer to an enforced norm. The basic proposal is for an incomes gains tax (IGT) which would be applied by the Inland Revenue to every individual. It would be levied at a rate of 100 per cent on any increase above a prescribed maximum percentage in any financial year. The permitted percentage could be made progressive, so as to allow larger increases on smaller incomes and smaller increases on larger incomes. Certain forms of additional income such as annual increments or higher pay due to promotion or a limited amount of earnings from voluntary overtime would be disregarded.

Applications for special treatment would come before a special exemptions board. These applications should be based on evidence that the workers concerned were paid less than others doing similar work, or that their work was undervalued as measured by some agreed standard of evaluation, or that the earnings in their industry were insufficient to attract as large a labour force as the national interest required.

Lydall's proposal

Lydall's proposal [17] is similar to a suggestion originally put forward by C. R. Ross, and later developed by Worswick [25]. Lydall proposes three rules as a basis of his new wage system. The first rule is that all wage and salary settlements should take effect on the same appointed day. The second rule is that the content of all wage settlements, whether made by collective bargaining, by wages councils, or in other ways should be reported in detail to the Department of Employment at least two weeks before the appointed day, only those settlements which were reported in time being eligible for implementation on the appointed day. It would be the responsibility of the Department of Employment to estimate the national average effect on earnings (including fringe benefits) of all the settlements reported to it within the time limit. This estimate would be passed to the Cabinet, which would then decide in the light of prospective changes in productivity, import costs and other factors, what average increase in money earnings was consistent with a tolerable rate of inflation. Comparison of the rate of earnings derived from the settlements with the rate consistent with a tolerable rate of inflation would yield a rate of discount sufficient to reduce the former to the latter. This may be called the inflation discount factor. The third rule is that on the appointed day there would come into effect (a) all duly reported wages settlements and (b) the inflation discount factor. The three rules together would constitute a new wage system.

In order to ensure observance of the rule, all large firms and government organisations would be audited each year, together with a sample of smaller firms. Heavy fines would be imposed on firms or organisations which broke the rules, and possibly also on their top officials. In these ways it would be easy to make rule-breaking unprofitable.

Elkan's proposal

This summary is based on Maurice Scott's summary of Elkan's proposals [22]. They are in some ways similar to those of Lydall, in that they allow collective bargaining to proceed as at present, but include a device for bringing down the average rate of increase in income from employment from an inflationary to a non-inflationary figure.

Let us suppose that average income from employment per employee is rising at 14 per cent a year at the beginning of the year, and that – with national productivity rising at 2 per cent a year – the requirement for price stability is that the rise of 14 per cent should be brought down to 2 per cent. The Elkan scheme requires the government to instruct all employers, public and private, to deduct 1 per cent from all wages and salaries in the first month of the scheme – say January – *and keep it.* In February the deduction is raised to 2 per cent, in March to 3 per cent, and so on, so that by December the deduction is running at 12 per cent. So employers' actual payment of wages and salaries will have risen by only 2 per cent on average during this year: this should result in stable prices. The tax (in much the same way as Lydall's inflation discount factor) merely replaces the role of price increases. Employers would have no incentive to evade the tax, since they would be keeping the proceeds. Free collective bargaining would proceed normally. It would be possible to superimpose on these arrangements an incomes policy dealing with *relative* incomes if the government so wished.

The scheme could embody safeguards against excessive profit increases if this was considered desirable. Scott suggests a 'watch-dog' institution to ensure that personal incomes from property after tax did not grow unduly; this could be helped by the reduction in interest rates which should follow the elimination of inflation. Scott also suggests that any group of workers that is prepared to take the option of abandoning collective bargaining, and in particular the right to strike, might be allowed exemption from the pay adjustment factor embodied in the Elkan scheme.

Conclusions

Many of the issues are more political than economic, and the main problem with any policy is to find one that works. The issue is not between market and non-market solutions. On the one hand, free collective bargaining as at present practised can hardly be said to represent the market. On the other hand, a number of incomes policy approaches are market-based.

A central question for those discussing these matters is to decide whether they want to change towards even more fragmented bargaining, and to a trades union system with less central control, or whether they would prefer a move in the other direction towards less fragmented bargaining, with stronger trade unions, and possibly more centralised negotiations. It is not internally consistent to want more fragmented bargaining and at the same time to want trade unions to exercise greater discipline over the behaviour of their members.

Tax-based policies are possibly more appropriate in countries where a smaller proportion of the workforce is unionised than is the case in the UK. The administrative difficulties of even a simple scheme would be fairly considerable. However, this approach might appeal to a government which considers it important to allow the existing system of free collective bargaining to determine relativities.

A number of bodies of very different political complexion have come to the conclusion that a national economic forum of some kind is desirable. There are unresolved questions about its functions. It could be simply educative, or it could be a bargaining forum. It could simply consider various alternative scenarios, or it could emerge with recommendations of some kind about numbers.

There are, in any case, policy problems to be settled in connection with pay in the non-market public sector. A system in which there is a large number of separate review bodies seems hard to defend. Some suggest that these review bodies should simply provide information; some that they should add recommendations; some that arbitral judgements should be accepted from them. The relative roles of collective bargaining and of comparability studies in the public sector are also questions at issue.

References

[1] *A Better Way* (published by the signatories), London, 1979.
[2] Basnett, D., 'A way out of warfare over pay', *Sunday Times*, 6 December 1977.
[3] Brown, E. H. Phelps, 'A workable incomes policy for Britain', in F. Blackaby, ed., *An Incomes Policy for Britain*, London, Heinemann, 1972.
[4] Brown, Wilfred, *Inflation and a Possible Solution*, London, 1971.
[5] Chiplin, B. and Doherty, N., 'Strike insurance for employers', *Lloyds Bank Review*, April, 1980.

[6] Colander, D. C., 'Incomes policies: MIP, WIPP and TIP', *Journal of Post Keynesian Economics*, Spring 1979.

[7] Colander, D. C., *Incentive Anti-Inflation Plans*, Washington D.C., Joint Economic Committee, forthcoming.

[8] Confederation of British Industry, *Pay: the choice ahead*, London, 1979.

[9] Council on Prices, Productivity and Incomes, *First Report*, London, HMSO, 1958, para. 102.

[10] Dildine, L. L. and Sunley, E. M., 'Administrative problems of tax-based incomes policies', *Brookings Papers on Economic Activity*, no. 2, 1978.

[11] Economic Affairs, Department of, *Productivity, Prices and Incomes Policy in 1968 and 1969*, Cmnd 3590, London, HMSO, 1968.

[12] Fogarty, M. D., 'Fiscal measures and wage settlements', *British Journal of Industrial Relations*, March 1973.

[13] Jay, P., *Employment, Inflation and Politics*, London, Institute of Economic Affairs, 1976.

[14] Jones, Aubrey, *The New Inflation: the politics of prices and incomes*, London, Deutsch, 1973.

[15] Jones, Aubrey, 'Can there be an economics of equality?', *Encounter*, 1976.

[16] Lerner, A. P. and Colander, D. C., *MAP, a Market Anti-Inflation Plan*, New York, Harcourt, Brace, Jovanovich, 1980.

[17] Lydall, H., 'A new wage system', *Oxford Bulletin of Economics and Statistics*, forthcoming.

[18] Maude, A., ed., *The Right Approach to the Economy*, London, Conservative Central Office, 1977.

[19] Meade, J. E., 'The fixing of money rates of pay' (mimeo), Cambridge, 1979.

[20] Okun, A. M. and Perry, G. L., 'Editor's summary', *Brookings Papers on Economic Activity*, no. 2, 1978.

[21] Pechman, J. A., *Brookings Papers on Economic Activity*, no. 2, 1978.

[22] Scott, M. FG., 'A new way to attack inflation', *The Banker*, April 1974.

[23] TUC, *The Economy, the Government and Trade Union Responsibilities* (joint statement by the TUC and the government), London, 1979, para. 27.

[24] Wootton, Barbara, *Incomes Policy: an inquest and a proposal*, London, Davis-Poynter, 1974.

[25] Worswick, G. D. N., 'Prices, productivity and incomes', *Oxford Economic Papers*, June 1958.

Comments on Chapter 4

I *H. Phelps Brown*

The suitability of the proposals that Blackaby has surveyed can usefully be considered in the light of recent experience. There are four features of this that seem relevant.

(1) In the private sector, management *has been taking the initiative* to develop orderly negotiation within the plant or firm. New bargaining units have been formed: their structure runs across the boundaries between trade unions, and they act independently of the employers' association. Within the firm, managers have been doing more to pass information down the line. In the recent round of settlements there has been less uniformity, and more response to the capacity of the particular firm to pay.

(2) The past decade has seen notable examples of *the great bargaining power* wielded by individual trade unions. A number of changes in technique and organisation have given small groups the power to hold up a whole industry. The extension of unionism among the white-collared has been accompanied by a willingness to use the disruption of the life of the community as a bargaining weapon. Occasional protracted struggles have been sustained with tenacity. About 1968–9 there appeared in this country as in many others the 'hinge' in the rate of rise of earnings, and this seems to have arisen from an upward shift in expectations and militancy among the rank and file.

(3) At the same time our trade unions have become less concerned with the aims of the labour movement and *are more like business unions*. The attitudes of business unionists stand contrasted with those of trade unionists of the old school, who feel themselves part of a labour movement, and accept the duty to defer their own gains to the interests of their comrades, and obey the ruling of a common leadership. So it was in May 1926, when they answered the call to come out on a strike of indefinite duration against a government that would not extend a subsidy to the mining industry. When in May of this year the TUC called for one day of absence from work in protest against

the government, the response in England – though not in Scotland or South Wales – was remarkably limited. There are many differences in the setting to account for the difference of outcome, but 14 May 1980 may be seen as a landmark because it revealed the extent to which English unionists had become business unionists. Part of the change has come about because the extension of trade unionism in recent years has been among the white-collared, and their motive for joining has been, not to build a new society, but to restore their relativities.

(4) But bargaining power has not yet been exploited to the limit. It has been used to make good *claims based on three basic principles* – maintaining the real wage by offsetting the antecedent rise in the cost of living; restoring relativities and differentials; protecting jobs against displacement by new equipment.

If these features of recent experience have been rightly assessed, some inferences follow for the proposed changes in the bargaining system.

(1) A first inference is that there is little future for the Social Contract. Even in the most favourable political setting, the requirements for it are increasingly hard to satisfy. One is that the General Council of the TUC should be able to commit its constituent unions to an undertaking of restraint, and hold them to it. Its ability to do this depends on their executives' sense of the allegiance they owe it out of their loyalty to the movement as a whole and on the executives' expectation of their ability to secure the compliance of their own members. But as the wider aims of trade unions recede and more self-regarding purposes take their place, the moral authority of the General Council is weakened; and the shift of power to the shop floor has been a shift also within the trade union, which has made the executive dependent on the acceptance of a Social Contract by a membership to whom the element of wage restraint may be more prominent as a cost than any political counterpoise as a benefit. The winter of 1978–9 shows how little restraint many unionists were prepared to accept to help a Labour government in its approach to a general election. How far any one Social Contract would prove acceptable would depend also on what it offered in return for restraint, and here again the business unionist is a more awkward customer – the old

considerations of social welfare, or getting unemployment down, may not attract him.

This negative first inference is that the possibility of restraint through the TUC, even in favourable political circumstances, has diminished. The problem then poses itself more sharply than ever of what sanctions can be applied to particular negotiations.

(2) The proposal that settlements in excess of a norm should attract a tax must be discarded as administratively impracticable – despite the quoted opinion of the two officials in the US Department of the Treasury. Any one firm's books would have to be checked in order to see how far a change in the total paid to employees was due to higher rates paid to an unchanged number of persons of unchanged grade, and how far to all other causes, such as changes in numbers of persons and types of work, upgrading, and overtime. Management that can get a settlement only for a rise that will attract a tax has to choose between the cost of a protracted stoppage and the cost of the tax. The extent of the stoppage and its outcome will be unknown: the managers are likely to prefer the tax. If competitors are under similar pressure, the tax will prove to be recoverable through price. Where there is monopoly, as in nationalised industry, it can simply be passed on. In a large sector of tax-supported employment, it has no application.

Measures that make striking less disruptive to business or more costly to strikers, or enable employers to support one another in resisting strikes, will keep down the settlements in particular cases, and so reduce the rate of rise of pay overall. But they do not promise to hold in the basic thrusts of bargaining power – the ability of tactically placed groups to stop wide sectors of the economy by withdrawing their own labour; and the confidence and determination with which the employees of today, acting it may well be without dependence on official union direction, formulate claims and pursue them. These measures have the further limitation of operating within the adversary system of industrial relations. Their application may be necessary and salutary, if we are to go on as we have been going, settling pay by what Sidney Webb called 'the arbitrament of private war': then we are bound to ask if the two armies are evenly matched for a fair fight. But a previous question is whether this is the right structure for pay fixing at all, and whether pay fixing cannot be lifted out of industrial relations and provided with a structure of its own. This question of structure is one of the first importance, to which I shall return in (4) below. But in the present context there is another form of sanctions to be noticed.

This is whatever sanction is to be attached to a statutory incomes policy. Similar to this is the sanction applied in a system of compulsory arbitration. What penalties can be prescribed that will prevent trade unionists from pressing for, and their employers from settling, for a pay rise in excess of the amount that incomes policy permits; or that will prevent a party to a dispute from refusing to submit it to arbitration, or, having submitted it, refusing to accept the terms awarded? Experience indicates the inadvisability of procedure against individuals which could have to result in their imprisonment. The practicable sanction has been taken to be the fining of trade unions – there will be a symmetrical provision against companies, but it is restraint of employees that is the crux. The first statutory incomes policy in this country, in the Labour government's Prices and Incomes Act of 1966, provided that any trade union that took or threatened to take any action, particularly by way of a strike, to put pressure on an employer to implement a settlement at a time when that was forbidden might be fined an unlimited amount. Under the legislation of the Australian Commonwealth, though there is no objection to the parties reaching agreement on rises in pay of any amount mutually agreed, it is an offence to strike or lock out without resort to the Board of Conciliation and Arbitration, or because of refusal to accept an award by the Board, and trade unions whose members have so struck in recent years have been fined by the Commonwealth Court. But two considerations limit the effectiveness of this kind of sanction. One is 'the dispersive revolution', the limited extent to which trade unions are effectively responsible for the actions of their members, and the increasing extent to which those members are able to sustain a strike whatever the depletion of coffers at headquarters. The other consideration is that a penalty that serves as a deterrent when it is incurred only by the occasional deviant ceases to deter, and is simply repudiated, when a large number of unions clash with the policy it is meant to enforce. In this field, more perhaps than in most, the enforceability of statute law depends on acceptance by the majority.

The conclusion here must be that there are no built-in or automatic sanctions capable of restraining cost push over a wide front, or the breakthrough of a determined norm-buster at a particular point. But this is not to say that there are no means of restraint. Our dependence in the last resort can be only upon the acceptance by employees themselves of rates of pay, and the arrangements by which they are reached, as fair and reasonable. The question is how such acceptance is to be obtained.

(3) One proposed step towards this is the national forum to discuss the prospects for the economy. Out of this discussion, it is hoped, a consensus will emerge for the guidance of negotiators; but then the fear arises too that this consensus will be expressed as a norm that will be seized on as a minimum entitlement for all.

That a norm of some kind should be formulated does seem necessary. The forum meets the need for spreading information about what the Dutch call 'the room in the economy' – what resources there are in prospect to honour additional claims from various sectors. But information about the national accounts provided in this way at the national level needs to be reduced to a compact form if it is to be carried down to the localities. It is in any case not expressed in the terms in which people think when they are assessing what they can fairly claim themselves. The message from the national level can hardly be conveyed in a form with a practical bearing over the whole field of employment unless it is expressed as some kind of norm.

But this norm does not have to stand as a single figure, or as a bracket of which the upper limit will be taken as the operative part. The exceptions which in the past it has been felt necessary to admit to the application of a norm should be seen not as departures from it but as part of its definition. Their administration should not breach it but strengthen it: by showing that regard is paid to particular circumstances and that special claims will be attended to, the procedure gives an assurance of fairness, and does much to secure acceptance of the norm itself. This holds in the many cases where no use is made of it: the machinery of adjustment is an integral part of the formulation of the norm. The norms agreed in the conferences of recent years between the central organisations of employers' associations and trade unions in the Irish Republic have owed their acceptance to their being linked with a procedure for obtaining permission for settlements greater or less than the norm: this procedure has not only provided a safety valve, but has implicitly enlarged and legitimised the concept of the norm. By analogy it may be remarked that the binding nature of the plant contract, accepted by the parties to it in the US, depends not only on the attitude towards the law in the American community but also on the effectiveness of the grievance procedure set up to deal with issues arising under it. The attitude of the individual towards the rule is shaped by the procedure to which he has access for administering the rule.

(4) The question remains of how the forum should be constituted. One immediately practicable gathering brings together the CBI, the TUC and the government: indeed meetings of this kind on a small scale already take place in NEDC. But there is a growing case for considering more radical proposals seriously.

The negative part of this case is that understandings reached between spokesmen of the CBI and TUC do not flow down quickly to the negotiating tables. Their influence takes time to percolate. The influence exerted by the centre has in any case diminished. Nor is either central body organised by negotiating unit. Here appears the positive case for convening a new type of consultative assembly.

It would be the essential principle of such an assembly that because it was intended to gain the confidence and assent of negotiating units, its members should be drawn from those units, and its constituencies should be formed of them. The bodies to be represented, that is to say, should be not the principal trade unions and employers' associations, but the principal negotiating units, whether they be Whitley Councils in the civil service, a council or meeting covering a sector of the employees of a nationalised industry, the representatives of employers and trade unions in a multi-employer bargaining unit, or the management of a large firm and the negotiators on behalf of their employees. The administrator's mind can only quail before the number and variety of those constituencies: how can they be enumerated and, in the private sector, delimited? The task is more complicated than when the writs first went out to two knights from every shire and two burgesses from every city. Yet the principle seems right. *Quod omnes tangit, omnibus approbetur* – what touches all must be approved by all, and the all are the negotiators. Their representatives, moreover, would be summoned not to vote taxes or legislate but to hear and discuss a statement of what pay movements the economic outlook calls for.

There are two considerations that warrant the present and active discussion of proposals of this radical kind. One is that they would help to *separate pay regulation from industrial relations*. The structure of industrial relations is made up of the cooperation, conflict, leadership, subordination, and group loyalties and rivalries, between those who work together workplace by workplace. Out of these internal relations, tensions and agreements there arises at present a certain aggregate movement of pay in the whole economy. There is no reason why the movement that emerges in this way should fulfil its proper functions. These should be to keep the economy in external balance by guiding the course of costs and prices, and to adjust domestic outlay to the available resources. How far the movements of pay have been from performing these functions in recent years confronts us with the consequences of housing pay regulation wholly within industrial relations.

That it is practicable to separate guidance of the national movement of pay from the direct relations between employer and employed is indicated by the experience of Australia. For many years the Australian trade unions have accepted the determination of changes in wages throughout the greater part of the economy by the national wage awards of the Conciliation and Arbitration Commission. This acceptance on the part of the unions is the legacy of a phase of economic history peculiar to Australia; it is far from unconditional, and it has been interrupted; but its persistence does show the practicability of a structure that provides for guidance of the national movement of pay as an object in itself from the first. Or again, to cite instances which are less persuasive in one way because they differ from the United Kingdom in so many more respects, but which command attention because of the comparative and striking success of the economies concerned in avoiding cost inflation – we can hardly suppose that this success of the Soviet-type economies has been achieved by continuous detection and repression of impulses towards bargaining. It must rest rather upon the existence of a structure that provides effective modes of action to meet the needs of the individual worker in his industrial relations, while fixing his pay as part of a system common to a whole economy.

These instances raise the second consideration concerning radical proposals for the development of institutions. Can the essentials of pay determination to which the individual employee in this country is attached be *safeguarded by some method of central or external regulation*, or do they include the need for the employee himself to have the last word? On the one hand there is the powerful tradition of voluntarism, and objection to compulsory arbitration, which maintains that for a man to be required to work on terms that he himself has not freely accepted is tantamount to serfdom. But against that it is pointed out that the freedom enjoyed under free collective bargaining is in practice highly qualified – it has sometimes been only the freedom to be starved out; and it is further urged that what concerns most persons in their pay is simply the maintenance of differentials and relativities, and the protection and, if possible, the improvement of their real earnings. This seems the attitude more likely to prevail once pay determination is removed from the possibility of being the dictate of the employer, which is intolerable as a matter of industrial relations. Blackaby has reminded us that in criticism of an earlier argument that incomes policy must be internalised to the bargaining unit it was remarked that 'very few people determine their own wages anyway; would there really be objections if relativities were settled by some central authority, so long as there was some general confidence that the central authority would try to be fair?' It is possible, then, that a centrally regulated pay system would prove acceptable to employees individually if it met their predominant concerns about their own pay.

Against this there must be set the continuing possibility that some groups, having become increasingly conscious in recent years of their bargaining power, will wish to continue to exert it for no limited aim but for 'more and more'. The effective resistance to this can come only from employers and, in the last resort but not unthinkably, from associated workers whose jobs are threatened. To justify the exploitative exertion of bargaining power, to oneself and one's neighbour, is one thing in a free-for-all of disordered relativities, but would be quite another when it was a generally agreed system of relativities that was being disrupted.

There is this to be said at the last about the radical plans, that it is hard to see what can be done that is practical at the present time by edging forward with existing institutions. Mr Len Murray is reported as having said recently (*The Times*, 16 May 1980) that 'the British disease ... was old age, old institutions, old industrial assets and old attitudes'. If we are agreed that restraint cannot be imposed by sanctions against incomprehension and resentment, we depend wholly upon a basic change of attitudes so long as we remain within the old institutions; but it is possible that people as they are would behave to different effect when placed within a different structure.

II *K. Sisson*

This paper draws on a number of the ideas and proposals outlined in Blackaby's review. However, it does not comment on them directly, but makes suggestions on the direction of the reform of pay bargaining and – perhaps more importantly – on the next steps which should be taken. These suggestions assume that collective bargaining will remain the predominant method of settling pay – even if in the short run expediency demands yet another statutory pay policy.

A reduction in inflation may be the dominant objective in the minds of those putting forward proposals for the reform of pay bargaining and yet it is difficult in practice to divorce it from the other two mentioned by Blackaby – especially the need to introduce greater equity. The present arrangements – massively decentralised and fragmented by comparison with most other countries – encourage the pursuit of comparisons and breed competitive bargaining. They are a major source of disputes – especially as the economy declines. They help to produce the dissatisfaction which fuels inflationary pay claims and contributes to inflation because the competitive bargaining adds to the upward movement of pay settlements. For this to happen it is enough that groups of workers seek to keep up with settlements negotiated elsewhere. There does not have to be a clear cut wage round; there does not have to be a recognisable key bargain. In brief, the crux of the problem is the lack of coordination which exists between pay settlements.

The Direction of Reform

Attempts to fragment pay bargaining still further are only likely to exacerbate the problem – unless they are accompanied by measures that so weaken collective bargaining that it is doubtful if they would be acceptable in a democratic society. The author (with William Brown) has already put on record proposals about the direction which the reform of pay bargaining should take [1]. These proposals are very much in the mould of the 'concerted action' or 'social contract' approach discussed by Blackaby. Perhaps the key difference is the emphasis which, in our proposals, is placed on bargaining. Our proposals explicitly provided for a three-stage bargaining process.

Stage one would involve the government and representatives of the TUC and CBI. It would not simply be a matter of relating general pay increases to the average increase of productivity or to the index of retail prices. The negotiations would be concerned with real incomes; and they would be concerned with net incomes after tax.

Stage two would involve the three parties in deciding how the share going to wages and salaries should be distributed between people of different pay levels: it would be concerned with the fundamental problems of adjusting pay relativities. In practice the main responsibility for formulating proposals under this stage would devolve upon the TUC.

Stage three would involve the negotiators in individual bargaining units in deciding how they are going to distribute the total package resulting from stage two within the bargaining unit. The process would be facilitated if there was some synchronisation or compression of the timing of negotiations.

There is little likelihood of these proposals being accepted in the short run. But this does not mean that nothing can be done. Perhaps one of the failings of recent years is that too much time has been spent on deciding the destination and not enough on the route. The suggestions which follow are designed to bring about greater co-ordination – without conflicting with the ultimate goal. The burden of responsibility for change is placed on government and employers.

The Role of Government

Every government has to have a pay policy; that is to say, it has to have a view about what it expects or wants the rate of increase in pay to be. It has to make some assumptions about pay in order to set realistic targets for the control of money supply or the setting of cash limits in the public sector. There would be considerable benefit if it made these assumptions explicit; in particular it would help to influence the general level of expectations. There is little point in talking about what the nation can afford if it is not spelt out – not necessarily in terms of a norm but in a number of possible economic projections.

There are a number of ways in which this could be done. It could pass legislation. In West Germany, for example, the 1967 Law on Stability and Growth requires the federal government to publish its reactions to the Council of Experts' Annual Report and to make a statement about its economic and financial policy. Or it could set up an economic forum as the CBI has suggested. Or it could quite simply take advantage of an existing institution like the NEDC to make a statement.

However, the most urgent task is for the government in its capacity as employer (or paymaster) to put its own house in order – especially in the public services or non-market sector. Some five million workers are involved; their pay accounts for approximately 70 per cent of total costs in organisations like the NHS and local authorities. Pay bargaining is highly visible. Unlike much of the private sector, it takes place at the centre and affects all the workplaces. Disputes are extremely damaging and the public are quickly involved. There is also a great danger that the public services sector and not the market sector becomes the pay leader – something especially dangerous for an economy which is so dependent upon international trade.

The government must resist the temptation to fragment pay bargaining – the prospect of individual local authorities, regional/area health authorities, and civil service departments negotiating independently is an industrial nightmare. Instead, it should take a closer look at Basnett's proposals in *The Way Out of Warfare Over Pay* [2]. In particular it should '... amalgamate into one all the existing review bodies; require the new body to produce information which would be available to negotiators, but not to make recommendations; bring together the starting dates of pay agreements of public service workers. (Currently, for example, manual workers in local authorities and the NHS negotiate in November; white-collar workers in July.) It should shift the starting dates of pay agreements of public service workers to the end of the pay round.' Under these proposals cash limits would return to their rightful place as financial controls. They would no longer be substitutes for a pay policy.

Implicit in these proposals is an acceptance that comparability will continue to be a major factor in the determination of public service pay. It is difficult to see how it could be otherwise: successive governments have recognised this. The Pay Research Unit, the various salary review bodies, the Standing Commission on Pay Comparability and numerous *ad hoc* bodies all bear witness to the recognition of the need to reach settlements which are regarded as fair. Experience suggests that governments can only break the link for limited periods before there is confrontation. The catching-up process which results threatens to set the pattern for the private sector. There is thus more chance of preventing the public sector from setting the pattern if the principle of comparability is allowed to operate systematically.

This is not to suggest that there could be no improvements in the present arrangements. Having one review body would be a step forward; it would mean that its findings would have to be on a comparable basis. A requirement to publish its findings in detail would be helpful too. There is also scope for clarifying the relative worth of particular elements of compensation – cars and pensions for example.

Nor does an acceptance that comparability will be a major factor mean that performance has to be ignored. Serious consideration should be given to the extension of work-study-based incentive schemes – especially into white-collar areas. Pay might be made up of a base rate negotiated nationally, together with a bonus element which depends on acceptable levels of performance.

The Role of Employers in the Private Sector

The CBI has already recognised that there is need for greater co-ordination of pay bargaining in the private sector. Indeed, it offers to its members a set of guidelines for reducing competitive bargaining. But guidelines do not go far enough. The CBI should discuss with its members – if necessary in special conferences – the *action* which is going to be taken. Two areas in particular demand attention.

First there is a need to resolve the dilemma posed by two-tier bargaining in many manufacturing industries. The farcical situation in engineering in 1979 – when many large employers were involved even though the multi-employer agreement had little impact on pay – can surely be avoided. One possibility would be for the larger employers to adopt non-conforming status much as ICI do in chemicals. The analysis of present bargaining arrangements in Brown's paper suggests that a dual structure is beginning to emerge. Perhaps this could be made explicit.

Secondly, in the case of those multi-plant employers who have opted for single-employer bargaining, there is a need to give serious consideration to the level at which pay is settled. If one of the CBI's main criteria is applied – that the bargaining unit should comprise all those employees who share a common interest and who would be able normally to claim comparable concessions from employers – then many are out of line. Many of these employers indulge in the illusion of plant bargaining; that is, they negotiate at plant level, but coordinate at the division/group/company level.

The CBI should also discuss how to secure greater coordination between its members – including the nationalised industries. Clearly, the coordination between employers which is found in most other countries on multi-employer bargaining cannot any longer be achieved in Britain; yet the need remains. The compression of the pay round is likely to have dire consequences if there is no provision for employers' coordination. There is a glimmer of hope in the fact that manufacturing industry has come to be dominated by large multi-plant employers – which, in essence, are employers' organisations in their own right. It should be possible for them to coordinate with one another. They might even go so far as to think in terms of coalition bargaining – much as employers in the US have done. Whether there is the will remains to be seen. If not, employers should not grumble if competitive bargaining continues.

The Role of Trade Unions

This paper has said little about the role of trade unions in achieving greater coordination. The reasons for this are simple. Trade unions are reactive bodies – and their organisation is what it is *because of* the present pay bargaining arrangements. To expect individual trade unions to exercise moderation when there is no guarantee that others will do likewise is totally unrealistic. Theirs is very much the prisoners' dilemma.

The burden of responsibility for change, then, rests with the government and with employers. A useful analogy can be drawn with some of the developments in workplace industrial relations. The rationalisation of payment systems, the application of job evaluation, the introduction of procedures – these reforms have come about largely as a result of employer initiatives. Not only have they done much in their own right to reduce competitive bargaining, they have helped to increase the authority of joint shop steward committees – which itself has contributed to a decline in fragmentation. It is a lesson which employers *collectively* would do well to learn.

References

[1] Brown, W. and Sisson, K., *A Positive Incomes Policy*, Fabian Tract 442, Fabian Society, 1976.
[2] Basnett, D., 'A way out of warfare over pay', *Sunday Times*, 4 December 1977.

III *R. Close*

In developing the British Institute of Management's ideas on pay bargaining the BIM's prime concern has been to find an alternative to bouts of temporary pay restraint and bursts of irresponsible collective bargaining; to explore ways of developing lasting proposals which will have a moderating influence on the level of pay settlements. We see the benefits of such a process in reduced inflation and improvement in investment, output, and, in the long term, employment. We do not see pay policy as a means of achieving greater equity. The priority guiding all pay negotiation should be to provide adequate reward for contribution in order to create the incentive needed to encourage the acquisition and practice of skills and knowledge.

The Social Contract: the Forum

The BIM believes that there should be an annual (or six-monthly) discussion and debate on pay in the context of economic trends and policy. The aim would be to move towards a broad consensus on, and understanding of, the economic situation; a broad agreement on the main lines of policy and strategy, and a common view of likely and desirable trends in pay, prices, and perhaps also, taxation. This would provide the context for the conduct of collective bargaining.

Essential background for informed debate will be economic analysis from sources broadly acceptable to all concerned, showing the range of economic possibilities, the likely implications for prices, unemployment, economic growth, and real income of alternative wage and salary growth patterns.

There is a strong case for involving forecasting expertise independent of government in this process. Nevertheless, the government must be involved in the presentation of the background analyses to ensure that the data base, the modelling and policy assumptions are consistent with those used by the Treasury. The arguments in favour of a debate on economic policy and pay supports the case for more open government and less Treasury secrecy about their analyses of economic policy options and their forecasts of the consequences of alternative developments.

It will not be easy to reach an agreement on likely future developments that will be broadly acceptable to all parties. In addition to the uncertainty associated with economic forecasting, there will remain a wide range of views on the desirability and likely consequences of alternative policy options. It is likely, however, that a good deal of common ground will be identified.

The central discussions should be seen as having a general educative value, providing better public understanding of the implications of attempting to obtain rapid increases in money wages in the context of firm monetary control – in particular, better awareness of the trade-off between pay rises and unemployment.

We are not suggesting that such a forum, meeting say twice a year, would solve all problems; merely that it would make a contribution to the understanding of inflation and of the ways in which living standards and job opportunities could be improved. It would be worthwhile holding such a public discussion even in the absence of formal TUC endorsement so long as some leading trades unionists take part.

Synchronisation

The BIM view is that the notion of 'synchropay' is worth considering. The possibilities include greater synchronisation at plant, company, industry or even national level. While accepting in principle that this might help to reduce the competitive leapfrogging of pay demands, we recognise that there are formidable difficulties – such as the problem of persuading unions to alter their settlement dates; the effect of placing new and different pressures on established bargaining machinery; and the extent to which synchropay would lead to synchronised price increases. The BIM has tended not to press this particular option, but recognises it as a proposition worthy of consideration as a long-term aim.

The Norm, with Exceptions

A variety of policies based on a pay norm, with or without specified criteria for exceptions, have been tried over the past twenty years and, in each case, have been effective for only a short period. Some periods of restraint have clearly checked the rise in average earnings in the short run. But this has been achieved at the cost of creating pay anomalies, distorting pay structures, narrowing differentials, and seriously eroding incentives. The build up of pressures for greater flexibility has been the principal cause of collapse. During the subsequent periods of relaxation the average level of earnings has risen sharply as employees have attempted to restore their levels of absolute and relative pay. The long-term effect of these alternating periods of restraint and relaxation on the rise in average earnings is uncertain.

There have been suggestions that periodic pay restraint followed by pay relaxation should be replaced by a permanent incomes policy. It is widely accepted that if an acceptable way could be found of reconciling the need to provide sufficient flexibility and adequate incentives with effective pay restraint, this might offer the prospect of faster growth and lower unemployment. Past experience suggests however that it is not possible to devise such a policy. A relatively simply pay policy, such as that under phases I and II of the Social Contract, is too rigid. A highly complex policy is likely to collapse either through evasion (as with the National Board for Prices and Incomes) or through confrontation (as with the Pay Board). In the improbable event that a complex policy could survive it would represent too great a degree of intervention in collective bargaining. However carefully constructed, it is highly doubtful whether any formal policy can offer sufficient flexibility. The responsible use of this flexibility is crucial in providing incentives to employees for improved performance, for coping with changing labour requirements, for the introduction of new products and processes, for promoting industrial restructuring and so on.

Relativities Board

While the BIM rejects a policy of permanent pay control, it believes that an impartial board or procedure is needed for helping to identify appropriate changes to the existing pattern of relativities and differentials; it would facilitate the necessary adjustments in a way which lessens the risk of competitive leapfrogging.

Such a board or procedure would have no formal powers; it would not replace existing processes; nor would it be called upon to arbitrate on particular disputes. It would instead seek to exert an influence by providing a source of impartial information, and analysis based on a national rather than local perspective. The board's principal concern should be to recommend a pay distribution that is conducive to improved economic performance.

The board would examine the general case for adjustments in relativities in the light of historic anomalies and of structural changes in the economy. It would identify groups of employees who on economic grounds appeared to warrant priority consideration and it would also indicate the degree of priority to be attached to individual cases. While not being involved directly with particular claims, the board, by providing an impartial source of information and analysis would reinforce the weight of public opinion against groups who sought to exploit their bargaining strength. On the other hand, relativity adjustments which appeared to be justified on economic grounds could, because of support from the board, be implemented with less prospect of counter-claims being made by others. Because of the imbalance of bargaining power, differentials of skilled, managerial and professional people will remain a source of concern. An essential role for the board will be to examine pre- and post-tax trends in differentials, and to look at the evidence about the consequences of the severe squeeze on differentials in recent years. The value of using job evaluation techniques to establish a series of bench mark jobs and rates across skilled and managerial grades could be explored. The main aim would be to increase the general level of understanding of the economic case for differentials, to move towards a degree of consensus on what constitutes adequate differentials, and to consider how best these might be achieved.

Other Proposals

The BIM has not explored tax-based incomes policies in any detail. Further, there is no relevant practical experience upon which to draw. The Institute would not support permanent pay control whether this was enforced by tax incentives/penalties or by other means. Of the more flexible tax-based incomes policy options (for example, those based on value added), it is clear even from the initial analyses provided by Blackaby's paper that such policies would be very complex. This would undermine credibility and must raise serious doubts about their suitability as a basis for a lasting policy on pay, which we believe can only survive if there is a general consensus of support. Another worry is whether such policies would offer sufficient flexibility. The other more 'radical' proposals discussed by Blackaby seem more of academic than practical interest.

While accepting that the imbalance of bargaining power is a contributing factor in inflation, the BIM's views on legislation to limit trade union power are based on broad industrial relations considerations. While changes in labour relations are not unimportant, the Institute does not believe in any easy way of restoring the balance of bargaining power. Managers attach much less weight to specific reforming legislation than to the importance of a broad improvement in the political and economic circumstances of the country as a whole, reinforced by continuous management efforts towards better labour relations, improved communications, and voluntary participation in the decision process.

IV *R. J. V. Dixon*

This comment summarises briefly the CBI's analysis of what is wrong with our present pay determination system and its proposals for reform, and reviews the progress that has been made. In theory, collective bargaining is an excellent way to determine pay. It should allow pay and conditions to reflect the economic circumstances of each enterprise. It should result in settlements which represent a fair compromise between the financial requirements of business and the aspirations of employees. But practice has been very different from theory and has driven every government since the war to try to limit pay in one way or another.

The CBI believes that improvements in three areas could make collective bargaining work better: in the balance of power in industry; in pay bargaining structures; and in attitudes towards pay bargaining. This comment first analyses the problems in these three areas, and then summarises CBI proposals and the progress which has been made.

In recent years, for a number of reasons, the balance of bargaining power has moved steadily in favour of organised labour. This situation is not unique to Britain; yet the problem of pay determination seems greater here than elsewhere. One reason for this is a framework of law uniquely favourable to trade unions, which have wide immunity from legal action. Another is the fact that employees can be cushioned from the cost of industrial disputes through the payment of supplementary benefit and tax rebates. Government subsidies to uneconomic operations in the private sector have served also to reduce the fear of unemployment as a counter to unrealistic pay demands, and in the public sector, the ability of some groups to cause a great deal of disruption has led to pressure for government to meet, rather than resist, large claims.

The structure of pay bargaining in this country is highly fragmented – both vertically (in that an employee's terms and conditions can be determined by agreements made at industry, company and plant level); and horizontally – with employees in the same company or industry, whose pay is compared with each other, split into several different bargaining units (Chapter 6). This fragmentation can be inherently inflationary when, for example, domestically negotiated bonus arrangements are eroded by nationally negotiated minimum rates; or when competition exists between bargaining units represented by different unions, so that each time one group gets an increase another group will try to restore its relative position.

Attitudes towards pay are often heavily influenced by factors external to the individual firm, notably the cost of living and comparability, and are too little influenced by immediate business realities. An employee, it is true, will naturally expect his pay to be comparable with that of others doing the same thing in the same industry; and employers will need to offer rates of pay which are competitive in the labour market. However, unreasonable comparisons are often drawn with workers whose situation is not at all similar, and if such comparisons are conceded, industrial efficiency can be seriously damaged.

Proposals: the Reform of Pay Structures

The CBI has urged its members, when appropriate, to make their bargaining structures more rational and coherent. This involves (a) reducing the number of bargaining units, so far as practicable; (b) including in each bargaining unit all employees sharing a common interest, who could reasonably claim comparable concessions from employers; and (c) where bargaining takes place at more than one level, ensuring that there is a clear separation of those items of the employment package bargained at each level, with only those items for which flexibility is required bargained at the lower level. The CBI has also proposed a compression of the annual bargaining round; this proposal is more fully discussed in Chapter 4. It appears that some progress has been made towards shortening the negotiating period.

A third area of structural reform is the system of pay determination in the public sector. A key principle is that there should be no discrimination against government employees. The nationalised industries should be treated as part of the market sector; their operating efficiency should be encouraged by setting financial targets, which should not be altered in the face of excessive pay demands. For the tax dependent public services which operate without the discipline of the market, cash limits should be established and maintained, and settlement dates should be shifted to the end of the bargaining round, so that the pay year and the financial year coincide.

The CBI's view was that the role and method of comparability in public service pay determination needs urgent examination. If it is to play a significant part, the various pay research bodies and review boards should be brought under one umbrella. The comparisons they make should take fully into account market factors such as recruitment and efficiency, and non-pay factors such as inflation-proofed pensions, job security, automatic progression, as well as a higher level of fringe benefits in the private sector. The CBI initially welcomed the establishment of the Standing Commission on Pay Comparability under Professor Clegg, but is disturbed by the inadequate timetable for dealing with the references, by the fact that the reports have been regarded as binding rather than advisory, and by some doubts about aspects of the Commission's methodology, in particular its failure to take market factors fully into account.

Attitudinal Change

The CBI is concerned to create a climate that encourages more responsible pay bargaining. It has called for an end to incomes policies, urged effective control of the money supply, and has proposed the creation of a national economic forum. (This proposal has not yet been taken up by the government in the form envisaged by the CBI.) The CBI also stresses the need for companies to improve inadequate systems of employee communications; it has published its 'Guidelines for Action on Employee Involvement', and has organised a number of conferences on this theme.

Changes in the Balance of Power

On the balance of power between employers and employees, the government's Employment Bill incorporates most of the CBI's thinking on the law with respect to picketing, the closed shop, and the finance of union ballots. On the finance of strikes, the Social Security No 2 Bill provides for substantial reductions in supplementary benefits to the dependents of strikers. This includes a new provision to ensure that the first £4 of PAYE tax rebates are no longer disregarded in the assessment of supplementary benefit entitlement.

The CBI has also done a good deal of preparatory work on a Mutual Strike Insurance Fund; however, the proposal is, for the time being, in abeyance.

5 Report of the Discussion
F. T. Blackaby

Unemployment

The conference began by discussing an important distinction between the 'level of unemployment associated with a given degree of labour shortage', and the 'natural rate'. It was strongly argued that the figure of unemployment corresponding to a given degree of labour shortage had risen – on the evidence, amongst other things, of the CBI series which gives the percentage of firms which say that their output is limited by shortages of skilled labour; other indicators of labour shortage also gave support to this contention (Metcalf, page 51). There were various questioning points. Some had a sense of *déja vu*: they remembered that in the 1930s there were also widespread complaints of labour shortage, and that partly for this reason in the late 1930s it was widely questioned whether it would ever be possible to run the economy with unemployment below 8 or 10 per cent. Whenever unemployment was high, there was always the temptation to find structural rather than 'demand deficiency' reasons for it. The CBI series, for management statements about shortages of labour, represented a succession of essentially subjective judgements about the degree of difficulty which could be regarded as a shortage; the subjective perception of difficulty could vary over time. It was also suggested that the decline in manufacturing industry might have led to lower investment in human capital as well as in fixed capital, so that the supply of skilled labour had come down together with the demand for it. If the demand went up, so would the supply. However, most people accepted that there had been some rise in shortage-related unemployment; the question was how much.

Why had shortage-related unemployment risen? A few tentative suggestions were made. It was argued that it was not the benefits–earnings ratio, but perhaps the laxer administration of the social security system. It was easier for people, when unemployed, to earn money in the 'informal economy'. It was also possible that, because of the increase in the number of women in employment, men could take longer over finding a new job, since the family could manage for a time on the wife's earnings.

Although shortage-related unemployment appeared to have risen, most of those present took the view that this was only part (perhaps a small part) of the apparent rise in the 'natural rate' of unemployment.

The natural rate

There was some discussion of the definition of this term. Some preferred an 'expectations' definition – the rate at which there were no systematic errors in inflationary expectations. The alternative view was that the question in which we were interested was this: at what level of unemployment would the rate of inflation stop accelerating and start to decelerate? We needed some phrase when we were discussing what this figure might be, and the 'natural rate' appeared to be as good a term as any. It was used at the conference more frequently than the alternative phrase – the non-accelerating-inflation rate of unemployment (NAIRU).

Those who put heavy weight on the effect of expectations accepted that there might be a temporary further rise in unemployment while expectations were adjusted, but saw no reason to think that the subsequent natural rate was higher than the present one. At the other end of the spectrum, there were those who suggested unemployment had very little effect on the rate of increase in earnings. Some declared themselves unimpressed by time series regressions of money earnings on unemployment – 'the observation of twigs floating together down the stream of economic history'.

There were a great many circumstances in which trade union negotiators could negotiate an increase in earnings which, although it would lead to some fall in employment, would not mean any involuntary redundancies. The turnover of labour was such that if the firm reduced its recruiting, the labour force would soon fall; and the experience of recent years had shown that quite a large number of workers volunteered to accept redundancy. They might indeed be unwise to do so, and it was difficult to explain why workers in regions with high unemployment voluntarily accepted rather small capital sums, in spite of the fact that they would have little hope of finding another job; none the less this is what in fact they did. (As a consequence, the unemployment which resulted was among the older, less mobile, less adaptable part of the population.) Even if there were involuntary redundancies, negotiations about pay tended to be conducted according to one set of rules in one compartment, and negotiations about redundancies according to another set of rules in another compartment. Trade union negotiators negotiated on behalf of members and not on behalf of the unemployed: the tendency was for unemployment to rise among school leavers, who obviously were not members of trade unions, and among the floating population of those who took casual employment. It was quite rational for negotiators to prefer a higher wage for a slightly reduced number of employees to a lower wage for the full existing complement of workers. Those who regarded economic behaviour as essentially selfish should not expect trade union negotiators to be much concerned with the unemployed.

Unemployment would be effective as a way of bringing down money earnings if the unemployed could offer to take the place of the employed for less pay. That might have been the case before the First World War, when blacklegs were quite common – even in South Wales, with police protection. It was not the case now.

How far did a firm's 'ability to pay' affect the increase in earnings? On the one hand Daniel's evidence about the experience of 1975 (Chapter 7) suggested that the effect was not large. Companies – whether their cash flow was good or bad – were extremely vulnerable to interruptions in production. For example, when overseas markets had been developed, and contracts with penalties for late delivery had been accepted, then if production was interrupted, the firm ran the risk, not only of paying the penalty, but more generally of losing all the investment which had been devoted to developing that particular market.

Indeed it was suggested that trade unions sometimes deliberately picked on firms with cash flow problems, on the grounds that they were less able to withstand a strike than firms with stronger cash reserves. The acceptance of a strike could be regarded as analogous to a capital investment – a firm paid money now in order to keep down labour costs in the future; and it was only firms which were in a good financial position which could do this.

Some doubted, however, whether this was a good picture of what went on in Britain – the examples quoted tended to be American.

Certainly in the car industry, the rise in earnings in financially weak firms had been significantly lower than in financially strong ones. The figures from the CBI's data bank for the 1979–80 wage round were cited to suggest some effect from ability to pay: throughout that wage round, the figure for the 'past rise in prices' had moved up fairly fast – and yet the awards in manufacturing industry at the end of the wage round were about the same as those at the beginning. This suggested that, whereas the effect of past price rises might have been exerting an upward pressure, the ability to pay had been exerting a roughly compensating downward pressure.

Econometric evidence was cited to suggest that there was some unemployment effect, but that it was shallow – that it would perhaps need an additional 1 percentage point in unemployment to reduce the rise in money earnings by 1 per cent. However, such relationships should not be linearly extrapolated to read off the effect on earnings of figures of unemployment which we have not hitherto experienced since the Second World War.

Rational expectations

The 'rational expectations' view of the labour market depends on the proposition that those engaged in offering, or accepting, given increases in money earnings are heavily influenced by their expectations of future trends in the economy; those expectations do not depend simply on extrapolations of the past, but take into account information they receive about, for example, government intentions. The medium-term money supply targets provide information of this kind; after a time, when people realise that the government is determined to adhere to these numbers, behaviour in the labour market will adjust to them. People will stop pricing themselves out of the labour market.

Various difficulties were suggested in the application of rational expectations ideas to the labour market. It was suggested, for example, that – although there were many areas (such as exchange-rate or interest-rate determination) where these ideas were useful, the bargaining process in the labour market was not one of them. It might be a more useful idea if pay bargaining was either atomistic, or alternatively if the trade unions negotiated as a block; in Britain we had 'fragmented labour monopolies'. It was not clear that those engaged in bargaining necessarily shared the particular rationality embodied in a monetarist view of the working of the economy. Even those around the table – who were presumably rational men – probably had different price and earnings expectations for the next few years. Expectations generally might be very gradually formulated, and might be very difficult to shift. Further, there was the question about the importance of the expectation of future inflation, as against the experience of past inflation, as a determinant of wage demands and wage settlements. Both the Daniel survey and CBI studies from the firms in their data bank suggested that the strong influences on wage settlements were past prices and comparability: negotiators looked at what has happened, and what is happening, to other people. Comparability was important partly because ideas of fairness were important: it was fair that there should be equal pay for equal work.

There was some discussion of the relative validity of 'asking people what they do' as against statistical inference: when people were asked why they did what they did, frequently they did not know, and sometimes they did not tell the truth. For example, it was suggested that the rise in earnings in 1975 – which was the subject of Daniel's survey – matched closely the rise in the money supply two years earlier. The counter-argument was that the exact transmission process of such a monetary effect had to be spelt out: 'some econometricians ascribe to workpeople motives which they do not have'.

The Real Wage

The discussion began with a distinction between the 'internal' and 'external' real wage. There is the internal problem when wage and salary incomes rise faster than profits, and profits are squeezed. There is the external problem, which is different – when all incomes, including profits, rise to a figure that is too high in relation to those in competing countries, at ruling exchange rates. (The first of these two problems could affect all countries at the same time; the second could not.)

Was the problem one of engineering a reduction in the real wage, in one of the senses described? Or was the problem simply one of discovering ways of getting both money earnings and prices to rise more slowly, leaving the movement of real wages substantially unchanged? (Of course the UK could have both problems – a wage–price spiral and also a need to reduce the real wage.)

Both views of the real wage problem had their proponents. It was certainly said that at ruling exchange rates the UK's 'external' real wage was now too high: the requirement was, therefore, that money wages should rise more slowly here than in competing countries, unless an effective devaluation could be engineered. The internal case was also argued – that profits had been squeezed, and capital investment consequently reduced, so that there was inadequate capital stock for the employment of all those who wished to work. However, one questioner asked why funds for capital investment had to come out of profits: was there no way in which the funds might be forthcoming from wage and salary increases, so that the employees collected the returns on the additional capital, rather than the rentiers?

There was a further real wage problem, arising from the target real wage hypothesis advocated (amongst others) by the Cambridge Economic Policy Group. On this view, money earnings started to accelerate if a real wage target had not been met. The government's reaction to accelerating inflation was to deflate the economy, reducing employment. A classical view of the behaviour of the economy might suggest that, as employment fell, smaller amounts of labour would be using the same quantum of capital, so that output per head (and consequently the real wage) could rise. On the CEPG view, because of the existence of a sizeable 'overhead' labour force, as employment and output fell, so also would productivity and the real wage: the real wage would fall even further behind the target, thus creating a vicious circle.

Others stressed that – whether or not there was a real wage problem in any of the senses described above – there could well be a wage–price spiral problem. Even if profit-margins had not been eroded, and even if the exchange rate moved in such a way as to preserve competitiveness, it would still be desirable – if wages were rising at 15 per cent and prices at 13 per cent – to find ways of shifting the numbers down towards 5 and 3 respectively.

However, for purposes of policy towards money incomes, it really made no difference whether the problem was seen as a real wage one or a wage–price spiral one: in either case the objectives must be to reduce the rate of increase in money earnings. It made no sense to urge workers to reduce the rate of increase in their real wages: all they could do in any case was to reduce the rate of increase in their money wages, and the consequences for their real wage depended on a multiplicity of other factors – the terms of trade, the length of the lag in the response of prices and government fiscal policy. If the government, by exhortation or incomes policy, succeeded in getting a deceleration in money earnings, then the best way of restoring profit-margins might be to combine this success with reflationary policies, so that the rise in output could accelerate the increase in profits. It was generally noted that deflationary policies tended to have a greater impact on profits than on income from employment – and that therefore such policies by themselves were hardly appropriate for reducing the 'internal' real wage.

Other Countries' Experience

In the discussion of Dean's paper (Chapter 8), there was a good deal of comment on pay bargaining in West Germany. 'Concerted action', it was suggested, might not be of central importance. It was more important, first, that there was powerful multi-employer bargaining – employers' associations were strong, and prepared for coordinated action; as a consequence any individual employer was also in a much stronger position than in the UK. Strong employers' associations had led to strong centralised unions; so the negotiations were at the centre, and unions were 'neutralised in the workplace'. There was no equivalent in West Germany to the strength of shop stewards in the UK. It was suggested that one reason why the trade unions in West Germany had been combative over the extension of co-determination was because they felt their power over pay was limited. A second important comment was that in a certain sense West Germany had an incomes policy which was settled by the negotiations in the metal and engineering sector, between the employers' association (the Verein Deutscher Maschinenfabriken) and the metalworkers union (I.G.Metall). The settlement came early and covered over two million workers; it was a large enough settlement for the union to be aware of the economic consequences of high figures.

There was some discussion of Japanese experience and the problems of flexibility that arose from lifetime employment. There was, it was suggested, a good deal of training within the large conglomerate firms, so the workers could be moved from declining to prosperous sectors. There was also flexibility in the retirement age. However, there was in many ways in Japan a dual labour market, with a great deal of subcontracting from the big firms with lifetime employment to the small firms which did not have this practice; firms with lifetime employment included only about 40 per cent of the labour force.

There was some general comment on 'concerted action', which appeared to be a fairly general feature of the more successful countries – more successful, that is, in their price–employment combination. Perhaps one of the reasons for the degree of social consensus in those countries might be that there was a certain general acceptance of the existing distribution of incomes in those countries. However, there did not seem to be any strong evidence that the distribution of incomes in the more successful countries was significantly more equal than in those countries which were less successful.

The situation in Australia was discussed with direct reference to possible policies for the UK (page 125).

What is Wrong?

There were rather different approaches to this problem. There were those who argued that the main problem was the distortion to the production pattern which arose from the fact that unionised labour gained at the expense of the non-unionised. They tended to see the problem simply as the problem of monopoly bargaining, and the preferred alternative system would be one which approximated more closely to atomistic bargaining, with each individual making his own bargain with his employer.

Others took the view that the UK system of pay bargaining had a great deal to do with our inflation – or, as alternatively phrased, with the high unemployment cost of bringing inflation down. Those who took this view argued that the reduction in profit-margins strongly suggested wage-push rather than demand-pull.

On this view, the problem was not one of simple monopoly, but of 'fragmented labour monopolies', which led to competitive bargaining. Many trade union leaders fully recognised the folly of high money wage increases and high price rises, and would much prefer 5 per cent for wages and 3 per cent for prices to figures of 15 and 13, or 25 and 23. However, they were confronted with the fact that what would be rational for the trade union movement as a whole, if it negotiated as a body, was not rational for the individual negotiator once others had set the example of a higher figure. It was the 'prisoner's dilemma' problem.

Because, therefore, of competitive bargaining, we had a highly unstable system, in which any shock easily set off a price–wage–price escalation. On this view, market discipline was not strong enough (except at excessive cost in unemployment) and some other external discipline was needed. The last thing that was needed was further fragmentation in bargaining, with even more competitive units; the move should rather be in the other direction.

What is to be Done?

The purpose of the discussion of the various proposals was not, of course, to pick a 'best buy'; given the composition of the conference, that would hardly have been practicable. It was rather to air the various arguments about the various suggestions. Some of those present were concerned to discuss the next appropriate move; others to discuss the arrangements which might eventually be arrived at after some years. These are some of the points which were made, on the proposals set out in Chapter 4. The section considers first the less radical changes, and then goes on to discuss the more radical ones.

Some discussants put a great deal of emphasis on the need for more employer solidarity. They noted the collapse of employers' associations in this country; they noted the importance of strong employers' associations in West Germany; and they looked for more coordinated action from the big conglomerate firms, possibly under CBI auspices. Without stronger employer coordination, they were doubtful whether it would be possible to moderate the consequences of the present system of 'fragmented monopoly bargaining'. They saw strong employer associations, leading to strong trade unions, as a good part of the answer. The relatively successful countries in Europe were those where negotiations were centralised; in this sense we needed more monopoly, not less.

A number of those present thought that public sector pay bargaining was in a chaotic state and in need of urgent reform. Governments had behaved like the most ramshackle Midlands engineering employers. There were three policies at the moment – the policy of cash limits, the Clegg comparability exercises, and a 'norm'. Some suggested that there had to be some kind of norm for the non-market public sector – in that governments had in the end to decide what average increase they would pay their employees. Others added that it was not practicable for any length of time to have a norm for the public sector which diverged markedly from the average increase given in the private sector. The views on what should be done differed a good deal. Some argued that with the growth of trade unions in the public services, and with their new readiness to use industrial action, comparability exercises should be abandoned, and negotiations should be local rather than national. Others took the opposite view: if any group of employees was willing to accept an arbitral process instead of 'the arbitrament of war', that was a gain which should not be lightly abandoned. The Clegg Commission, on this view, had made a considerable advance in ironing out some of the anomalies in pay between those employed in the National Health Service and those employed by local authorities. There was no reason why comparability exercises should not look at the market position for the various jobs – though those advocating this should be aware that it is not an easy thing to do. On the second view, local negotiations by individual local authorities and regional health boards would lead to a chaotic situation.

There was some support for other suggestions of Mr Basnett and of the CBI (page 76) – that public non-market sector negotiations should come at the end of the pay round, and that the various review bodies which consider the pay of particular employees in the public sector should be brought under a single umbrella. As it is, each review body tends to become an advocate for its particular group, and so there tends to be a kind of institutional leapfrogging in the pay of the professional people whose salaries are set by review boards of one kind or another.

There was not a great deal of discussion of further measures to limit trade union power, though the general argument was certainly put forward that the original function of trade unions – to prevent the exploitation of workers – was a function which was no longer needed. One comment, on the provisions then going through Parliament to reduce social security payments to strikers' families, was that the objective here was not so much to reduce trade union power as to persuade the trade unions to raise their subscriptions, so that they would become both more responsible and more professional. Some took the view that the power of organised labour would continue to be formidable so long as the right to strike remained; the trends of technology and increases in capital intensity served to strengthen the power of organised labour. In any case in Britain it did not seem very promising to hope that the trade union movement would wither away; it was in fact booming.

There was a basic choice to be made between a policy which attempted to weaken the power of trade unions, and a policy which tried to devise arrangements by which they would take more responsibility for the economic consequences of their actions; for the second of these two approaches, it would be better to have strong rather than weak unions.

Proposals for compressing the wage round – or, in its more extreme form, for 'synchropay', were also discussed. It was suggested that any such moves would increase trade union power; it would be much easier for them to arrange simultaneous industrial action. The counter-arguments were that an additional 1 per cent would be a small price to pay for being free of wage negotiations for most of the calendar year; that synchropay was a good way of making apparent the real position – that trade unions were essentially negotiating against each other for a share in a given rise in national output; and that a general strike was in any case not an effective form of industrial action.

The idea of a forum of some kind to discuss economic prospects and wages is, of course, part of a number of the proposals put forward. There were different views about the composition of such a forum, and about what it should do. The common proposal is that it should be tripartite – with representatives of the government, the CBI and the TUC. Some people were afraid that this would simply produce a set of conflicting views, with no consensus. The conference was reminded that the National Board for Prices and Incomes had on the Board both employers and trade unionists, but was none the less able to produce agreed reports. One suggestion was the forum should get closer to those actually engaged in negotiation, and should be closer to the consortium which Phelps Brown had suggested (page 86).

There was then some debate about whether the forum should simply be educative, or whether it should also have a bargaining function. Some were emphatic that it should limit itself to education; however, there was the difficulty here that there was no economic consensus about the way the British economy functioned, and that might make it difficult for the forum to agree on the consequences of various alternative assumptions or policies. The economists present were rebuked by the non-economists for not getting their act together.

Those who favoured an educative function only suggested that the forum should concern itself possibly with alternative scenarios on certain alternative assumptions; one remark was that it would not matter if the forum did not explicitly discuss wages at all. Others took the view that the forum should be a bargaining forum. First of all, it was suggested that the two sides would hardly bother to turn up if its purpose was solely to instruct them about British economics. Secondly, it was perfectly reasonable for the government to suggest certain bargains in exchange for wage moderation – the common practice in Norway, in Sweden, with some tentative experiments in Britain as well. Thirdly, sets of alternative scenarios would only lead to confusion: some single number ought to emerge.

The norm

The problems of any norm are well known: the fact that it will tend to be treated as a minimum, and the problems of flexibility which arise. However, it is sufficiently specific to affect individual negotiations, whereas any general agreement about restraint is unlikely to do so. The norm should apply not to wage settlements but to the average increase in actual earnings per head of the plant or firm; this would have the advantage of adding some flexibility.

Its proponents suggested that institutional provision for dealing with exceptions was the most important part of any such arrangement; reference was made to the provisions in Ireland (Chapter 8) and to the Anomalies Conference in Australia. However, there was some discussion about the amount of flexibility that was needed. The Saunders paper (Chapter 9) was cited to suggest that under free collective bargaining not many groups registered substantial gains or losses. During the 1970s, up to 1978, one of the main changes was the rise in women's relative pay, which was the result not of bargaining or the market but of legislation, and which did not prevent a very big increase in female employment.

On the criteria for exceptions to any norm, one suggestion was that exceptional treatment should be accorded only on two grounds – either because labour could not be obtained for that particular job, or as partial reward for success in exceeding a target figure for value added. How far should there be any criteria of equity, or social justice, for exceptional treatment? Most of those who talked about the norm doubted whether low pay should be a criterion: past incomes policies which had attempted redistribution in this way had been wholly unsuccessful. Fiscal policy should be used for any desired redistribution.

The Americans present were clearly more disturbed than the British by the possibility that any wage restraint might lead to excessive increases in profits; the British view in general appeared to be that profit-margins were so low that a substantial shift to profits was in any case desirable.

However, there was one suggestion for introducing a greater degree of 'equity' into relative incomes. The government, it was suggested, could encourage firms to develop job evaluation schemes; firms should also be required to notify the nature of these schemes to a central authority of some kind, which should gradually work towards harmonisation of the criteria.

The advocates of more job evaluation accepted that it could not be demonstrated that the importance given to the various elements – responsibility, dirty jobs, etc. – was in any sense objectively right; the argument was about acceptability – that the proposal would produce a set of differentials which was more acceptable than those prevailing now. However, some felt that once job evaluation was let loose, on for example comparisons between white-collar and blue-collar jobs, a whole Pandora's box would be opened. All kinds of valuations hitherto accepted would be questioned – why should not pay for blue-collar jobs rise with age, as it tends to do with white-collar jobs – and so on?

A number of those who wanted to impose some kind of discipline on the bargaining process accepted that, if trade union powers were to be limited in the area of pay, they should be given some other functions: the most common suggestion was more industrial democracy.

It was suggested that the medium-term monetary targets which the government had announced fulfilled all the valuable functions of a norm, without the disadvantages: it was not difficult for any economist employed by a trade union to work out the order of increase in money earnings which was compatible with any given money supply target. This proposition was disputed: it would be difficult for such an economist to predict how rapid the rate of deceleration was in fact likely to be: he would find himself concluding, for next year, that the figure might be as high as 15, or might be as low as 9.

There was some comment on those proposals which embodied

sanctions – and this included those tax-based incomes policies in which excessive increases in incomes were then partly or wholly taxed away. The argument was as follows: if trade unions had been given the power to extract excessive increases in incomes in the first place, what reason was there to think that they would then acquiesce in the removal of this power by fiscal means? One answer – which applied to a number of the proposals – was that they would certainly only work if there had been some fairly general acceptance of the principles involved: that is, they required some prior consensus. There was no reason to think that trade unions would break laws if these laws had been fairly generally accepted.

Other suggestions

There was some discussion of the Australian example; those who wanted to draw the attention of the conference to the Australian arrangements emphasised the advantages which arose when questions of pay, and relative pay, were separated from issues of industrial relations. Certainly the Australian Arbitration and Conciliation Commission had a problem which was probably more political than economic in making decisions which were generally acceptable; their use of partial indexation had been effective in bringing down the rate of inflation in Australia. It was an important point that their system of indexation was retrospective, rather than the prospective provisions which have increasingly been incorporated into wage agreements in the United States and, to a lesser extent, in Britain.

The conference listened to a short exposition by Professors Lerner and Colander of their Market Anti-inflation Plan. One of the points stressed was that the proposal should be much more acceptable to the trade union side than many incomes policy proposals, since it was based on value added per unit of input, and not exclusively on wages, so that profits were covered as well as wages. Further, whereas with tax-based incomes policies there is a problem in trying to decide what tax rate to set, in the Lerner–Colander proposals the market solves this question. One comment was that, in spite of the claimed advantage for value added, none the less it might be conceivably more practicable to operate on the income side; this would avoid the problem of valuing capital input. The idea of saleable permits to exceed certain increases in hourly labour costs, or dividends, was perhaps a more comprehensible concept. The public sector would be a problem; there would have to be a separate scheme for the public sector. Most discussants found it difficult to imagine circumstances in which such a scheme might be introduced: it was suggested that it might perhaps just be possible if it followed on a cruder policy in which there had been a uniform limit on the increase in the wage bill per head.

There was some discussion of role assignment – the assignment of particular policies to particular objectives – mainly in connection with Meade's proposals (Chapter 4). The discussion was conducted, using the standard quantity theory of money abbreviations – M(money), V(velocity), P(prices), T(output). Meade argued that the neo-Keynesian idea was to use control of MV to get the desired movement of T, and that incomes policy then had to be used to control P. His view now was that MV – that is, fiscal and monetary policy – should be used to keep PT on a steady path, and wage-fixing arrangements should be used to divide PT in an appropriate manner. When asked whether the objective really should be to keep PT on a steady path, irrespective of developments in other countries, he indicated that in his view this should be the case; interest-rate and exchange-rate policy could be used to make the adjustments with the rest of the world. He agreed that T was more important than P – that is that economic growth, and full employment were more important than inflation – but that he considered it was impossible to run an economy with inflation accelerating indefinitely.

Some discussants were not sure about the reality of this assignment problem. A macabre story was told about someone giving two children two pennies and telling them that the first penny was to be spent on milk, and the second penny on candy, and that if they failed to do exactly what they were told, they would be killed. They came back and said that they had done what they were told – except that they actually used the second penny to buy the milk and the first penny to buy the candy. So they were killed.

6 The Structure of Pay Bargaining in Britain

W. A. Brown

Pay determination in Britain is dominated by the use of collective bargaining. Over a half of employees are trade union members and over three quarters are covered by some sort of collective agreement. Perhaps the most distinctive feature of the British scene in international terms is the extensive involvement of shop stewards in the pay fixing process, an involvement that contributes to the considerable variety and fragmentation of the bargaining arrangements in use. This paper sets out to describe this far from orderly picture and to account for the substantial changes currently underway.

The starting point is a description of the principal pay fixing arrangements in use and an attempt to quantify their coverage. This is followed by an outline of current developments in methods of payment. In order to place the discussion in the wider context of industrial government it is then necessary to describe the rapid transformation taking place in the organisation of both employers and of trade unions. Some concluding observations are made about the implications for future incomes policies.

Types of Bargaining Arrangement

The term 'bargaining structure' has, in recent years, acquired considerable technical complexity and should strictly be considered in terms of several different dimensions (Clegg [3]). For present purposes, however, the focus of concern is on the one issue of pay and the organisational levels at which negotiations over pay occur. These levels, whether those of the departmental manager or the industry-wide employers association, are closely linked to the pattern of bargaining units: that is, to the groups of workers covered by particular agreements. Bargaining units are, however, considerably more complex than can be deduced from a description of bargaining levels alone. It is, for instance, almost universal for there to be separate negotiating arrangements for manual and non-manual employees and, within these broad categories, there may be separate negotiations for sub-groups such as maintenance workers or junior managers.

Rather than use the imprecise notion of a bargaining 'level', it is preferable in the first instance to distinguish arrangements by whether or not they involve collaboration between employers. 'Multi-employer' agreements where employers act in coalition or association are thus to be distinguished from 'single-employer' agreements negotiated by the individual employer for his own workforce and no one else. The former strategy has been seen as offering a chance to 'take wages out of competition' and present a united front to the unions, while the latter may be preferred by employers desiring greater freedom in their labour policy. Some implications of the two different strategies will be returned to later.

Multi-employer bargaining, industry-wide at either district or national level, developed strongly in Britain in the nineteenth century and was reinforced after the First World War. A series of bodies, most often called National Joint Industrial Councils, permitted negotiations between employers' associations and groups of trade unions to determine pay and conditions of work for specific industries. For want of a better phrase, these will be referred to as 'industry-wide' arrangements.

In industries where trade unionism was weak, successive governments this century have sought to encourage the development of independent industry-wide bargaining arrangements through the creation of wages councils (originally called trade boards). On these the balance of votes is held by individuals held to be independent of management and of trade union representatives, and the awards made are statutorily enforceable through a Wages Inspectorate. In practice most wages councils have failed to 'evolve' into agencies for free collective bargaining, and both the late Commission on Industrial Relations and the Advisory, Conciliation and Arbitration Service have sought to apply pressure in this direction, the latter using provisions from the 1975 Employment Protection Act to recommend new statutory joint industrial councils, stripped of independent members but still with wages inspectorate support (Sharp [15]).

On the continent of Europe, multi-employer industry-wide pay bargaining has remained supreme. But in Britain, with longer traditions of workplace bargaining and less commitment to employer solidarity, industry-wide agreements began to crumble with postwar full employment. Under pressure from both the labour market and their workforce, local managers became accustomed during the 1950s to augmenting industry-wide wage rates with payment-by-results bonuses, overtime and all manner of supplements. By the time the Royal Commission on Trade Unions and Employers' Associations reported in 1968 [14], the realities of wage bargaining were so remote from the formalities, particularly in much of manufacturing industry, that a fundamental change was recommended. The only way to gain control over wage drift and disputes was through formal factory agreements unhindered by commitments to industry-wide rates. In the terms of this discussion, the Commissioners proposed that much of industry should shift from half-hearted multi-employer to whole-hearted single-employer arrangements.

Before moving on to demonstrate how far this shift has been achieved, there are two observations to be added. The first is that, since 1968, the character of many multi-employer industry-wide agreements has altered fundamentally. Those covering the engineering and chemicals industries (and thus over half the trade union members in manufacturing) are among several whose minimum wage rates have been altered from providing 'floors', whose raising affects the earnings of everyone covered by the agreement, to providing 'safety nets', whose raising affects only the lowest paid in the industry. Put another way, in much of manufacturing, multi-employer agreements have been weakened to prevent their inhibiting the freedom of single-employer bargainers in their industry (Brown and Terry [1]).

Secondly, single-employer bargaining arrangements are very varied. Single-establishment bargaining, whether or not in the context of a multi-plant firm, has a special significance because it is the locus of operation of most shop steward organisations. At the other extreme there are some multi-plant organisations – Ford, CEGB, ICI and the civil service are examples – where single-employer arrangements cover all points of employment uniformly. Between these extremes the degree of centralisation of pay bargaining varies considerably. Perhaps the most common pattern for a large multi-plant concern is to have bargaining at the level of the product division, as does Unilever, but few large companies exhibit total internal consistency.

Table 6.1 Principal arrangements for pay-determination in 1978 (percentages of employees)

	Total employment	Trade union density[b]	Employees concerned[a]					
			Multi-employer		Single-employer			No bargaining
			Wages council	Industry, regional	Corporate		Single estab.	
					State	Priv.		
Ag., forestry, fish	1.6	23	95	2	3	—	—	—
Mining, quarrying	1.5	90		10	85	5	—	—
Food, drink, tobacco	3.1	51	7	24	—	32	25	8
Coal, petrol products	0.2	51	3	11	—	27	46	8
Chemicals, etc.	1.9							
Metal manufactures	2.1	69	1	11	30	8	46	4
Mechanical eng.	4.2		3	5	—	18	69	6
Ships marine eng.	0.8							
Instrument eng.	0.7		—	3	—	19	62	13
Electrical eng.	3.4							
Vehicles	3.5		1	3	—	39	53	1
Metal goods n.e.s.	2.4		1	8	—	19	63	8
Textiles	2.1	41	19	36	—	10	27	6
Leather, etc.	0.2	47	26	32	—	19	16	7
Clothing, footwear	1.6	64						

	Total employment	Trade union density[b]	Employees concerned[a]					
			Multi-employer		Single-employer			No bargaining
			Wages council	Industry, regional	Corporate		Single estab.	
					State	Priv.		
Bricks, pottery	1.2	60						
Timber, furniture	1.2	35	9	24	—	18	39	8
Other manufactures	1.5	(50)						
Paper, printing	2.4	72	3	68	—	3	16	8
Construction	5.5	27	—	70	—	—	—	30
Gas, water, elec.	1.5	92	—	—	100	—	—	—
Transport	6.4	93	—	20	65	5	—	10
Distribution	12.0	11	40	10	—	20	—	30
Insurance, banking	5.1	45	—	—	—	50	—	50
Professional	16.3	73	—	—	85	5	—	10
Misc. services	10.2	(10)	35	25	—	5	5	30
Public admin., defence	7.1	88	—	—	100	—	—	—
TOTAL	100	50	12	15	29	13	15	15

[a] Excluding the 15 per cent of manufacturing employees who work in establishments with fewer than 50 employees. This probably leads to a slight understatement of members covered by no bargaining or by multi-employer arrangements, but it cannot be more than 2 percentage points on the total figures.

[b] Percentage of total employees in that industry in trade unions in 1974.

Sources: Price, P. J. and Bain, G. S. 'Union growth revisited', *British Journal of Industrial Relations*, November 1976; Brown, W. A. (ed.) *The Changing Contours of British Industrial Relations*, Blackwell, forthcoming; NBPI, CIR, and ACAS reports.

It is a question to which this discussion will return. In what follows, the acute problems of defining organisational structure will be evaded: any single-employer arrangement affecting more than one establishment will be referred to as 'corporate', with the strong proviso that this does not necessarily mean the arrangement covers all of the employer's establishments.

The Coverage of Different Arrangements

Using the categories discussed in the previous section, Table 6.1 makes a first attempt to 'map' the British bargaining structure. The total manual and non-manual labour force of each industrial SIC category is broken down according to which arrangement provided the principal increase in earnings during 1977–8. Overall, single-employer arrangements cover around 57 per cent of the labour force, half of which is accounted for by the public sector and the remainder fairly evenly divided between the establishment and corporate bargaining. The rest of the labour force falls in roughly equal proportions between wages councils, industry-wide arrangements and no bargaining of any sort. These results are in close accord with Daniel's pioneering survey of 1975 in terms of the most important level of bargaining [5]. They differ principally in that he found more supplementary levels of bargaining in play; it is probable that both institutional reform and the existence of an incomes policy had led to a tidier pattern of bargaining by 1978.

In the public sector there are strong organisational reasons for corporate arrangements covering the whole of a service; and in broad terms, the last decade has seen increased centralisation of control both within the public sector industries and between them and the government (Clegg [4]).

In private manufacturing industry there has been a more fundamental change in bargaining structure since the war. Multi-employer arrangements, which in the 1930s were the principal source of pay increases for almost all manual workers, now play this role for only 27 per cent of manual workers in 36 per cent of establishments of 50 or more employees. Wages councils cover 7 per cent and industry-wide and regional agreements 20 per cent of the manual manufacturing workforce in establishments of 50 or more employees. It is negotiations with their own employer alone that principally affect the pay of 68 per cent of manual employees (in 53 per cent of establishments). For 46 per cent of employees these are at establishment level and for the remaining 21 per cent at some corporate level involving more than one establishment.

The particular wage-fixing arrangement used appears, as Table 6.2 shows, to depend substantially upon the size of the establishment concerned. It is the small establishments, particularly those with fewer than 100 employees, that either have no agreement covering them

Table 6.2 Bargaining arrangements for manual workers in manufacturing industry by size of establishment[a] (percentages)

	Number of full-time employees					
	50–99	10–199	200–499	500–999	1000+	Total
Wages Council	22(25)	12(13)	5(6)	3(4)	2(1)	14(7)
Industry-wide	21(21)	16(15)	23(24)	18(19)	12(10)	19(17)
Regional	1(1)	5(5)	4(5)	2(2)	1(0)	3(3)
All multi-employer	44(47)	33(33)	32(35)	23(25)	15(11)	36(27)
Corporate multi-plant	7(8)	11(12)	15(14)	16(18)	32(38)	11(21)
Establishment	32(32)	48(47)	45(45)	54(52)	52(49)	42(46)
All single employer	39(40)	59(59)	60(59)	70(70)	84(87)	53(68)
Other	0(0)	2(2)	1(1)	2(2)	1(1)	(1)
No bargaining	17(13)	5(6)	6(5)	4(3)	0(0)	10(4)
Total	100	100	100	100	100	100

[a] Percentage of establishments with percentage of employees in brackets.
Source: Industrial Relations Research Unit survey.

or use wages councils' awards. Use of industry-wide and regional arrangements also tends to decrease with increased size. Single-employer arrangements, on the other hand, are strongly preferred by larger establishments, being almost universal among those with more than 1000 employees. The sharp increase in the popularity of corporate arrangements as one moves to very large establishments arises in part from their disproportionate tendency to be part of multi-plant firms. Using discriminant analysis on these data, Deaton and Beaumont [7] have concluded that: 'high regional concentration, high union density and multi-unionism are associated with multi-employer bargaining, whereas larger establishments, multi-plant firms, foreign owner firms, high concentration industries and firms with (specialist) industrial relations management tend to have single-employer bargaining'.

Largely because they were later in joining trade unions, non-manual workers in manufacturing have never had much reliance on multi-employer pay fixing arrangements. Today all but 15 per cent of non-manuals (in 25 per cent of establishments of 50 or more employees) are covered by some sort of collective agreement and they are predominantly single-employer agreements. Industry-wide arrangements cover 7 per cent of non-manuals and wages councils 2 per cent, whereas establishment arrangements cover 45 per cent and corporate arrangements cover 29 per cent of non-manuals. Once again, the very few establishments that use multi-employer arrangements for the pay of their non-manual workers tend to be the smaller ones.

There are substantial differences between industries. Table 6.1 combines manual and non-manual employees. The engineering and chemicals industries are outstanding for their reliance upon single-employer arrangements. At the other extreme, paper and printing stands out as an industry where (outside newspapers) the industry-wide agreements have retained their control. Multi-employer arrangements also dominate textiles, clothing, footwear, leather and fur, the small establishments encouraging dependence upon wages councils. The catch-all bricks, pottery, glass, cement, timber, furniture and miscellaneous category is similar to food, drink and tobacco in that both have about a third of their workforce on multi-employer arrangements. But they differ interestingly in their reliance upon corporate agreements, which are particularly important in food, drink and tobacco, a point to be returned to.

Turning to non-manufacturing, the private sector is generally characterised by a far lower dependence upon collective bargaining. Agriculture relies on wages boards. In building and construction the larger firms generally observe the basic rates of industry-wide agreements. Insurance and banking has perhaps half its workforce covered by corporate single-employer agreements. The very large categories of distribution and miscellaneous services, covering over a fifth of the workforce, are collective bargaining wastelands. There are some pockets of powerful bargaining, such as in television, and corporate agreements are currently spreading rapidly among chain stores and large hotels. But most of the industry-wide arrangements, such as that for motor repair workers, are so weak a form of collective bargaining that they must be little different in operation to the wages councils upon which the highest proportion of employees depend.

Methods of Payment

The importance of methods of payment to a consideration of bargaining structure lies in the differing implications that different methods have for the control of pay. The more complex the rules of payment and the more they leave to managerial discretion, the less likely it is that the authorised negotiating body will have control over actual earnings.

The principal basis of payment is by time, and there has been a tendency for the minimum time period of accounting to increase in length, with manual workers' wage rates, for instance, increasingly being expressed in weekly rather than hourly terms. The spread of job evaluation has generally simplified and stabilised job payment grades. Among white-collar workers, increased unionisation and recurrent incomes policies have brought more rigid salary structures with greater use of incremental pay increases. In these respects pay structures are becoming simpler and more sharply defined.

One feature of payment by time that does not change is the British addiction to overtime working. Outstandingly among European countries, we are accustomed to our male manual workers being paid, on average, for over six overtime hours per week. As Table 6.3 shows, non-manuals and women are far less dependent upon overtime. Among manual men, however, its use is widespread across most industries, although in some it is common for overtime to be paid without the hours necessarily having been worked. Particularly notable about British overtime working is its stability over the years: throughout the 1970s the proportion of operatives working overtime kept between 28 and 37 per cent and they were paid, on average, for between 7.8 and 9.2 hours per week. So narrow a range of fluctuation reflects the extent to which overtime is institutionalised. It is a stable component of pay rather than a significant source of pay increases. Its relevance to the present discussion lies more in the importance which the overtime ban has come to have as a cheap but effective collective sanction;

one quarter of all incidents of industrial action in manufacturing take the form of overtime bans.

Payment by results of some sort, as can be seen from Table 6.3, contributes to the earnings of 44 per cent of manual men, 34 per cent of manual women and a much smaller proportion of non-manuals. Payment fairly directly related to physical output continues to be the most widespread basis (Lloyd [10]). There are, however, a number of changes in preference apparent. Individual piecework is tending to give way to group incentive schemes. The variable component of the wage is tending to diminish. There is more experi-

Table 6.3 Overtime and payment by results in April 1979[a]

	Men		Women	
	Manual	Non-manual	Manual	Non-manual
Overtime				
Hours per week	6.3	1.6	1.1	0.4
Per cent of employees	44.0	20.3	17.5	10.3
Pay as per cent of total	15.0	3.5	3.5	1.2
Payment by results[b]				
Per cent of employees	44.0	12.9	33.6	7.7
Pay as per cent of total	9.4	2.9	10.1	1.0

[a] Adult full-time employees; all industries and services.
[b] Encompasses commission and profit-sharing bonuses as well as more conventional incentive schemes.
Source: *New Earnings Survey* 1979.

menting with incentives based upon profits, value added and other non-physical measures. Perhaps most important of all, it has become normal to have payment-by-results schemes based at least nominally upon fairly rigorous work-study techniques. Work study is in use in 50 per cent of manufacturing establishments, having spread substantially during the 1970s. All these developments assist managerial control over bonus and thus inhibit 'drift' away from agreed rates of pay.

Studies over the past few years agree that, overall, there is no very substantial change in the proportion of the workforce covered by payment by results, but that this conceals considerable change both between and within industries (NBPI [11]; Lloyd [10]; Brown *et al.* [2]). While its extent and significance of payment by results has declined substantially in vehicle assembly, port transport and shipbuilding (where it dominated industrial relations as recently as the 1960s), it has spread rapidly through the public services. In gas, electricity, local authorities and the health service, incentive schemes have been a key instrument in attempts to increase labour productivity. Although these schemes are generally based on work study, there are exceptions and the tight centralised control over bonus that has been maintained in electricity supply contrasts with the very varied bonus earnings to be found in different local authorities.

A development that has particularly far-reaching implications for bargaining structure is the increased use of job evaluation techniques. These are systematic methods for establishing the relative pay rates for different jobs within a bargaining unit. By its nature, job evaluation is applicable to one bargaining unit at a time and, with a very few exceptions, its use has been confined to single-employer bargaining units. Job evaluation has tended to undermine multi-employer industry-wide agreements because managements find that they cannot maintain the integrity of their newly established pay structures if multi-employer negotiated rate increases have to be imposed subsequently. It is not possible to reconcile even half-hearted adherence to industry-wide pay rates with an effective factory or company job evaluation scheme.

When the NBPI surveyed the question in 1967 it concluded that 23 per cent of all employees in manufacturing were covered by job evaluation; in 1978 the IRRU survey suggested a figure of 55 per cent, and the rate of growth implied is consistent with intervening surveys (NBPI [12]; Brown *et al.* [2]). Although it appears that the Equal Pay Act provided a stimulus, there is evidence that job evaluation is continuing to be introduced, particularly among small establishments. A study conducted in 1976 suggested it is both widespread and developing in distributive trades, banking and finance, miscellaneous services and much of the public sector (Thakur and Gill [16]).

In summary, there is good evidence that employers have done much to rationalise and control payment systems over the past decade. Although payment by results has been introduced to much of the public sector even as it was being eased out of many other industries, there can be little doubt that it is no longer the generator of unnegotiated wage drift that it was in the 1960s. Job evaluation, by permitting bargaining units to maintain coherent internal pay structures, has done much to reduce fractional bargaining and leapfrogging. By making earnings more amenable to control by management and the negotiators, these changes have made pay more accessible to national policy-makers.

Employers' Organisation

It will be evident from the earlier description of the bargaining structure that employer solidarity, at least at the industry level, is in a state of collapse. It is true that there are industries such as building and construction, electrical contracting, hosiery and printing, where multi-employer agreements are still effective, but they are unusual. Although a large proportion of employers follow multi-employer agreements in some way (and the employers of three quarters of the manufacturing workforce say they do), they do so primarily for provisions such as hours of work, disputes procedures and shift premia. After the unsuccessful attempt by the largest employers' association, the Engineering Employers' Federation, to resist the erosion of the 40-hour week in the face of repeated strikes during the summer of 1979, even this degree of support of multi-employer agreements must be in jeopardy. Employers are increasingly looking after pay bargaining for themselves.

Paradoxically, however, there are no signs of any exodus from the membership of employers' associations. In manufacturing, 75 per cent of establishments (employing 72 per cent of the workforce) report themselves to be members of an employers' organisation, and they are evenly distributed across different industries. However, firms now appear to belong to employers' associations not for the strength of concerted action but as a source of advice for them as individual collective bargainers. Employers' associations, to put it more extremely, have changed their primary role from being brokers between employers and trade unions to being brokers between employers and the government.

It will be evident from what has been said so far that the move to single-employer bargaining has been accompanied by an increase in the professionalism of company industrial relations policy. Besides substantial reform of payment systems, the last decade has seen the introduction of procedures which have clarified the bargaining process in the majority of establishments. Probably the principal force behind these developments has been the great increase in governmental intervention through incomes policies and legislation on, among other things, redundancy, training, unfair dismissal, the closed shop, and health and safety. By obliging employers to cope with a host of fresh liabilities, recent governments have stimulated the growth of company industrial relations departments and have unwittingly encouraged the development of single-employer bargaining.

Just how the single-employer bargaining is taking shape is still a matter for speculation. Three quarters of all employees in manufacturing – and probably more elsewhere in employment – work in establishments that are part of multi-plant organisations. Probably about half of all employees in the whole economy and about 40 per cent of all employees in manufacturing work in organisations with workforces greater than 20,000. Britain is distinctive, as Prais has shown, in the extent to which giant companies dominate its private sector, and this concentration has increased steadily since the war (Prais [13]).

Much depends upon how these giant companies construct their internal bargaining structures. Because they differ in their degree of financial integration and in their product and industrial homogeneity, the giant companies have adopted very different structures. If we consider the twenty largest employers in manufacturing, which all have workforces of over 40,000 and employ approximately a quarter of the total manufacturing workforce, only two depend mainly upon multi-employer industry-wide arrangements, another two have genuinely company-wide comprehensive agreements, and another six rely almost exclusively on single-establishment arrangements. The remaining ten have a mixture of divisional agreements, 'two-tier' arrangements with some discretion delegated to the establishment, and establishment bargaining with varying degrees of central co-ordination. The diversity of practice reflects the fact that, within certain constraints, firms appear to have considerable discretion in their choice of bargaining structure.

There are, however, signs that companies are tending to raise the level of bargaining and, in particular, to move away from a reliance upon single-establishment arrangements for fixing pay. A number of factors appear to contribute to this. Perhaps because it facilitates financial control, foreign-owned firms show a preference for corporate agreements. Where there has been a series of mergers and takeovers, corporate bargaining appears to assist organisational adjustment; the relatively high level of corporate bargaining that was earlier noted in the food, drink and tobacco industries is likely to reflect this. There are also trade union pressures. As unionisation spreads up into those echelons of management which are mobile between plants, so there are growing pressures to harmonise terms and conditions between plants. Finally, there is the stimulus of the government's growing intervention in industrial relations. Companies find they have to 'police' their subsidiary plants if they are to avoid being penalised for pay settlements that breach incomes policy or for inept dismissals that may be judged unfair.

In summary, although the control of employers' associations over pay negotiations has, with some exceptions, all but vanished, this does not mean that the employers' forces are dispersed and powerless. On the contrary, even putting aside the fact that nearly half the membership of the Trades Union Congress is employed directly or indirectly by the government, a large proportion of trade union members are employed by a relatively small number of employers. In both public and private sectors the big employers are tending to move away from fragmented bargaining and to raise the level of control over pay. There is the basis for an unusually compact pattern of employer cooperation over pay bargaining, albeit far removed from the traditional industry-based associations.

Trade Union Organisation

The most outstanding fact about contemporary British trade unionism is its rate of growth. After years of stagnation, the percentage of the labour force in trade unions rose from 43 per cent in 1968 to 54 per cent in 1978. This has occurred despite the contraction of many industries which were traditionally union strongholds, and there are no signs of it abating.

There are also strong indications that trade unions are less likely to lose members than has previously been the case. The causes of trade union growth are varied – inflation, legislation and governmental attitudes play an important part – but there are two developments which have helped consolidate union security. The first is the rapid recent growth of the closed shop, which is now estimated to cover one worker in four as compared with one worker in six in 1964 (Gennard *et al.* [9]). This growth has been particularly rapid in industries such as food manufacturing and clothing where hitherto the institution was unusual. Of note is the fact that three quarters of closed shops in manufacturing are maintained with explicit managerial support. The second contributor to union security has been the spread of 'check-off' arrangements whereby employers deduct union dues from their employees' pay. Almost universal in the public sector, these now cover over two thirds of union members in manufacturing and over 90 per cent of arrangements have been introduced since 1968.

Another feature of contemporary trade unionism has been the spread of the office of shop steward throughout almost the whole of employment. In the public services this has been encouraged by the recent introduction of payment by results. In private non-manufacturing it has seemed natural to adopt the patterns of organisation proved in manufacturing. In manufacturing, three quarters of all establishments with 50 or more employees (and virtually all those with unions recognised by management) have shop stewards for manual workers and one third have shop stewards for non-manual. In all but the smallest of workplaces it is normal for management to recognise one or more senior stewards and for stewards to hold regular meetings among themselves.

Perhaps the most eloquent statistic on how totally managements have come to live with shop stewards is that of the number of stewards paid by management to spend all their working hours on trade union duties. Both union and management sources suggest that the number of full-time stewards in manufacturing quadrupled between 1966 and 1976 so that now it stands at between four and five thousand, with possibly an equal number in the public sector. Since the overall number of full-time trade union officers paid by union funds has increased only slowly and has not exceeded 4000, it will be evident that we have recently witnessed a fundamental change in trade union organisation.

This development has been a natural consequence of the increased professionalism of industrial relations management. Job evaluation, single-employer bargaining, procedural reform and the management-sponsored closed shop have all given strength and authority to the shop steward's role. Perhaps surprisingly, this has not brought about serious conflict within trade unions. Full-time officials and stewards generally work well together, having complementary rather than competing interests. In the three largest unions, with some prompting from the leadership of Jones, Scanlon and Basnett, it has proved possible in the last decade to involve shop stewards in all levels of union government. Because of this trade union leaders generally had a surer political touch in the 1970s than in the 1960s and were able to deliver a degree of compliance to the Social Contract incomes policy, for instance, that would have been unthinkable a decade earlier. There may still be problems, but, in terms of predictions being made twenty years ago, unions have accommodated the rise of the shop steward remarkably smoothly.

Although it has brought many advantages to union members in terms of protection at the place of work, however, this growing dependence upon shop stewards is beginning to appear increasingly inappropriate to the problems of the 1980s. In the first place, it is ill-suited to deepening unemployment. As Turner [17] once observed: 'other things being equal, the more decentralised the bargaining system, the faster wages are likely to move in whatever direction they are moving anyway. This is why national agreements were so important in the inter-war depressions; because they reacted less promptly than wage-rates determined at the workplace level, they set a "floor" to the general tendency of wages to fall.' There are already signs of increasing variation between establishments in the size of wage settlements and of an increased inability of shop stewards to combat redundancies.

Secondly, a pattern of trade union organisation based upon the factory is proving ill-equipped to cope with corporate bargaining. Many efforts have been made to form 'combine committees' linking the shop steward organisations of different establishments in multi-plant companies. Some sort of inter-plant link is reported in over a third of multi-plant establishments. But their bargaining achievements have been slight. Factory chauvinism and an unwillingness to make sacrifices on behalf of far-off sister factories have made it difficult for stewards to grapple with corporate decision-making. Designed to win factory battles, shop steward organisations are tending to lose the increasingly important company wars.

Thus, while at first sight the trade union movement might appear to be thriving, its bargaining effectiveness may be flagging. Its current growth owes more to the administrative convenience of employers than to some sort of grass-roots movement. Its heavy reliance upon shop steward organisation may be particularly ill-suited to a rise in both the level of unemployment and the level of bargaining. On the other hand a steady rationalisation of trade union structure in recent years has eased some problems of union cooperation. Three quarters of the country's thirteen million union members are in only twenty unions. In addition, reflecting the increase in governmental intervention in industrial relations, the status of the Trades Union Congress until recently has risen substantially. It is hard to exaggerate its achievement in negotiating and maintaining the Social Contract. After three decades in which fragmented rank-and-file activity has been pre-eminent, there are signs that larger coalitions are returning to the fore.

Conclusion

Collective bargaining will continue to be the dominant means of pay determination in Britain for the foreseeable future. But the structure of coalitions within which this occurs is likely to change as much in the future as it has in the past. This paper has attempted to describe the current structure, how it has changed and continues to change, and the underlying redeployments taking place among employers and trade unions. In any discussion concerned with incomes policy the central remaining question must be how far the present structure might be changed to permit greater coordination of bargaining across the economy as a whole. An enduring incomes policy cannot depend upon the unilateral action of government without the democratic process suffering unendurable damage. It can only come from reform of the bargaining structure.

One question that arises is how far the present bargaining structure, for all its institutional diversity, is coordinated in practice. How far are pay settlements interlinked? Three observations cast some light on this. First, there are no clear-cut 'wage rounds' in terms of regular sequences of settlements of similar magnitude, although there may be small constellations of related settlements (Elliott [8]). Second, there is evidence in private manufacturing industry that single-employer bargainers may set the pace for manual wage settlements which multi-employer bargainers follow; in the 1977–8 phase of bargaining, 55 per cent of single-employer agreements had been completed by the end of 1977 compared with only 29 per cent of multi-employer agreements (Brown *et al.* [2]). Third, manual wages in the public sector, while keeping slightly below their private sector counterparts throughout the 1950s and 1960s, surged ahead during the 1970s (Dean [6]). In short, it appears that while settlements may be related to each other, the links are not simple, clear-cut, or permanent. Although it would be unwise to overlook the increased use of comparability in the public services, in general terms the bargaining structure is not trussed up with strings of comparability.

In two important respects the bargaining structure is altering in a way that will facilitate greater coordination of bargaining. In the first place, those arrangements which claim to determine pay increasingly do so in practice. The old notion of 'wage drift' is obsolete because the industry-wide multi-employer wage rates against which it was measured generally lay no claim to be the bases of actual earnings. Employers increasingly have pay more under control both by having explicit negotiations with representatives of their own employees and by doing so within the framework of job evaluation and work study. In the 1960s no incomes policy could have much impact upon earnings for any length of time because earnings were out of the control of the approved negotiators. Now, and increasingly, there is less ambiguity over pay fixing arrangements. Negotiators are more accessible to argument and they are more able to make their agreements stick.

Secondly, chances are improving for forming the large coalitions from which the economy-wide coordination of collective bargaining might develop. At the same time as the economic and organisational tide is running against their success as workplace bargainers, shop stewards are being more closely involved in the industrial and national policy-making of their unions. But, throughout the western world, trade unions ultimately have to respond to employer initiatives rather than create fresh structures on their own. There are many signs that the government is, albeit reluctantly whichever the party, increasingly coordinating its own policy as the country's largest employer. The most important question for the future of the bargaining structure is how far private sector employers will do likewise. For without the emergence of employer solidarity there is no chance of Britain achieving coordinated collective bargaining and, consequently, a long-term incomes policy.

References

[1] Brown, W. A. and Terry, M. A., 'The changing nature of national wage agreements', *Scottish Journal of Political Economy*, June 1978.

[2] Brown, W. A., ed., *The Changing Contours of British Industrial Relations*, Oxford, Blackwell, forthcoming.

[3] Clegg, H. A., *Trade Unionism under Collective Bargaining*, Oxford, Blackwell, 1976.

[4] Clegg, H. A., *The Changing System of Industrial Relations in Great Britain*, Oxford, Blackwell, 1979.

[5] Daniel, W. W., *Wage Determination in Industry*, Political and Economic Planning, 1976.

[6] Dean, A. J. H., 'Public and private sector manual workers' pay 1970–77' *National Institute Economic Review*, November 1977.

[7] Deaton, D. and Beaumont, P., 'The determinants of bargaining structure: some large scale survey evidence for Britain', *British Journal of Industrial Relations*, forthcoming.

[8] Elliott, R. F., 'The national wage round in the United Kingdom: a sceptical view', *Oxford Bulletin of Economics and Statistics,* August 1976.

[9] Gennard, J., Dunn, S., and Wright, M., 'The extent of closed shop arrangements in British industry', *Department of Employment Gazette*, January 1980.

[10] Lloyd, P. A., *Incentive Payment Schemes*, British Institute of Management, 1976.

[11] National Board for Prices and Incomes, *Payment by Results*, Report No. 65, HMSO, 1968.

[12] National Board for Prices and Incomes, *Job Evaluation*, Report No. 83, HMSO, 1968.

[13] Prais, S. J., *The Evolution of Giant Firms in Britain*, Cambridge University Press, 1976.

[14] Royal Commission on Trade Unions and Employers' Associations *Report*, HMSO, 1968.

[15] Sharp, H., 'Wages councils, a way forward?', *Department of Employment Gazette*, September 1978.

[16] Thakur, M. and Gill, D., *Job Evaluation in Practice*, Institute of Personnel Management, 1976.

[17] Turner, H. A., 'Collective bargaining and the eclipse of incomes policy', *British Journal of Industrial Relations*, June 1970.

7 Influences on the Level of Wage Settlements in Manufacturing Industry

W. W. Daniel

This paper focuses on the influences over the level of settlement during one annual round of periodic negotiations over rates of pay at the level of the plant (formally the establishment) in manufacturing industry. Our starting-point was a probability sample of 254 establishments employing 200 or more people in manufacturing industry selected with probability proportionate to the number of people employed. We carried out initial background interviews with management respondents at the 254 plants, during which we established whether they had formal periodic negotiations over rates of pay. In cases where they had such negotiations we sought separate interviews with the principal management negotiator and the principal trade union negotiator who had been concerned with the most recent set of negotiations. We achieved 148 interviews with management negotiators and 98 interviews with trade union negotiators. (Daniel [2] gives a fuller tabular presentation of the propositions in this chapter.)

In summary, the main results to emerge from the study were as follows. First the ability of employers to pay according to their financial circumstances, as measured by trends in product demand, labour intensity, cash flow and the changing size of the workforce, appeared to have little influence over the formal, periodic increase in rates of pay that was agreed. Secondly, financial circumstances influenced management priorities and the degree of difficulty associated with the negotiations rather than the outcome. Thirdly, the major influences over the level of pay settlements were social and administrative considerations, represented essentially by the notions of compensation for increases in the cost of living and of comparability with levels of increase received by other groups of workers doing similar kinds of work. Fourthly, these notions were backed by trade union bargaining power, which was more likely to be invoked to protect members from receiving a level of increase below that appropriate to the increase in the cost of living and to the increases received by others, than to exploit fully the advantages of favourable financial circumstances.

Of course, these findings cannot necessarily be generalised to all levels of bargaining, to sectors of the economy other than those with which we were concerned or to bargaining at other periods of time. As will be apparent from Chapter 6 a distinctive characteristic of the British system of pay determination is the multiplicity of levels at which bargaining is conducted. That is especially the case for manufacturing industry. We were concerned with negotiations at only one level. The wage round to which our analysis relates concerned the year 1974–5. That round followed a period of formal incomes policy and took place when the cost of living was increasing very rapidly. On the other hand our study did concern an important level of bargaining within an important sector of the economy and we do suggest that its findings have general implications.

The Role of Plant Bargaining

Within manufacturing industry plant level bargaining represents one of the most important levels at which periodic negotiations over rates take place. Management responses to our initial interviews showed that there were periodic negotiations over rates of pay at the establishment level in approaching three quarters of our plants. In slightly over half the cases respondents reported that their plant level negotiations were those that had most influence over rates of pay. Plant bargaining was clearly most important in the engineering and metal working industries. In such industries three quarters of managers said that their establishment level negotiations had most influence over rates of pay. In other sectors the proportion dropped to around a third.

Negotiations at plant level also appeared to have a high level of autonomy. Union negotiating teams were normally led by a lay officer such as a convenor or senior shop steward. In less than half the cases had a full-time officer of the union been involved in the preparation of the union case. Rarely was a full-time officer attributed much influence over the claim. Indeed our findings strongly suggested that one of the major roles of full-time officers was to be brought in as conciliators when local management and lay officers could not agree.

On the management side negotiating teams were normally led by someone from the labour relations function in conjunction with someone from works or general management. Generally management negotiators were accountable to the chief executive on site. In a quarter of cases, however, they were accountable to someone outside the establishment at divisional, company or group level. Accordingly, local management, too, appeared to enjoy a high level of autonomy. Indeed, the level of local management autonomy proved to be critical to the degree of disruption associated with the negotiations. In circumstances where management negotiators were accountable to someone outside the establishment there were strikes or threats of strike action associated with the negotiations in the majority of cases. Where local management was plenipotentiary strike issues tended to be less than half as frequent. There were clear indications of strikes or threats of strike being used to enable local union negotiators to talk directly to the people who had the real power. The findings indicated not only that local negotiators generally enjoyed a high level of autonomy but also that such autonomy was conducive to orderly bargaining.

Management Considerations and Priorities

Initially we asked management negotiators an open-ended question to establish what had been their considerations in drawing up the first offer they made to the union team. Answers to such questions provide an indication of the range of considerations and the overall salience of different issues. They do not provide a measure of the proportion attaching importance to a particular issue for which purpose more direct questioning is appropriate. We used such questioning for our second-order analysis of management priorities described below. First, however, Table 7.1 shows management answers to the initial question.

The most frequently mentioned batch of items related to the capacity of the establishment or enterprise to pay. Where that type of answer was amplified mention was made of the effect of any wage increase on prices, profits, cash flow or investment. The second most common set of items mentioned by managers were independent of the employers' ability to pay. These were items concerned with

Table 7.1 *Main considerations of management negotiators*

	Number employed		
	All	200–500	501 +
Percentage of negotiators mentioning:			
Ability to pay	61	58	64
Comparability with other groups	51	52	51
Cost of living	36	40	34
Change in payments system	30	27	31
Company/national agreement	11	4	14
Social contract/guidelines	11	10	11
Easing recruitment	6	10	4
Other (including cannot say)	9	10	7
Number of negotiators	*148*	*52*	*96*

the increase in the cost of living and the comparability of the earnings of workers covered by the bargaining unit with the pay and pay increases of other groups. It is instructive that managements had so frequently incorporated such considerations into their planning for the negotiations. For instance, issues concerning comparability were mentioned with a similar order of frequency to issues concerning ability to pay. It appeared that managers either accepted the legitimacy of pay increases being made on grounds separate from the employer's capacity to pay or they had become reconciled to the inevitability of increases being made on such grounds. Thirdly, there was a substantial number of other considerations that managers had taken into account when preparing for negotiations. Those items illustrate the range of issues with which periodic negotiations are concerned and the variety of functions they are required to fulfil.

In order to provide a basis for a more systematic analysis of management priorities in negotiations we asked a series of direct questions on the importance managers had attached to a list of items. These included the implication of the negotiations for prices; interruptions to work; the establishment's cash flow position; other sections of employees; investment; redundancy; labour shortages and the shareholders' dividends. Answers revealed a general set of priorities as reflected in the order of the list. The more instructive aspect of answers, however, was the way in which management priorities varied according to the financial circumstances of the establishment. For instance, as Table 7.2 shows, there was a marked difference in management priorities in relation to the establishment's product market. In circumstances where product demand had been rising over the previous twelve months top priority was attached to the avoidance of any interruptions to work (effectively strikes or other industrial action) and less importance was accorded to the effect of any increase upon prices. Where demand for products had been falling management attached the highest importance to the effect of the level of any pay increase upon prices. It was secondly concerned about its cash flow

Table 7.2 Rank order of items rated by management negotiators as very important

	Total	Product demand in previous 12 months			
		Rising	Stable	Falling	Fluctuating
Effect on prices	1	2	1	1	3
Avoiding interruptions	2	1		3	1
Effect on cash flow	3	3	3	2	2
Effect on other sections	4	4	4	4	4
Effect on investment	5	5	5	5	6
Avoiding redundancy		8	7	8	5
Easing labour shortages	6	6	8	6	7
Maintaining dividend		7	6	7	8
Number of negotiators	*148*	*30*	*28*	*64*	*26*

position. It attached relatively little importance to the avoidance of interruptions to work. In labour-intensive plants, management was most concerned about its cash flow position, was secondly concerned about its product prices and again was much less concerned about the possibility of interruptions to work. This pattern of variation in management priorities is much as would be expected by economists. The analysis suggests that measures to reduce the general level of demand in the economy and the availability of funds to companies would lead management to be more disposed to resist wage claims, and to risk strike action or other interruptions to work in order to achieve pay settlements that were tolerable to the financial position of the firm. The pattern, however, reflects only management priorities when entering negotiations and takes no account of union priorities or the ensuing negotiations between the two parties.

Trade Union Considerations and Priorities

Our questioning of trade union negotiators about their considerations in preparing their claim followed a similar pattern to that for management negotiators regarding their preparation for bargaining. First, we asked a parallel open-ended question. Secondly, we asked union negotiators to rate the importance of a range of specific items. Table 7.3 shows the answers of trade union negotiators to the general

Table 7.3 Main considerations of union negotiators

	Number employed		
	All	200–500	501 +
Percentage of negotiators mentioning:			
Cost of living	75	78	71
Comparability with other groups	51	44	76
Change in payments system	41	34	62
Ability to pay	15	22	15
Company/national agreement	10	6	17
Social contract/guidelines	5	6	7
Equal pay for women	4	3	7
Improved fringe benefits	23	16	38
Number of negotiators	*98*	*33*	*65*

question. The items covered were similar to those mentioned by managers. There was a marked difference, however, in the frequency with which they were mentioned. For union negotiators the increase in the cost of living and comparability formed the foundations of their claim. These were followed by items associated with the system of payment. The establishment's or enterprise's ability to pay ranked much lower among the considerations of union negotiators than had the cost of living and comparability among those of management negotiators.

Again, however, it was the analysis of variations in the answers of trade union negotiators to direct questions on the importance of particular items that provided the more revealing insight into their priorities. Table 7.4 shows the rank order of ratings in relation to the product demand circumstances in which trade union negotiators found themselves. A number of points warrant attention.

First, the concern of management negotiators to avoid any interruptions to work resulting from the negotiations was matched by a similar concern to an only slightly less marked degree on the part of trade union negotiators. It is particularly noteworthy that trade union negotiators were especially concerned to avoid interruptions in circumstances where product demand had been rising. That priority again mirrored the management priority in similar plants.

Table 7.4 Rank order of items rated by union negotiators as very important

	Total	Product demand in previous 12 months			
		Rising	Stable	Falling	Fluctuating
Cost of living	1	1	1	1	1
Avoiding redundancy	2	4	2	2	4
Avoiding interruptions	3	2	3	3	2
Competitive position	4	6	4	4	5
Earnings of others	5	5	6	5	3
Profits	6	3	5	6	7
Investment	7	7	7	7	6
Number of negotiators	*98*	*21*	*18*	*42*	*17*

Secondly, trade union negotiators attached a high priority to the avoidance of any redundancy resulting from the pay settlement. Our studies of redundancy policies and practices indicate that for union negotiators the avoidance of redundancy generally means 'no redundancy other than voluntary redundancy' (Daniel and Stilgoe [3]). The voluntary redundancy strategy provides management with a powerful tool for running down workforces in a way that is acceptable to trade union representatives and seen to be painless to the parties within enterprises.

Thirdly and most importantly there was a clear indication of trade union negotiators having, in a wholly reasonable way, chosen their arguments to suit their ground. The increase in the cost of living was clearly of prime importance for all. At the same time, 98 per cent of union negotiators in circumstances of falling demand said it was very important compared with 76 per cent of counterparts in circumstances of rising demand. Where demand had been rising union negotiators attached a relatively high priority to the profitability of the company or establishment. Where demand had been falling they attached little importance to profits.

Issues and Problems in Negotiations

We asked management and union negotiators separately, first, what arguments the other party had used to press its claim or resist the claim as the case might be, and secondly, which of those arguments it found most persuasive. The respective rehearsals of the other party's arguments showed that generally there had been no failure on either side to make its points. Each account of the other side's case generally mirrored that side's own account. There appeared to be no failure of communications. Table 7.5 shows the aspects of the other party's case that each side had found most convincing. It is clear that managers had had very considerable sympathy for the union position

Table 7.5 Arguments by the other side that each party had found most persuasive (percentages)

	Management negotiators
Cost of living	52
Comparability with other groups	15
Change in payments system	3
Low pay	2
National/regional agreement	1
Profits	1
Others	8
None/don't know	19
	Union negotiators
Ability to pay	29
Effect on prices	7
Comparability challenged	5
Cost of living challenged	—
Productivity arguments	5
Threat to jobs	4
Other	—
None/claim accepted	42

regarding the increase in the cost of living. Of course managers tend to be salary earners and consumers too, and experience, along with all wage and salary earners, the way that inflation reduces the purchasing power of earnings.

On the trade union side there was less general indication of any of managements' arguments having been found to be particularly powerful. The inability of the firm to pay, however, was mentioned more frequently than any other among the points that union negotiators had felt to be persuasive. That point raises a general issue in our findings. Managers had attached the highest priority to the capacity of the business to pay in preparing for negotiations. They had concentrated upon that capacity in negotiations with unions. And yet all our evidence suggested that managements were disinclined to provide trade union officers with information on the financial position of the business. We had asked union negotiators to rate their employer generally as an employer, to evaluate the facilities with which they were provided at the plant, and to assess the information with which they were furnished on the financial position of the firm. Around 90 per cent rated as generally satisfactory both their employer and the facilities with which they were provided. In marked contrast about half the union negotiators said that the information they were given on the firm's financial position was less than satisfactory. The evaluations of union negotiators were consistent with managers' own accounts: 38 per cent of managers said they gave little or no information to union officers on the financial position of the firm. It becomes a little difficult to see how managers could expect effectively to deploy arguments about the financial position of the establishment in periodic negotiations over rates of pay when they denied union negotiators the basic information on which they could assess such arguments. Certainly our findings showed clearly that where managements were more inclined to provide financial information then union negotiators were markedly less likely to have found no aspect of managers' arguments persuasive and more likely to have paid attention to their points concerning ability to pay.

When we asked both parties separately what were the main issues that divided them during the negotiations, we found again, first, that the separate accounts were remarkably consistent. Secondly, we found that surprisingly high proportions on both sides said 'nothing' or 'not very much'. Of course our interviews were retrospective and it may have been that what had seemed to be substantial issues at the time had subsequently come to be seen as not very important with the passage of time. Nevertheless it is instructive that a quarter of management negotiators said that nothing had really divided the parties during the negotiations when we were talking about the wage round that contributed to the most rapid annual rate of increase in inflation that there had been in Britain during this century. Thirdly, both parties agreed that ultimately the sticking point had simply been the question of how much. It appeared that whatever issues of principle either party had felt to be involved, and whatever its frame of reference for determining an appropriate level of increase, differences had tended finally to centre on the pragmatic point concerning the size

Table 7.6 Variation of main issues dividing the negotiators (percentages)

	Nothing	Just the money	Ability to pay
Labour as % of total costs:			
0–20	36	29	10
21–30	28	32	16
31–40	12	69	4
Over 40	14	38	29
Trend in product demand:			
Rising	40	30	13
Stable	25	25	14
Falling	22	41	11
Fluctuating	12	62	19

of the increase. Fourthly, the most interesting feature of the pattern was the way it varied in relation to the plants' financial circumstances. We saw above that where managements had found themselves facing falling product demand and where they were operating relatively labour-intensive plants they had been more concerned about the effect of pay increases upon prices and cash flow and less concerned about avoiding interruptions to work. When it came to the issues that had divided the parties in negotiations there were clear indications that there had been fewer difficulties the more favourable had been the establishment's product market and the lower was its level of labour intensity (see Table 7.6). Accordingly problems had been concentrated in labour-intensive plants and those where demand had been falling or fluctuating. It was in such circumstances that management priorities generated conflict relative to those of trade union negotiators.

The Outcome of Negotiations

The chief feature of our findings on the outcome of negotiations was that, while the financial circumstances of plants had influenced management priorities and had influenced the degree of difficulty associated with negotiations, they appeared not to have influenced the level of settlement reached. For instance, Table 7.7 shows that the median level of increase was similar whatever had been the product market position in the previous twelve months and whatever was the level of labour intensity. Similarly increases had been of much the same level whether the workforce had been increasing or decreasing in the previous period and whether or not the plant had experienced redundancies. Of course this by no means implies that the earnings of workers were the same regardless of the market or financial circumstances of plants. In fact earnings were higher the more favourable were plants' market circumstances. It can be assumed that such variations arose from differences in levels of overtime and wage drift brought about by bargaining at lower levels. Our findings concerning levels of settlement suggested, simply, that there were influences upon the outcome of formal periodic negotiations over rates other than the market and financial circumstances of plants and that the other influences prevailed.

One particular other influence worthy of note is the association between the level of settlement and the deployment by union representatives of strikes and other sanctions during negotiations. Where there had been strikes and threats of strike during negotiations the level of settlement tended if anything to be marginally less than in circumstances where there had been no question of strike action. Consistent with that picture there was a more marked tendency for union negotiators to express less satisfaction with the final outcome of negotiations in circumstances where there had been strikes or threats of strikes. The general pattern suggested strongly that the use of withdrawals of labour in negotiations had tended to be more a reaction against relatively low offers than a cause of relatively high increases.

Conclusions

As we made clear at the beginning of the paper it may not be possible wholly to generalise the findings of our study of influences upon bargaining at one level, in one major sector and over one wage round. It may be, for instance, that the rate of increase in the cost of living was so great over that particular wage round that it swamped all other considerations in a way that does not always happen [1]. Equally we would be inclined to feel that issues of comparability operate as a more coercive force in national negotiations. On the other hand we would suggest that it is possible to extract from our findings principles of general relevance that help to explain the wage-push element in inflation. Essentially the study underlines the part that ideas of social justice play in the level of wage settlements. Secondly, it highlights the role that organised labour plays in enforcing ideas of social justice. Both these forces operate independently of market or financial circumstances. At the same time market forces and financial circumstances continue to play some roles in pay determination. We would suggest that it is the simultaneous operation of social and market forces that provides the dynamic for the wage-push element in inflation.

Table 7.7 Variations in median settlement agreed (percentage increases)

Trend in product demand		*Labour costs as % of output*		*Disruption to work*	
Rising	14	20 or less	15	No threat	15
Stable	14	21 to 30	15	Threat, no action	15
Falling	15	Over 30	15	Some action	15
Fluctuating	13				

Employees in favourable market or financial circumstances derive the benefit from their good fortune. There is a favourable market for their products, sales and profits increase and they share in the benefit. Productivity increases and the workers involved receive a share. There is a shortage of people with particular skills and pay is increased to attract people with the skill or to encourage people to acquire the skill. At the same time wage or salary earners in less favourable circumstances receive comparable increases on the basis of social equity or on administrative grounds. Their pay system is linked to that of other groups or increases are agreed on the basis of comparability. Organised bargaining power plays a part in reinforcing and promoting both sets of criteria. We saw how trade union negotiators sensibly and understandably tended, in promoting their case, to adopt the criteria that were suited to their circumstances. Profitability was invoked where establishments were profitable. Equity was invoked where they were not. Management negotiators tended in practice to accept the dual system of criteria. If, however, wage and salary earners in favourable market or economic circumstances receive the full benefit of their good fortune while those in less favourable circumstances are insulated from their ill fortune by notions of equity strongly backed by bargaining power, then the result must be wage-push inflation. According to our findings the chief role of trade unions in that process was to protect the levels of earnings of those in less favourable circumstances by seeking to ensure that they received the norm despite the market and financial positions of their employers. The idea that unions largely fulfil a protective and defensive role in relation to members' pay was supported by our findings on the relative net pay of trade union members and non-members in a parallel survey (see Chart 7.1). Generally within each occupational level both the relatively very high earners and the relatively very low earners were not trade unionists. The distribution of the pay of trade union members was generally much less wide. The pattern is consistent with the idea that trade unions serve more to insulate members from the very low earnings they might suffer if fully exposed to market forces than to maximise earnings in the most favourable market circumstances.

Clearly a resolution of the inflationary dynamic built into the dual system of pay determination requires that one set of criteria prevails. Either market forces predominate or social forces prevail. The implication of the above analysis is that measures to restrain the earnings of members in favourable circumstances would be more acceptable to trade unionists than measures that depress the relative pay of members in less favourable situations.

The present government strategy in Britain relies upon market forces. Whatever reservations might be held about that strategy it will certainly represent an invaluable test case. Inflation is to be reduced by strict control of the money supply. That process is to be aided by reducing the bargaining power of trade unions through

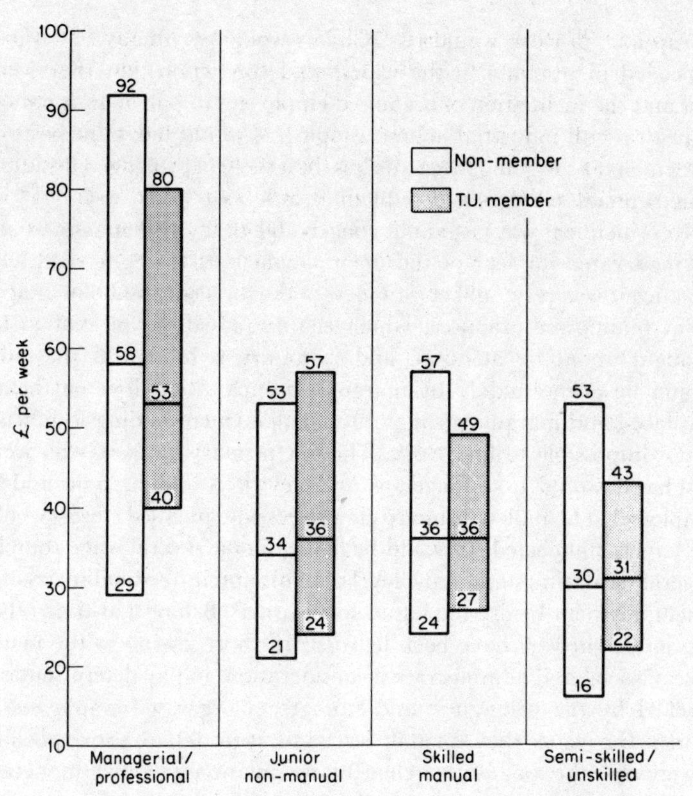

Chart 7.1 Net earnings of union and non-union members

increased unemployment and industrial relations law reform. Our predictions of the results of that strategy based on the findings and analysis of the study reported here have been as follows. The strategy was introduced at a time when the rate of increase in the cost of living was rising and that rate of increase was giving a further boost by an increase in indirect taxation. Organised employees would seek and gain compensation for those increases. In some sectors where demand, productivity and profitability were rising employees would achieve higher increases. Others in less favourable financial circumstances would seek comparable increases on the basis of equity. Employers would often resist claims owing to depressed product demand and monetary restraint. The incidence of disputes and disruptions to work would rise. Claims would eventually be largely conceded in response to the widespread conviction that they were just and the inclination of organised employees to pursue that notion of justice with industrial action. Employers would judge the costs of settlement at the going rate to be less than those of prolonged disputes. Bankruptcies, closures and reductions in labour would rise.

In principle it was just about conceivable that pay demands would be moderated for fear of the unemployment that might result. In practice it was very unlikely. In view of the sophistication of management manpower practices, which enable reductions in staff to be brought about by attrition, and voluntary redundancy, the costs would be borne mainly by marginal groups in employment being displaced and marginal groups out of employment finding it difficult if not impossible to find work. The few primary workers who were displaced would take longer to find new jobs and become underemployed. The bulk of primary employees who pursued claims would be largely unaffected. It would be likely to take several wage rounds, several escalating steps in the level of bankruptcies, redundancies and unemployment before the lesson was learned. Before that time other lessons might well have been learned. In short, owing to the major role of social and administrative considerations in pay determination, backed by the willingness and strength of organised employees to pursue the justice they see in those claims, it would not prove possible to control the wage-push element in inflation through monetary measures alone. Or rather a prolonged attempt to do so would lead to levels of industrial disorder and unemployment that have hitherto been considered intolerable.

References

[1] Coutts, K., Farlington, R. and Wilkinson, F., 'Wage bargaining and the inflation process', *Cambridge Economy Policy Review*, No. 2, 1976. (Using a different method they came to a very similar conclusion.)

[2] Daniel, W. W., *Wage Determination in Industry*, PEP No. 563, 1976. (This contains full details of the study and fuller versions of the tables published here.)

[3] Daniel, W. W., and Stilgoe, Elizabeth, *The Impact of the Employment Protection Laws*, PEP No. 577, 1978.

8 Roles of Governments and Institutions in OECD Countries

*A. J. H. Dean**

Although the inflationary record of the OECD area was substantially worse in the 1970s than in the 1960s, the experience of individual countries has been varied. The dispersion of inflation has been far more pronounced since 1970 than before, coinciding with the move from an era of fixed exchange rates to one of floating rates. The purpose of this chapter is to examine whether variations in institutional arrangements and the degree of government involvement in the pay determination process have contributed to the contrasting inflationary records. The chapter also looks at the way in which experience elsewhere might suggest improvements for British procedures.

The Economic Background

Inflation has concerned governments throughout the postwar period, but it is a problem that has become particularly serious and apparently much more difficult to cope with since the late 1960s. For the OECD as a whole the inflation rate averaged 3 per cent in the 1960s but 9 per cent in the 1970s, being in double figures in the mid-1970s and again at the end of the 1970s. Even where the inflation record seems to have been more moderate, performance in the 1970s was much less satisfactory than in earlier years. Indeed, there is not one OECD country where the rise in prices through the 1970s has not been

* The views expressed in this paper are those of the author and do not purport to represent in any way the views of the OECD. The original paper submitted to the conference included a description of the pay bargaining arrangements in Denmark, Finland, France and the United States. For reasons of length, it was not possible to include them in the book; they are available from NIESR on request.

substantially higher than in the 1960s. For the OECD as a whole the rise in consumer prices in the first half of the 1960s averaged only 2½ per cent a year, but it then accelerated to 5–5½ per cent in 1969 and 1970. For a time there was a slight abatement of inflation, the OECD rate coming down to 4½ per cent in the first half of 1972. But there followed, in 1972 and early 1973, a remarkably strong and area-wide surge in growth and this, when taken with the explosion in commodity prices which the rapid growth engendered, led to a rapid deterioration in the inflation performance through 1973.

The enormous oil price rises in October and December 1973 were therefore superimposed on what was already a serious rise in the underlying rate of inflation, so that the OECD annual rate of inflation went up to 10 per cent in the second half of 1973 and climbed to almost 15 per cent in the first half of 1974. In that period every OECD country except Germany had an inflation rate in double figures. The rate of inflation subsided only slowly after that surge, despite three half-years of declining GNP in the OECD area, with prices still rising by 11½ per cent year-on-year in 1975. In the following years the area inflation rate only came down to 8 per cent – in 1978. Inflation subsequently accelerated again, being pushed up in part by further increases in oil prices, even though the wage response seems likely this time to be more muted.

The general increase in the inflation rate in OECD countries in the 1970s has been accompanied by a greater *dispersion* between countries. Differences in price performance are even more striking if account is taken of the employment situation. In some countries where price performance has recently been quite a bit better than average, unemployment has been low (Austria, Germany, Japan and Switzerland), and in some other countries with an average price performance this has been achieved in conditions of very low unemployment (Norway and Sweden). Although there is some relationship between the average level of inflation and the degree of dispersion of inflation rates, the relationship is far from precise. Inflation differentials rose sharply (about three or fourfold) between 1972 and 1974 at a time when the area inflation rate was doubling, but those differentials have remained high even after the inflation rate subsided. The spread of inflation rates amongst the major seven and the other OECD countries is shown in Table 8.1. Several features are noteworthy. First, particular countries can remain as the leaders or laggers in the

Table 8.1 Inflation and its dispersion in OECD 1970–9[a]

	All OECD		Major countries		Other countries[c]	
	Rate	Dispersion[b]	High	Low	High	Low
1970	5.6	1.9	Ja 8	Ca 3	No 11	Gr 3
1971	5.3	1.9	UK 9	Ca 3	NZ 10	Gr 3
1972	4.8	1.4	UK 7	US 3	Ir 9	Gr 4
1973	7.9	1.8	Ja 12	US 6	Gr 16	Sw 7
1974	13.4	5.3	Ja 25	US 11	Ir 17	No 9
1975	11.4	4.8	UK 24	Ge 6	Ir 21	Sz 7
1976	8.6	4.9	It 17	Ge 5	Ir 18	Sz 2
1977	8.7	6.3	It 17	Ge 4	Sp 25	Sz 1
1978	7.9	5.1	It 12	Ge 3	Sp 20	Sz 1
1979	10.0	5.2	It 5	Ja 4	Gr 19	Sz 4

[a] Annual percentages change in consumer prices.
[b] Standard deviation of percentage rates of change in 20 OECD countries.
[c] Excluding Iceland, Portugal and Turkey. In 1970–5 figures for Greece may not give an accurate measure because of incomplete coverage of the price index.
Source: OECD *Main Economic Indicators*.
Note: Ja: Japan; It: Italy; Ca: Canada; Ge: Germany; No: Norway; Ir: Ireland; Gr: Greece; Sp: Spain; Sw: Sweden; Sz: Switzerland.

inflation rankings for periods of several years, suggesting that virtuous or vicious circles can become established; secondly, notwithstanding that, a particular country can undergo radical changes in its inflation ranking and move from a very low relative inflation rate to a very high one (such as Greece) or vice versa (such as Norway, and indeed the UK); thirdly, in spite of the high figures that have persisted for the area as a whole since 1973, the experience of Germany and Switzerland shows that it is possible to get back to very low rates of inflation.

It is clear that the move to floating exchange rates in the early 1970s has had a most important impact. In the era of relatively stable exchange rates it was not possible for the inflation rates as between countries to move far out of line over a period of years. For if they did so, then either the exchange rate would have to give or automatic equilibrating mechanisms would operate, through changes in monetary demands transmitted internationally, to bring those inflation levels closer together again. Brittan and Lilley [3] have argued that in the era of fixed exchange rates the more open economies, whether they had incomes policies or not, were effectively forced to accept a strong impact of foreign prices on domestic wages and costs; it is therefore only since the era of floating rates that an independent role can be assigned to incomes policies.

It would, however, be wrong to think that incomes policy is irrelevant in a period of fixed exchange rates. If incomes policy can successfully contain inflation, then a country with a tendency to above-normal inflation, which is hence susceptible to recurrent balance of payments crises and subsequent restrictive action, may be able to avoid such developments, thereby enjoying a higher level of growth than otherwise. Nevertheless, in principle, it is in an era of floating exchange rates that there may be more scope for incomes policies.

Institutional Procedures for Pay Determination

The different institutions developed in the industrialised countries for pay determination and the degree of government intervention vary widely. The way in which present institutions have developed in a number of countries over the postwar period is reviewed below. This section draws on that review and attempts to assess the effectiveness of the different systems.

The review leads to few strong conclusions, for it soon becomes clear that what is feasible and successful in one country may be inappropriate or counter-productive in another. The perfect recipe in one country may fail in another either because of important missing ingredients or because the chef is ill-equipped or ill-trained. Some lessons can nevertheless be drawn about the nature of the successes.

Perhaps the place to start is with a country which has arguably been the most successful in forging a collective bargaining system – Austria. The Austrian voluntary tripartite system of *sozialpartnerschaft* has existed since the early 1950s. The tripartite system depends on fairly strong central control of their members by the two main union and employers' organisations, a government willing to support a central agreement with appropriate economic policies, and a social consensus that a reasonable centralised voluntary agreement is a necessary prerequisite for successful economic and social development.

Since centralisation seems to be an important ingredient in the success of Austrian policy, it is worth enquiring whether it is more generally successful. In categorising different bargaining systems one of the most important aspects is whether the system involves centralised negotiations. In a comparative study of the interaction between collective bargaining and government policies Blyth [1] has plotted his subjective view of the degree of centralisation in each country's trade union and employer federated organisations, against the level of bargaining, finding that in general a high level of national bargaining in Austria, Norway, Sweden and Denmark is associated with a high degree of centralisation, whilst at the other extreme the US and Canada are low on each count. A second diagram plots the level of bargaining against the degree of unionisation and finds a fairly strong correlation, supporting the argument by Clegg [6] of an important connection between the two. Centralisation may take the form of bipartite bargaining between union and employer representatives or it may be tripartite, with government involvement. Other parties may also be involved (for example separate representation for farmers) and the coverage of particular industries and occupations may be more or less comprehensive; as a basic minimum such centralisation must include the representatives of the major industrial unions and the leading employers. Centralisation has been a feature of collective bargaining in Austria, in all the Scandinavian countries, in the Netherlands and in Ireland. It might also be argued that there is a certain amount of centralisation in Australia, even though it is a federal country, because the Arbitration Commission has legal powers and provides a formal forum for negotiations amongst the interested parties.

Centralisation, or coordination, is achieved in very different ways in different countries. In Norway it is the central labour and employer organisations which are usually the negotiating partners, whereas in Austria coordination is achieved by a body consisting of representatives of the authorities, the unions and management who supervise and approve each individual settlement. In Norway all unions negotiate at the same time (since it is the centralised unit which is negotiating), whereas in Austria negotiations are spread out throughout the year.

Countries with rather more decentralised bargaining systems are the US and Canada, Japan, France, Belgium and Switzerland. This does not mean that there are not large industrial unions in these countries – rather it indicates that those unions are involved only in industry-wide bargaining at national level, and not in economy-wide bargaining. In Italy the degree of centralisation is a matter of interpretation, but despite some moves towards coordinated agreement and despite the *scala mobile* (system of indexation) it should probably also be classed as having a decentralised system.

Germany is a case on its own. Although there are only a small number of large industrial unions, and concerted action involves discussions on the feasible growth of incomes, negotiations are decentralised and none of the unions is bound by any central accord. Hence, whilst the system involves a certain number of centralised meetings, the outcome is determined by major autonomous union negotiations and is to that extent still decentralised. Nevertheless some German industries are acknowledged pace setters, so that an important lead is often set by key settlements for groups such as the steelworkers. Furthermore, concerted action has been virtually on ice over the last three years and moves back to it are only just now being made.

Amongst countries with centralised systems there are many differences in coverage, in institutionalisation of the procedures, in the degree to which such procedures are enshrined in law, and in the degree of government involvement. Also, even where the system is geared to regular centralised agreements, it has often not proved possible to conclude a settlement, and if anything this has been increasingly the case in the 1970s. Such problems have been particularly acute in the Netherlands, where an arguably very successful national wage policy disintegrated in the 1960s. Since then only one central agreement has been successfully concluded (in 1972). In other years agreements have either been made at industry level or the government has stepped in with wage limits, or with a wage freeze as in early 1980. Failure to reach a central agreement has also occurred in some years in Sweden and Norway; in Norway there has been a fifteen-month freeze on wages and prices which ended only at the end of 1979. There have been increasing problems in reaching a central agreement in Sweden and attempts to reach a settlement in Spring 1980 led to a series of widespread disputes. The serious problems which arose in Sweden indicate how difficult it has become for the Swedish government to maintain a hands-off policy. In Denmark, with perhaps the highest degree of centralised bargaining in OECD, each of the last two agreements has had to be legislated by parliament. Ireland moved to a system of national pay agreements in 1970. The length of these has varied substantially, and each has included several different phases and sometimes a government-imposed period of pay pause. In recent years reaching agreement has proved increasingly difficult.

In all these countries where central negotiations play a key role, the system works (if it does) only because the negotiating parties – the union and employer representatives – exercise a certain amount of control over their members. This factor of control over either constituent member unions/companies, or indeed over individual workers and managers, is a prerequisite for satisfactory central negotiations. This is not to say that central pay increases cannot be supplemented at company or plant level. A certain amount of wage drift may even be encouraged, if it adds a necessary degree of flexibility, but if supplementary movements become too large the system breaks down – not only will inflation be seen to be far higher than implied by the central agreement, but also leapfrogging claims may well develop. In some countries drift accounts for 50–60 per cent of total wages. Significantly, however, in Austria, where the *sozialpartnerschaft* is a voluntary arrangement and bargains are ultimately made at a decentralised level, there has been very little drift.

Synchronisation of settlements occurs most frequently together with centralisation. Negotiating groups settle at one time, although local negotiations may subsequently take place (and not necessarily within the national guidelines). The advantage of synchronised settlements is that many of the problems of leapfrogging disappear. The need to guess the outcome of other settlements is avoided. If all settlements are synchronised, the negotiations are recognised as a *bellum omnium contra omnes*; if one group is to receive an excessive award then this can be achieved only at the expense of others.

Centralisation and synchronisation are clearly much easier to operate in a small economy where the number of negotiating bodies is limited, either because of strong centralised unions or because of a limited mix of industries. The Scandinavian countries are ones where negotiations with employers (and increasingly with governments) have developed over many years. However, a wage policy of this kind may be self-defeating if it leads to a high degree of wage drift, often following the attempted restoration of differentials, if it hampers labour mobility and thus raises unemployment, or if it leads to an inflationary leapfrogging of settlements when agreement cannot be reached. In recent years the difficulties in reaching agreement have led more frequently to government-imposed solutions, especially in the Netherlands and Norway.

The successful implementation of centralised agreements depends partly on the surrender of a certain amount of autonomy by individual unions and employers. In Sweden the degree of autonomy granted by unions to the *Landsorganisationen* is probably much greater than would be accepted in many countries, almost certainly including Britain. Employers also have to agree to a certain degree of compliance with the system, otherwise wage drift in particular will undermine any centrally determined settlement as firms attempt to bid labour away from competitors. In some countries a limit on the amount of wage drift beyond the centrally agreed figure is negotiated.

It has been pointed out by Saunders [18] that in all the countries where centralised bargaining takes place social democratic or other left-inclined parties have been in power or in coalitions for much of the postwar period. Such parties may be more predisposed to central agreements and their involvement may have encouraged a cooperative response from unions. But Saunders also points out that these countries are mostly small, where the degree of social cohesion may be greater and where the economic realities may be more clearly perceived. There is perhaps a greater awareness in the more open economies that one of the main determinants of high employment is the ability of industry to compete internationally, the achievement of which is made easier if wages and prices are not growing markedly faster than those of competitors. In Austria for instance, where trade plays a major role, and where competition from close neighbours such as Germany is intense, trade unions have always been aware of such constraints, and have cooperated in policies to achieve price stability.

Centralised bargaining may involve government participation or governments may be excluded. In several of the countries surveyed governments have been involved closely in the wage bargaining process. In some cases, this has involved only back door pressure (such as mediator of last resort in Norway and Denmark, and in emergency situations in Belgium and Holland). Where negotiations are centralised the government often provides forecasts of the economy. In

Sweden the employer and union organisations are actually involved in the production of the government's forecasts; they see these forecasts, and so know by how much national incomes can be expected to increase. In some countries the government is represented in the central negotiations, either on its own account or as an employer. The government may also have a role to play in offering a *quid pro quo* for wage restraint. Governments have used various measures to influence bargaining – for instance public sector policies, the reduction of indirect taxes and direct tax concessions. In Norway in particular the unions have, on several occasions, agreed to less-than-full compensation for price rises in return for alleviating fiscal or social measures; this has also increasingly occurred in Sweden. In both Denmark and Norway there are specific mechanisms for government intervention with statutory wage and/or price controls, so that there is an incentive for negotiators to reach agreement amongst themselves rather than to be subject to an imposed solution.

Although the notion of some trade-off between wage restraint by the unions and fiscal and social policy concessions by the government became popular in Britain in the mid-1970s, the idea has also come in for criticism. To the extent that organised labour and business are not representative of society as a whole, such arrangements may appear to jeopardise the democratic process; and the concessions made may be inimical to the proper functioning of the economy.

Attempts to try to make wage decisions consistent with the economic situation and with economic policy targets have occurred in a number of countries. The danger is that agreement may not be reached on the economic consequences of a particular set of wage bargains; the government's information may not be believed, or different participants may draw different conclusions from that information. A prerequisite must therefore be a broad consensus on present economic conditions, economic prospects and the mechanisms of the system itself. Countries where government discussions with negotiating parties most frequently appear fruitful are those where there is some degree of consensus about the workings of the economic system – as, until recently, with the 'EFO model' used in some of the Scandinavian countries. The economic experts' contribution to negotiations in Austria and Germany is also thought to be influential.

In several countries incomes policies have been given a bad name by the way in which they have been introduced in short bursts in an emergency fashion. This has happened even in countries, such as the Netherlands and Norway, which have had fairly well established long-run incomes policies but have had to resort to wage and price freezes as an expedient. Temporary freezes have rarely proved popular with workers. They have frequently been introduced at a time of rapidly accelerating price rises and consequently have led – if successful – to a sharp squeeze on real income. Very often the reaction to restraint has been a sharp catch-up in wages once controls have been lifted, so that the whole painful policy appears to have little or no long-run effect. This criticism has been raised against pay controls in the US and the UK in particular. Some people have argued, however, that the problem has been that controls have generally been phased out rapidly rather than gradually, a factor that was certainly true with the sudden ending of the Nixon pay controls in the US. On the other hand, gradual decontrol might prove extremely difficult to engineer, especially once people are aware that controls are to be removed. Although, as Braun [2] points out, short-term intervention may be used to check the development of inflationary price expectations, such measures have frequently proved counter-productive, not only because of catch-up problems, but also because of the hostility they have engendered.

Summary

It is not easy to draw any general conclusions about the relative efficacy of differing institutional procedures and of incomes policy periods during the 1970s. What does seem clear, however, is that no policy of wage and price restraint can operate properly unless the monetary and fiscal policy stance is tied in with it in a logical and consistent way. Hence the usefulness of a national forum or a set of economic experts to indicate whether or not any particular wage outcome is consistent with the state of the economy and the government's current economic policies. The use of independent economic advice has been an important ingredient of both the German 'concerted action' and the Austrian *sozialpartnerschaft*, as well as in some of the Scandinavian systems. It is nevertheless interesting that even 'concerted action' has run into problems in recent years, and that several other previously successful bargaining systems or policies have apparently come under considerable strain in the 1970s.

One reason is that the economic environment of the industrialised

economies has changed in the 1970s: for reasons which are still not absolutely clear, there was a great surge in cost pressures, which strained the existing fixed-rate system. The repercussions of the commodity price boom in 1972–4, the effects of the 1973 oil price shock, the large increases in world trade and liquidity, as well as internal changes in the industrialised countries, have all combined to make the economic environment very different. The 1970s have been a period of transition and change in collective bargaining procedures in a number of countries. In nearly all of them the adjustment to the 1973–4 oil price rises, and the implied real income loss, proved extremely difficult. In some countries, previously harmonious relationships between negotiating parties were strained and even broke down. In some the government felt obliged to step in, often with direct pay or price controls. In others the crisis led to new systems of pay determination, as in Australia where the Arbitration Commission returned to indexation after a break of over twenty years.

Some of the European countries appeared to adopt as their form of incomes restraint a 'hard-currency' policy, in most cases tying their currencies to the Deutschemark, in the hope that the element of imported inflation would be kept to a minimum, while export industries would have to keep unit labour costs down in order to remain competitive. Indeed it was only Italy and the UK amongst European countries, both of whom had weak and deteriorating balance of payments situations, that did not attempt to keep their currency in line with the Deutschemark. Such a link, if held, could be expected to exert a powerful restraining influence on price rises in the trading sector of the economy, and itself provide a rationale for policies of wage restraint. However, since it is logically impossible for all countries to pursue a 'hard-currency' policy, this particular means of restraining incomes cannot be advanced as a general prescription.

The conclusion to this review is that there is no unique prescriptive answer. The various countries are so different that generalisations prove difficult to make. It would be wrong to think that the Germans' concerted action or Austria's *sozialpartnershaft* could be neatly applied to the UK. The evidence from past attempts to import some of the elements of each into the British system is that there is not the degree of social cohesiveness or of union control over its own members for such a transplant to be immediately successful.

What appears to be of fundamental importance is that the negotiating parties should be able to recognise clearly the effect of their decisions on the economy. Incomes policy, at the least, might be viewed as an information system. Collective bargainers have heard many times that if only they would all demand less pay, then more growth would be possible. The results of polls indicate that workers would willingly forgo wage increases if all others would do the same. In this sense incomes policy is a public good, and one that governments might consider providing. If the institutions themselves are adequate, governments may not need to be involved in an explicit incomes policy. It is clear that government intervention in some countries is counter-productive. The most successful form of government involvement appears to be the sort of arms-length involvement characteristic of Austria and Germany. The government sets out the economic framework with its monetary and fiscal policies, and discusses prospects with the social partners. It is then up to the social partners to reach agreement with each other within the bounds of some broad consensus on the economy.

It is an open question whether any arrangement of this sort could happily be transplanted into Britain. It is very difficult, if not impossible, to operate an incomes policy in a country where people do not generally have a feeling that they get reasonably fair treatment. That is why governments have as far as possible avoided embarking on an incomes policy in countries like France and Italy. While in income distribution and social policy the egalitarian profile in Britain may be more like the Scandinavian countries or Austria and Germany than France or Italy, it is possible that social antagonisms may be rather pronounced and therefore make the operation of some form of social partnership difficult. The sort of centralised collective bargaining procedures which have at times been successful in some of the European countries have succeeded because of a broad social consensus. One must therefore ask whether such a social consensus exists or could be brought about in Britain and, if so, whether the development of a more centralised or coordinated system of wage determination would indeed be a desirable development.

In the matter of centralisation as against decentralisation, the balance of the country evidence is by no means clear. Centralisation, which at one time seemed to work rather well in some of the Scandinavian countries, has not been so successful in recent years and has frequently led to rather unsatisfactory forms of government intervention. The one great unsolved problem of centralised agreements has been the drift of wages at company and plant level beyond nationally agreed pay increases. On the other hand, an entirely decentralised system, whilst it may appear to be able to cater better for changes in relative prices, may tend to give too inflationary an outcome if leapfrogging settlements begin to occur. In the case of Austria and Germany, there does seem to be an underlying understanding amongst the negotiators about what the country can afford, while in Japan negotiations over productivity bonuses at least make it clear that bargaining is concerned with increases in real output and not with what may simply turn out to be paper money. In the end, therefore, it may not be the particular institutional structures that are important, whether centralised or decentralised, but whether there is some awareness, whether it be some social consensus or just a general acceptance of the need to remain competitive, of the realities of the economic situation. Where such awareness is absent then the government may have an important educative role in explaining the trade-offs between inflation and employment and in underlining the way in which such monetary and fiscal policies as it is necessarily pursuing must inevitably impinge on the labour market and circumscribe the feasible growth of real incomes. The use of a national forum to discuss the general economic situation would appear to be a useful aid in promoting such an aim.

Varieties of National Experience

Australia

Since the end of the nineteenth century all states and federal governments have had legislation for conciliation and arbitration in industrial relations issues (Dymond *et al.* [7]; Brown [4]). This system is unique in western industrialised economies with the exception of New Zealand. Legislation was originally introduced following a series of major strikes. The arrangements generally involve some form of independent tribunal for settling those disputes which cannot be resolved by the negotiating parties. These tribunals issue awards covering minimum conditions of employment for around 90 per cent of workers. Besides federal legislation, four of the states have their own tribunals, while the other two have tripartite wages boards. The linchpin of the system is the Australian Conciliation and Arbitration Commission; decisions on national wages made by that body lead to awards to other groups, since there are strong interconnections between various groups of workers. The decisions of the Commission and of tribunals are backed by law, so that the whole system of industrial relations in Australia is quasi-judicial.

The Australian system of wage fixing has run into problems in the 1970s. In the first place it was only minimum conditions of employment that could be fixed by law. This therefore led to numerous 'over-award' payments. The Australian Council of Trade Unions came out in favour of negotiation in preference to state-provided arbitration, and certain groups effectively moved outside the control of the arbitrators, so that by the mid-1970s the Arbitration Commission seemed to be acting only as a rubber stamp for previously agreed settlements. The system began to be criticised for encouraging the escalation of inflation and for the leapfrogging of settlements in 1974 which led to wage increases of around 30 per cent in that year. After much discussion the Arbitration Commission came out in favour of an indexation system whereby wages would be adjusted each quarter in line with movements in the consumer price index (thus reviving a system which had been abolished in 1953 after 32 years). The indexation was later amended so that as from 1976 there was less than full compensation for changes in the cost of living.

Australia has a long history of protecting wages against inflation. When indexation was readopted in 1975, awards were first made quarterly and later half-yearly. Less than half the awards have involved full compensation for the rise in the cost of living, with the rest giving only some partial indexation. Although the government has not been fully in favour of the arrangements, the Commission only pushed ahead with indexation after the fullest consultation with negotiating parties. The Commission is bound by law to take account in its awards of the state of the economy with particular reference to inflation and unemployment. It is also charged with a conciliation role so that it considers the degree of industrial unrest and judges the effects of its awards on the industrial climate. The Commission's functions therefore may be in conflict and in the end no body administering an incomes policy, which is what the Commission has now become, can afford to overlook market forces.

Austria

There has been an informal and voluntary tripartite system of social and economic partnership in Austria for over twenty years, although there was a short hiatus in the early 1950s (Mire [12]). The first national agreement on wages and prices was signed in 1947 by the Federation of Trade Unions and the Federal Chamber of Trade and Industry, and though it was regarded as a temporary expedient a further four annual agreements followed. With renewed price stability, there was a return to free collective bargaining in 1952, but a resurgence of inflation led to the formation in March 1957 of a Joint Commission on Wages and Prices. This body has been in existence ever since and is the central link in the *sozialpartnerschaft*. The original instigator of the Commission was not the government but the Federation of Trade Unions. Organised labour in Austria has been willing to cooperate and support a centralised system of wage bargaining.

The Commission is composed of four interested parties and the government. The four groups are the Chamber of Labour, the Chamber of Trade and Industry, the Chamber of Agriculture, and the Federation of Trade Unions. Each has two representatives and the government has four (including the Chancellor), but government members have not used their votes since 1966. The mandate of the Commission has always been to review all requests for higher wages and prices. A sub-committee examines all wage negotiations on two grounds: first, the likely effect of the negotiated package on the economy; and, second, the way in which such claims tie in with the overall wage policy of the Federation, the trade union body. Decisions must be unanimous and claims are passed backwards and forwards until unanimity is reached. A similar sub-committee meets weekly to examine requests for price increases, although only about a third of consumers' expenditure is covered, since imported goods, restaurant meals, government controlled prices and other items are excluded. Price rises have to be justified by those increased costs which cannot be offset by higher productivity. Problems which prove insoluble can be taken to meetings of the presidents' conferences for the presidents of the four groups to attempt some compromise.

Since 1963 there has also been a joint meeting of the relevant parties on the general state of the economy, at which members of the economics ministry, the central banks and the Austrian Economic Research Institute present their views on the economic outlook and economic policy. Economic forecasts are published and discussed and the Economic and Social Advisory Board makes recommendations on monetary and fiscal policy and on the labour market, these recommendations being passed to the Joint Commission.

The government naturally works closely with these various bodies, so that economic policy is to a large extent determined in conjunction with the social partners. The decisions made by the Joint Commission are usually adhered to, partly because all the major interest groups are involved in the decision-making process and partly because there is a general consensus that the *sozialpartnerschaft* is a sensible arrangement. Furthermore, the main four interest groups have considerable power over their members; in the case of the unions, although they are in principle autonomous, in practice they are affiliated to the Federation, a centralised trade union structure having been introduced after the Second World War.

Although the institutional arrangements are formal, participation in the system and adherence to its decisions are voluntary. That the system has held together and apparently served so well probably owes a great deal to the social consensus on the need for wage and price restraint which has now lasted so long that it seems to be permanent.

Germany

Germany is one of the rare countries where governments have not intervened *directly* to try to influence wage settlements in the period since the war. It has also been one of the most successful of the industrialised countries in achieving a high level of employment yet a relatively low level of inflation. The bargaining autonomy of employers and trade unions has been regarded as sacrosanct, and the 'social partners' have been given the responsibility of ensuring that settlements are consistent with the country's general economic policy. This has not meant, however, that the government has had no influence on incomes; indeed its monetary and fiscal policies have been specifically addressed to the problems of inflation. Since the 1960s there have been formal arrangements by which the government and others could make known their views on the scope for increases in incomes.

In 1963 an independent Council of Economic Experts was set up to report to the government on the economic situation, including in particular wage bargaining; this body was made up mostly of academic economists. Then in 1967 'concerted action' was formally established by federal law. This was not intended as an institutional arrangement, but rather as the expression of a four-pronged policy goal encompassing price stability, full employment, the foreign trade balance and economic growth (Clark [5]). This policy was set out in the Act on the Promotion of Economic Stability and Growth. In practice the unions and employers meet at regular intervals with the economic experts, the government and the central bank to discuss the macroeconomic framework within which bargaining must take place. The procedure is facilitated by the fact that the control of the union and employer organisations over their members is fairly tight. This is aided in Germany by the fact that there are only seventeen industrial trade unions which are members of the German Federation of Trade Unions, having seven million members, with a further one million-odd members of the two other main union organisations – the salaried employees and the civil servants. Although there are far more employers' organisations, they are mostly affiliated to the Confederation of German Employers' Associations. These employers' organisations are very powerful bodies; they not only coordinate their negotiating strategy but are also prepared to use lock-out tactics to support their position. Some agreements are made at national level, whilst others are made at works council level. However works councils are legally bound by a peace obligation and national collective agreements are legal contracts, with adjudication on matters of dispute being subject to labour courts. There are also nationally agreed conciliation procedures. Labour court decisions are said to have dissuaded unions from acting too much at a decentralised level and have thus encouraged the unions to look more to the national negotiations. Under this system there is no guarantee that the centrally agreed policy will be translated into a consistent set of individual settlements, but in general this has been the case. The settlement in the metal industry, where the Metalworkers' Union has 2½ million members, is always a crucial agreement, since other groups watch keenly for the outcome in determining their own stance.

The 'concerted action' system has been fairly successful, judged over the longer period and when relating the level of settlements to those in other countries, but it has not been without its problems. In 1973–4, for instance, it came under strain when, despite the stress on the need for wage restraint, actual settlements were fairly high, and the government was particularly unsuccessful in containing public sector pay following several major strikes. In contrast the unions' behaviour in 1979 was moderate, with union leaders in the steel industry, for instance, agreeing not to push for higher wages on the grounds of higher oil prices. Such moderation is an example of the educative role of the national forum and the sensitivity of the social partners to economic realities.

Over the years however there has been a growing dissatisfaction with 'concerted action'; from the union side because they increasingly felt that they were being exploited by the system, by the employers who resented the increased government use of tax and expenditure policies from the mid-1970s onwards in order to influence agreements. The unions' reluctance to settle in 1974 was repeated in 1977 when the union representatives withdrew for a time. The number of meetings which had averaged about five a year in the first five years dwindled to only about three a year in the later 1970s. The annual negotiations on pay have proved more protracted and agreement more difficult to reach as time has passed. Nevertheless an advantage over many other systems is that the negotiating process takes place over a short period, with a common starting date. Although the system has run into some difficulties in recent years, the rate of inflation has been successfully held down. The reason is that there is a strong underlying belief in the merits of the market economy, together with a deep-seated fear of a return to the sort of inflation and unemployment witnessed under the Weimar Republic. Whether this indeed still has a strong influence on the bargainers' behaviour is not clear, but it has undoubtedly influenced successive governments in keeping to a fairly strict monetary policy throughout much of this period.

Japan

The labour market in Japan is organised in a very different way from those in the other industrialised countries (OECD [14]). Wages increase in line with age and the length of service. This means of payment is directly connected with the Japanese system of 'lifetime' employment, under which, workers, at least in the major firms, generally stay with the same firm throughout their life, being virtually assured of employment until they reach a certain age (Seki [19];

Suzuki [20]). Another feature is that within industry the great majority of workers, both manual and non-manual, are organised in enterprise unions, many of which are affiliated (usually through industrial unions) to one of four main national trade union centres. About a third of all employees are members of trade unions. One of the major employers' organisations is concerned with labour matters (whilst another is responsible for commercial matters).

Although collective bargaining takes place between each enterprise union and the management, the main influence on wage bargaining is the 'Spring wage round' in which the national unions and employers separately concert their approaches, the result being expressed in key bargains which establish a going rate for wage increases. For, as in Germany, one or two major settlements, especially that in the iron and steel industry, are taken as the lead by other groups, although how closely the lead is followed depends on the industry or enterprise and in particular on the profitability of the enterprise in question. Once the major agreements have been made in the Spring wage negotiations most other settlements follow fairly quickly, so that the negotiations are in general completed in a short period. These negotiations are bipartite; the government does not interfere in the process although as the OECD report points out '... [the government] naturally ensures that information about the economy is available to all' and 'both the 1975 and 1976 wage rounds showed a statesman-like regard for the public interest on the part of the negotiators' (OECD [14]). The latter, which might be regarded as the same sort of social consensus that is seen to be so important in Austria and Germany, is supported by a national forum, the Industry and Labour Round Table, which exists for the discussion of major labour issues by unions, employers, the government and independent experts.

One facet of the Japanese system which is especially important is the exceptional identification of the worker with his enterprise, due not only to the lifetime employment system, but also the fact that remuneration depends importantly on the profitability of the enterprise, although there are suggestions that this attachment to the firm may be beginning to weaken. It is still true to say, however, that '... the duty of the employer to provide employment and generally look to the well-being of employees is matched by willing acceptance by employees that their energies should be devoted to furthering the efficiency and prosperity of the enterprise' (OECD [14]).

There are several reasons why, except for 1974, this system has proved very successful in keeping inflationary pressures in check. The fact that earnings are likely to rise each year, largely irrespective of the actual work being done, may reduce the worker's aspirations or expectations of additional wage increases. Furthermore, since additional increases in pay are geared closely to the profitability of the enterprise, the workers have a vested interest in ensuring improvements in efficiency and avoiding any disruptions. Arguments along these lines have been put forward to support greater worker participation and profit-sharing schemes in many European countries. The union, being centred on the firm, also has a vested interest in the enterprise, so that there is perhaps less hostility between workers and management than in other countries. Most workers receive semi-annual bonuses which may supplement the basic rate by substantial amounts. These bonuses vary in amount depending on the financial circumstances of the enterprise, and are themselves the outcome of collective bargaining. The weight given to seniority has been reduced somewhat over recent years as starting rates have moved up (due in part to earlier difficulties in recruiting sufficient workers) and age differentials have thus narrowed. Nevertheless the fact that most workers can usually expect an automatic yearly increase plus some sort of bonus will continue to be an important factor, alongside the importance of Round Table talks and of enterprise unions, in tending to ease the pressures for inflationary increases and to reduce the tension in wage negotiations.

Netherlands

There has been a long history of state intervention in collective bargaining in the Netherlands, although the formal system of 'guided wage policy' which has been instituted in the 1950s came to an end in 1967 (OECD [13]). Since then there has been no permanent statutory incomes policy but governments have intervened from time to time with wage and price controls, including a temporary wage freeze in early 1980. Wages policy has been supported by controls on prices, a variety of different formulae being used over time, but generally providing for limits to the extent to which cost increases, especially labour costs, can be passed on into prices.

The earlier statutory wages policy was a centralised wage-fixing system. Wage increases were determined by changes in the cost of living and the share of wages in national income. For many years the system worked well, but in the 1960s the system began to come under strain and was ended in 1967. The Social Economic Council, which was established under the 1950 Act on Industrial Organisation, consists of union and management representatives plus a number of independent experts appointed by the government as crown members. The Council acts as a consultative body on all matters of social and economic policy. This body has proved less effective in recent years because of the frequent failure to reach any unanimous recommendations. The other organisation is the Foundation of Labour, which is a bipartite body made up of union and employer representatives only, where most of the present central negotiations on wages take place. An important role in negotiations is played by the Central Planning Bureau, which provides detailed forecasts of the economy including an analysis of the scope for wage increases.

In the mid-1960s a strong surge in wages had led the government to introduce a wage pause in 1966 and then to set very strict wage limits in 1967. An easing of wage pressures resulted in the requirement for prior government approval of collective wage agreements being abolished at the start of 1968, but the government then pushed through a Bill which gave it the power to invalidate certain collective agreements in special circumstances, to freeze wages by decree or, as a last resort, to reintroduce the earlier system of prior approval of agreements. The measure met strong parliamentary and union opposition and was only passed, in heavily amended form, in conjunction with a vote of confidence. Several central union bodies withdrew from central negotiations in early 1970, but the government had already had to resort to a general price freeze in April 1970. Since 1970 the determination of wages has in principle been in the hands of the two sides of industry, but the government has always retained this right to intervene if there are serious economic or social problems, and it has frequently done so.

There has only been one successfully negotiated central agreement since the change in bargaining practices. That was the 1972 voluntary tripartite social contract. With the advent of the oil crisis negotiations broke down on a voluntary agreement in 1974, the government again stepping in with its own package, under a Special Powers Act, which once again enabled it to control wages and other incomes. The new package provided for indexation plus some gain in real incomes. The pattern since then has usually been failure to reach central agreement followed by individual industry settlements and occasional freezes, as happened again in 1975–6. Agreements in the 1970s have mostly included indexation clauses, although there has been much dispute about them. Despite the fact that wage agreements in the Netherlands are enforceable by law, there have been several recent bouts of strikes, including a whole series in the Autumn of 1979 which preceded the imposition of the latest wage freeze.

Norway

In Norway there has been an orderly system of collective bargaining since the end of the war, which has resulted in legally enforceable two-year centralised agreements on two occasions out of every three (Korsnes [9]). In those years when the unions and employers have failed to come to an agreement – for instance 1956, 1961 and 1974 – the number of days lost through strikes has been exceptionally large. The system is a tripartite one between unions, employers and government, which has progressively been coordinated with and incorporated in macroeconomic policy. Until 1952 wage disputes were investigated by a tripartite wage board. Then for a time wage settlements were left to the unions and employers, but from 1956 the government began to meet informally with the negotiators, recommending guidelines and being willing to subsidise price stability. A settlement of 10 per cent in 1961, which resulted in a sharp jump in prices, led to the formation in 1962 of the unofficial Contact Committee – a body where the Prime Minister and his economics ministers could meet with representatives of the unions, employers, farmers and fishermen to consider incomes questions. Although successful in securing a low settlement in 1963, negotiations broke down in the following year, despite mediation, and the Arbitration Board was reconvened. In June 1965 an independent expert committee – the Aukrust Committee – was set up to provide an independent review of the economic situation. The Committee provides an assessment of what will happen to prices, *real* wages and other incomes, and the balance of payments, on the basis of alternative increases in *nominal* wages and incomes, and these are generally accepted as a realistic basis for subsequent negotiations. The Aukrust Committee was broadened in 1967 to include specialists from the two negotiating parties, and was made permanent in 1969. An additional feature in

Norway is that the tripartite negotiations take place at the same time as the government is negotiating with the farmers and fishermen on income developments and government support; both sets of negotiators keep each other informed in order to avoid subsequent leapfrogging between farmers and wage and salary earners.

Since 1973 a new phase of wage policy has developed (Inman [8]; OECD [16]). The government has been more deeply involved, with taxes, subsidies and other economic policies becoming part of the wage settlement. An era of what became known as 'combined settlements' was initiated. These developments were strongly influenced by the work of the government-appointed Skaanland Committee to consider future policies on prices and incomes; its report, published in 1973, came out strongly in favour of greater government participation in a permanent form of wages policy. The recommendation of a new Council of Prices and Incomes Policies, which would replace the Contact Committee and have wider membership and deal with all matters of prices, wages, all other incomes, taxes and subsidies, was rejected by the Federation of Trade Unions (LO) as too rigid an arrangement, and in 1975 it was rejected by the government also although the need for a closer liaison between the social partners and the central authorities was accepted. Tax concessions were a feature of the agreements between 1975 and 1977 and these have involved the *quid pro quo* of less than full compensation for rises in the cost of living.

During the 1970s there have been certain problems with the system of central bargaining. On several occasions it has proved difficult to reach agreement and recently, from September 1978 to December 1979, the government was forced to resort to a general wage and price freeze. This proved very successful in the short term – prices rose by $4\frac{3}{4}$ per cent compared to the target of 4 per cent – but, as with nearly all experiments with temporary controls, problems have arisen with the return to 'normal' bargaining. In the early part of 1980 there were local claims for large awards. In March, an official bus drivers' strike in Oslo lasted several weeks, despite being ruled illegal by the Labour court and despite the LO calls for the workers to return to work. The Spring negotiations were made especially difficult because of a sudden surge in prices, due in particular to the rise in the price of oil and some other commodities. This follows a period when real disposable income has fallen for two years. So while the freeze proved successful in sharply reducing inflation, the after-effects may be less favourable. The eventual agreement, made in April, was for a general pay rise of 5.2 per cent from the start of the month, including large rises for the low paid. A ceiling of 3 per cent will be placed on wage drift over the next year. The government has conceded substantial tax reductions and increases in children's allowances as a *quid pro quo*. On this occasion the tax measures have been combined with public expenditure cuts to avoid overheating.

The reason why central agreements have at times played an important role in damping down inflationary pressures, allowing a higher use of productive resources than in many other countries, is that both of the central organisations, the LO and the National Federation of Employers (NAF) have wide powers over their constituent members, even though individual industries make their own agreements. There appears to be a consensus that centralised wage determination procedures are a fair and sensible part of the economic system. Agreements have generally been in the form of overall norms – often in flat-rate form with extra for the low paid. However, wage drift has often meant that earnings have risen more than intended, even though this element of flexibility has effectively operated as a safety valve for the system, and drift has helped to avoid too great a squeeze on differentials.

Sweden

The collective bargaining system in Sweden is unique in that both the unions and employers are involved in centralised bargaining, while the government is virtually totally excluded from the process. Since the 1950s collective bargaining has been conducted centrally by the two major labour organisations, the Swedish Employers' Federation (SAF) and the Swedish Confederation of Trade Unions, the *Landsorganisationen* (LO). The present arrangements grew out of an LO report [10]. The proposed policy was not simply a policy for wages but rather a wider plan for a comprehensive macroeconomic strategy. There were several strands in the policy concerned with obtaining a fair share of the national income for wage earners, the establishment of fair differentials, and the consideration of the effects of wage rises on the economy in general (Robinson [17]; OECD [13]).

The trade unions aimed to keep the government out of the collective bargaining arena and developed a bipartite approach with the employers which would take account of general economic conditions and would therefore give no particular excuse for government intervention. In this they were generally successful. The employers' organisation, SAF, was generally sympathetic to the LO suggestions and thus from 1952 onwards a central framework for wage settlements was devised by SAF and LO representatives.

Central negotiations were facilitated by the existing centralisation of both parties. There had been a centralised employers' federation since early in the century; no firm is allowed to sign a collective agreement without SAF permission. On the other side, since 1941 the LO has supervised and attempted to coordinate the wage policies of the different unions; furthermore LO approval is required for any but minor industrial action and the LO also acts as an arbitrator in inter-union disputes on wages.

The LO has built up this highly centralised system not just because they hoped to achieve wage restraint but because of a strong political desire to achieve a fairer income distribution. Many of the central agreements have therefore included flat-rate elements, low-pay kitties or similar devices intended to narrow differentials. The difficulty is that such attempts to raise the pay of low-income groups may lead to a large amount of wage drift for higher-income groups; it is clear that something of this sort has in fact occurred. To the extent that this has happened, the wage policy may even have added to cost inflation at times. The problem is that a policy to narrow differentials may fly in the face of economic forces; wage drift will reflect market forces which may well equate demand and supply for particular labour skills at a price which is above the centrally agreed one.

The central agreement is first agreed by the LO and SAF. At the top level there is a certain consensus that income claims must be reconciled with general economic and social policy. Since the early 1970s, the EFO model has been the basis for discussions on the economy and has been used to investigate the consequences of different wage outcomes. The model is named after Messrs Edgren, Faxen and Odhner, the economists of the TCO (the main white-collar union), SAF and LO, who jointly developed a model of economic policy in an open economy where wage developments in the shielded sector are dominated by developments in the competitive (traded goods) sector. In principle, the central agreement is made in full cognisance of its likely effect on inflation, employment, real incomes and other key variables. The central agreement only sets the framework for settlements, however, since there are then a number of separate collective agreements for each branch of industry. Although representatives from each industry have played a part in reaching the central agreement there is nevertheless considerable room for manoeuvre at plant level and wage drift can be both large and general. Yet once an agreement has been made, there is a 'peace obligation' attached to the parties to it, and furthermore the employers themselves are reluctant to see fellow members of their Federation settling outside the limits.

Although it was certainly the original intention of the trade unions to try to keep the government out of collective bargaining, during the 1970s there has been an increasing degree of government involvement in and influence on the central agreement. There had always been informal contacts between the government and the negotiating parties. In 1971 the government brought forward public sector settlements and declared that low-income groups should get higher percentage rises and that the rise in incomes should be close to the proposals of the government's arbitration committee (Lindbeck [11]). Then in 1973 the government cut income taxes in an attempt to persuade the unions to accept lower wage settlements. This initiated an era in which the government began using all sorts of devices – direct and indirect taxes, transfer payments, investment funds – to try to influence the central agreements, with various concessions being conditional on an outcome acceptable to the government. These moves broke a long tradition of government non-intervention in centralised wage negotiations.

The Swedish system has not prevented large rises in prices and earnings when external conditions have been adverse, as in 1976 and 1977. However, the problems engendered by the high settlements at that time were soon realised and resulted in a low settlement in 1978 which entailed a fall in real incomes for many union members. This led to problems with the 1979 settlement, the introduction of a temporary price freeze and many months of deadlock and bitter dispute in the Spring of 1980 involving overtime bans, strikes and lockouts. Disputes during the currency of an agreement must be settled in the Labour court which has existed since 1928, but the legalistic approach is not liked by either unions or employers so that adjudication by law has usually been regarded as the last resort.

The Swedish experience has therefore been rather mixed. Although government intervention was resisted for a long time, it has become increasingly common in the 1970s. The flexibility built in to the central agreements has meant that the incidence of labour disputes has been lower than it might otherwise have been, but high wage drift has meant that the centralised system has not avoided rapid cost inflation. The central agreement also seems to have become increasingly more difficult to negotiate.

References

[1] Blyth, C. A., 'The interaction between collective bargaining and government policies in selective member countries', in [15].

[2] Braun, A. R., 'The role of incomes policy in industrialised countries since world war II', *IMF Staff Papers*, 1975.

[3] Brittan, S. and Lilley, P., *The Delusion of Incomes Policy*, London, Maurice Temple Smith, 1977.

[4] Brown, W., 'Antipodean contrasts in incomes policy', in J. Bowers, ed., *Inflation, Economic Developments and Integration: Essays in Honour of A. J. Brown*, Leeds University Press, 1979.

[5] Clark, J., 'Concerted action in the Federal Republic of Germany', *British Journal of Industrial Relations*, July 1979.

[6] Clegg, H. A., *Trade Unionism Under Collective Bargaining*, Oxford, Blackwell, 1976.

[7] Dymond, W. R., Kellgren, N. and Weisz, M., *Manpower Policy in Australia*, Paris, OECD, 1975.

[8] Inman, J., 'Wages policy in Norway', *British Journal of Industrial Relations*, November 1979.

[9] Korsnes, O., 'Duality in the role of unions and unionists: the case of Norway', *British Journal of Industrial Relations*, November 1979.

[10] Landsorganisationen (L.O.), *Trade Unions and Full Employment*, Stockholm, 1951.

[11] Lindbeck, A., *Swedish Economic Policy*, London, Macmillan, 1975.

[12] Mire, J., 'Incomes policy in Austria under a voluntary partnership', *Monthly Labour Review*, August 1977.

[13] OECD, *Socially Responsible Wage Policies and Inflation: A Review of Four Countries' Experience (Sweden, Netherlands, Germany and United Kingdom)*, Paris, 1975.

[14] OECD, *The Development of Industrial Relations Systems: Some Implications of Japanese Experience*, Paris, 1977.

[15] OECD, *Collective Bargaining and Government Policies* (papers and report on July 1978 Washington conference), Paris, 1979.

[16] OECD, *Wage Policies and Collective Bargaining Developments in Finland, Ireland, and Norway*, Paris, 1979.

[17] Robinson, D., *Solidaristic Wage Policy in Sweden*, Paris, OECD, 1974.

[18] Saunders, C. T., 'Lessons for Britain from European experience', in F. T. Blackaby, ed., *An Incomes Policy for Britain*, London, Heinemann, 1972.

[19] Seki, H., 'Employment problems and policies in an ageing society: the Japanese experience', *International Labour Review*, May–June 1980.

[20] Suzuki, H., 'Age, seniority and wages', *International Labour Review*, January–February 1976.

9 Changes in Relative Pay in the 1970s

*C. T. Saunders**

The question to which this paper attempts a few answers – far from all the answers that might be given – is: what groups of employed people in Britain have been doing better, or worse, than average during the 1970s – a period in which average wages and salaries, in money, were multiplied by a factor of about 3·7 and consumer prices by a factor of about 3? The answer may illustrate some of the results of competitive pay bargaining, allowing for the constraints placed upon the bargaining process by incomes policies. There have been winners and losers in the pay Olympics; it is not wholly true to say that everyone has been running hard to stay, in real terms, in the same place – 'say not the struggle *naught* availeth'. The big question is whether the *sizes* of the gains, attempted or achieved, are in reasonable proportion to the cost to the economy; unless one takes the view that competing pay pressures bear no significant responsibility for inflation – a view which strains belief – then inflation is a large part of that cost.

A second question, which the present paper does not attempt to answer, is whether the specific gains and losses can be justified by economic, or welfare criteria. Comparisons between the beginning and end of the 1970s are obviously affected, but by no means wholly invalidated, by the influence of pay policies: effective and comprehensive pay restraints were in force for only about half of the ten years 1970–9.

* The paper is partly based on a research project, financed by SSRC, dealing with pay inequalities in the European Community. Acknowledgements are due to Mr David Marsden for much of the substantial work used in this paper, but he is not responsible for all the glosses put upon it. A full report, *Pay Inequalities in the Community*, is planned for publication by Butterworth in 1981.

Comparative British Experience

Comparison will be made, at various points, with developments in some other Western industrial countries. Institutional differences were, of course, apparent long before the 1970s. So is it differences in formal institutions that play a part in the faster rates of inflation in Britain? Or is it a difference in what are conveniently called 'attitudes', or in the unstable balance of pressures on the bargainers from the participants in the bargaining process: the government (in one way or another), employers, and the three levels of participants on the employees' side – the union leadership, the local shop stewards and the various sections of the 'rank and file'?

It may, then, be useful to suggest, as a background, how far Britain's experience in some relevant quantitative respects has differed from that elsewhere. Accurate international comparability of the statistical series cannot at present be assured. However, certain general conclusions can be drawn. These suggest that Britain over the 1970s, taking the period as a whole, stands out among fourteen Western industrial countries with:

(a) almost the biggest increase in *average nominal pay* in industry (in national currency), but exceeded by Italy and Ireland while Denmark was not far behind,
(b) about the biggest rise in *consumer prices*, again along with Italy and Ireland,
(c) almost the smallest increase in *average real pay* in industry – 19 per cent over nine years; but Sweden and the US did worse,
(d) only a slightly smaller fall in *industrial employment* (14 per cent) than the unweighted average for the fourteen countries (16 per cent),
(e) among the smallest increases in *industrial production*, but not very different from Sweden or Switzerland.
(f) among the smallest increases in *labour productivity* in industry, but not very different from Italy, and greater than Sweden and Canada.

The expected cross country rank correlation is found between increase in nominal pay and in consumer prices (Spearman correlation of 0.91, significant at 99 per cent). But the hypothesis that the strongest pay pressures produce only the smallest increases in real pay – through the process of deflationary reactions and loss of competitiveness – cannot be firmly asserted by simple deduction from these indices alone. The rank correlation between the increase in nominal pay and in real pay is certainly negative, at 0·65 (just significant at 95 per cent). But Italy managed to combine the fastest rate of nominal pay increases and price inflation with the largest increase in real pay (if the rather surprising figures are to be trusted). And the relatively small increases in nominal pay in Switzerland and the US accompanied very small increases in real pay. It must, of course, be remembered that many other influences play on consumer prices besides industrial pay; it is not suggested that these simple comparisons take us very far. And the comparisons concern only the first and last year of the 1970s; a more careful review of developments during the decade might create different impressions of performance.

What does appear from these figures, with all the qualifications that must be attached to them, is this: if increasing real pay is the expected benefit, and price inflation the cost, of the bargaining process, then the special feature of the British experience is almost minimum benefit from almost maximum cost. However, within the British pay structure, some have done better than others.

A host of differentials exists in every pay structure. First, we examine, in general terms, changes in the structure of differentials between industries; they depend in part – quite a large part – on the occupational and sex composition of the various industries; differentials between men and women are influenced by the differences in occupations, and so on. This is one reason for following the Department of Employment and the EEC Statistical Office in analysing separately when relevant the pay of men and women and of manual and non-manual workers, thus creating, for some statistical purposes, four 'labour markets'. The term is convenient but possibly misleading; while the four 'labour markets' are by no means wholly non-competing groups, yet there are barriers between them, established by qualifications, education, the history of pay determination, or by conventions about appropriate pay relativities. These barriers may be weakened, or strengthened, even during a decade.

Secondly, we look at changes in relative pay in rather more detail, using as our main classification the major groups established for collective bargaining. This is intended to suggest, in terms more closely related to the actual organisation of the British bargaining machinery, which groups have made gains and losses during the 1970s.

Trends in Differentials in the 1970s

Industry differentials

The general impression is one of remarkable stability over time in inter-industry pay differentials – a stability to which the forces of tradition and comparability have contributed. To render this impression rather more precise, the relative pay for manual men (adults only) in each of the 26 SIC Orders in April 1979 has been regressed against the corresponding figures for April 1970. The result is a correlation (R^2) of 0.72; that is 72 per cent of the relative pay structure in 1979 is explained statistically by the structure holding in 1970. The stability of the industrial pay structure, it may be noted, is not peculiar to Britain. It also applies to Belgium, France, West Germany, Italy and the Netherlands, as well as to Britain (see Saunders and Marsden [5]).

Returning to the 1970–9 comparison for Britain, we find that the pattern of overall stability leaves room for a number of changes in relative positions. Some important industries – taken from over 100 minimum list headings – may be classed as winners or losers as in Table 9.1. The criterion is a gain or loss of more than 5 per cent in relative pay.

Apart from coalmining and, perhaps, motor manufacturing and printing these are not very large changes over a period of years (especially bearing in mind that earnings in a single week are subject to various accidental influences). But they might suggest, at first sight, a certain narrowing of the dispersion since the significant gainers, with one exception, were all industries with less than average pay in 1970, and the losers were all earning above average. Comparisons with some other EEC countries (1977 compared with 1972) show some similarities. Relative pay in coalmining increased dramatically in Germany and moderately in France and Belgium. Printing declined considerably in France and Italy. Motor manufacturing declined in Italy but improved its position in Germany (see Saunders and Marsden [5]).

Over the nine years as a whole, no marked contrast appears between the private and public sectors in Britain. Of the seven gaining

Table 9.1 *Changes in relative average weekly earnings of manual adult men,*[a] *1970–9 (percentages)*

	April 1970	April 1979	Change 1970–9 (per cent)
MLH winners			
Coalmining	97	130	+34
Electricity supply	94	102	+9
Water supply	91	99	
Insurance, banking, etc.	85	91	+7
Shipbuilding	108	114	+6
Educational services	71	75	+6
MLH losers			
Printing and publishing[b]	114	108	−5
Air transport	128	121	−5
Man-made fibres	113	105	−7
Motor vehicles	123	111	−8
Posts and telecomm.	105	95	−10

[a] Expressed as percentages of average earnings for manual adult men in all industries and services.
[b] Excluding newspapers.
Source: *New Earnings Surveys*.

industries, four are mainly in the public sector, as are two of the five losing industries.

As a second approach to the changing pattern of inter-industry differentials, we can see how far the leading industries of 1970 were still in position in 1979. The *leaders*, or high-wage industries, may be defined as those in which average earnings were 15 per cent or more above the average for all manual men (all industries and services). Eight such industries appear in 1970. Of these, five survived as high-wage industries in 1979. They are (their percentage to the average in 1979 being given in brackets): printing and publishing of newspapers (137); mineral oil refining (126); port and inland water transport (122); air transport (121) and industrial (including process) plant and steelwork (115). But three disappeared from the top league: general chemicals (112); motor vehicle manufacturing (111) and printing and publishing (excluding newspapers) (108). And these three were replaced by coalmining (130); brewing and malting (116) and glass (115). In addition, three industries appear in the top league in 1979 for which earnings were not reported in 1970: wheeled tractor manufacturing (127); insulated wires and cables (115) and sea transport (122).

The laggers, or low-wage industries (with earnings 15 per cent below average) numbered twelve in 1970. Of these, nine remained in the bottom league in 1979, namely: catering (71); agriculture (72); educational services (75); national government (79); clothing (79); retail (excluding food and drink) (79); local government (84); medical services (85) and wholesale (non-food) (85). But three climbed a little way out of this low-wage group: woollen and worsted (86); timber (88) and dealing in coals, building materials, etc. (89). In addition, the 1979 survey shows three low-wage industries not reported in 1970: sport and other recreations (79); other miscellaneous services (82) and cotton spinning and doubling (85). On balance, it appears that there was rather more movement at the top than at the bottom of the list among manual men.

We turn now to the question of whether there has in fact been any overall widening or narrowing of the industry differentials. The statistical evidence suggests only a very slight narrowing over the nine years. Taking now approximately 70 minimum list headings for manual men in all industries and services, we find the coefficient of variation (unweighted) falling, but only from 13.9 per cent in 1970 to 13.3 per cent in 1979. However, there is some sign of a reversal of trends during these years. The coefficient of variation fell to 12.6 per cent in 1976 and then increased again. In view of the apparently rather wide spread of rates of increase announced in settlements since April 1979 – although the announced terms of settlements are not necessarily reflected in actual earnings – it may be that overall measures of the dispersion of inter-industry earnings differences would now show something like the extent of dispersion which held ten years ago.

The narrowing of inter-industry differentials is not, once again, unique to Britain. The narrowing during the mid-1970s was of similar dimensions in Britain, Belgium, France and the Netherlands, and even more significant in Italy, where union policy has been rather vigorously and successfully directed towards reducing the quite large differentials. On the other hand, inter-industry differentials in Germany have distinctly widened. At the same time, the inter-industry dispersion in Britain is not exceptional; in Germany and the Netherlands there was less inequality between industry averages; in Belgium, France and Italy more inequality. The trends during this period suggest a certain convergence.

It is difficult to find any close connection between the bargaining system and the magnitude of these dispersions. Is there any ground for suspecting that the elements of central pay bargaining in Germany and the Netherlands, and in Britain (through the 'norms') for part of the period covered, is a partial explanation of the higher degree of equality, while the more decentralised systems in Belgium and France are partly responsible for the greater inequality? Italy is a more difficult case: the marked erosion of the very wide differentials accompanied a decentralisation of bargaining from the national to the local or plant level, and a growth in the influence of shop stewards.

Occupational differentials

We come now to the differential by occupation. To give a detailed statistical story of developments in the 1970s is unfortunately impossible; in 1973, at a time when the battle of differentials was growing hot, a new interdepartmentally agreed occupational classification was introduced, sufficiently different from earlier classifications to destroy, at many important points, comparability with previous years, except by often precarious estimates. (See the latest – and regrettably the last – *Report* of the Royal Commission on Distribution of Income and Wealth [4].)

We begin with the socially and economically important distinction between white-collar and blue-collar workers, which the new classification has not disturbed. There was a clear narrowing of the differential: in 1979 the mean weekly earnings of non-manual men had fallen to 122 per cent of that of manual men, compared with 125 per cent in 1976 and 134 per cent in 1970. For women the corresponding figures were 120, 124 and 133 per cent.

We must, of course, bear in mind that the proportion of white-collar workers in the labour force has been continuously increasing, for well-known reasons on both the demand and supply sides. Thus the ratio of non-manual to total workers (full time adults only) in the *New Earnings Survey* sample has risen from 34 per cent in 1970 to 39 per cent in 1979; the percentage for women has risen from 62 per cent to 70 per cent. The diminished pay advantage of white-collar workers as a group may be attributed, *selon choix*, to increased supply, or to an increasing demand resulting in an erosion of qualifications, or to equalising incomes policies, or to increasing relative strength of the manual worker unions to which the growth of white-collar unions is, on balance, an ineffective reaction. But it is certainly not just a new trend of the 1970s. The Royal Commission *Report* [4] linking NES data with Routh's work [3] shows a downward trend in the relative pay of the major groups of white-collar workers throughout the postwar periods and, although not continuously, for some white-collar, especially higher professional, occupations since before the First World War.

Nor is the decline in the white-collar pay differential in the 1970s peculiar to Britain. It occurred even more strongly, at least in industry, in France and Italy, where, however, the differential was, and remains, much greater than in Britain. In Germany and Belgium, however, the differential – again rather wider than in Britain although a good deal narrower than in France and Italy – widened somewhat (see Saunders and Marsden [5]).

The non-manual 'labour market' includes, of course, a much wider spread of occupational pay levels than that for manual workers. And

Table 9.2 Relative median earnings by occupational groups,[a] 1971 and 1978 (percentages)

	Men		Women	
	1971	1978	1971	1978
Professional				
Higher	141	133	207	163
Lower	119	117	138	133
Managers	132	120	132	138
Clerks	88	82	104	98
Foremen	115	105	125	113
Manual				
Skilled	101	97	89	90
Semi-skilled	89	89	84	86
Unskilled	81	80	83	83
All employees	100	100	100	100

[a] Expressed as percentages of median for all employees in relevant year.

Source: Royal Commission on Distribution of Income and Wealth. *Report No. 8*, 1969, Table 6.9.

there is a substantial overlap; however, just over half the non-manual adult men earned over £100 a week in 1979 as against a third of manual men; among women, a third of the non-manuals earned over £70 a week, against only 15 per cent of the manuals.

Some very clear distinctions emerge between the broad categories for which continuous estimates can be made (leaping as well as may be over the obstacles set up by changing classifications), and these are shown in Table 9.2. The general pattern is the well-known narrowing of the differentials due mainly to compression at the top, particularly for the higher salaried professions and for men managers (but not for the small but increasing number of women managers). Industrial earnings within each occupational group also show a narrowing dispersion of individual earnings within each of the non-manual groups during the 1970s, due more to a marked reduction of relative pay at the top decile point within each group than an increase at the bottom. The dispersion within the manual groups appears to have changed less.

Table 9.3 Differentials by skill grades in average earnings in engineering and related industries,[a] 1963–79 (percentages)

	1963	1971	1976	1979
Skilled				
Maintenance	112.5	116.4	114.3	115.7
Toolroom	111.6	109.5	107.0	110.2
Other	105.2	105.5	102.8	104.7
Semi-skilled	97.6	96.9	97.7	95.6
Unskilled	76.3	76.9	81.9	82.7

[a] For adult men (including overtime) as percentages of the mean for all grades in June of each year.

Source: *Department of Employment Gazette* (various issues).

The shift to a new classification system since 1973 renders doubtful any precise comparison between skill grades among manual workers. A reliable analysis of the much publicised erosion of the skill differential can, however, be got for the engineering industries – where the erosion has caused most difficulty and the changes are shown in Table 9.3. The skill differential was widening in the 1950s and 1960s, following a marked compression during the Second World War (as in the First). During the 1970s movements have been rather diverse; they suggest a decline in the advantage of the skilled grades up to about 1976 (especially, as Dean [1] notes, in 1974–5 which was effectively a period of free collective bargaining), but there has been some restoration since then. We have here measured differentials in terms of the relationship of each grade to the average for all manual men in the industry; this seems more appropriate than the more commonly used relationship between skilled men and unskilled men in view of the very small numbers now classified as unskilled (about 6 per cent). The main changes have been the improved relative pay of the unskilled group at the bottom end of the range, but also of the skilled maintenance men at the top end. Another change is the fall in relative pay of the skilled toolroom grade – a fall which caused considerable trouble in the motor industry in 1976.

The two principal movements in occupational differentials are thus the decline of the relative pay of the managerial, professional and supervisory groups, and a decline in the skill differential of some manual workers offset by a certain improvement for the lower paid unskilled. These movements appear to be a continuation of earlier trends rather than new developments fostered either by inflation or by the direct effects of incomes policies.

Moreover there have been similar – in some ways more striking – developments in France (where the minimum wage regulations have played a part in improving the positions of the least skilled manual workers) and in Italy (associated with effective union pressures). On the other hand, in Germany, changes in differentials appear to have been quite small among manual workers, but, as elsewhere, some decline seems to have occurred in the relative pay of managers and supervisors.

The sex differential

In Britain, the major and clearest change in pay differentials affecting large numbers of workers (apart from the big rise in relative coal-mining pay) is the narrowing of the male/female pay ratio; and for this development of the pay structure it is public pressures leading to the Equal Pay Act of 1970 (rather than the enthusiasm of the trade union movement) which – belatedly by comparison with most other industrial countries – has produced effective results.

The long series of earnings statistics for manual workers shows average women's earnings at close to half those of men since 1939, with intervening fluctuations but no general trend (Routh [3]). In 1970 the stability of the relationship was broken. During the 1970s, the overall average of women's weekly earnings, both for manual and non-manual full-time workers, rose from 50 per cent to 58–9 per cent.

There are, of course, many reasons why the average woman earns less than the average man. Among the measurable ones are: (a) women normally work shorter hours than men, especially in the manual occupations: thus the percentage of manual women's to manual men's hourly earnings is about 10 points higher than for weekly earnings; the difference for non-manual workers is much smaller; (b) working women are generally in their jobs for a shorter time than men, and are younger; chances of promotion and of benefitting from service increments are smaller; (c) more important, the occupational and industrial distribution of women is very different from that of men (see Catherine Hakim [2]). Thus an unweighted average for 27 manual and non-manual occupations yields a percentage of women to men's pay of 75 per cent against 63 per cent on the weighted average. Moreover a more detailed breakdown of each of the occupations statistically recorded would no doubt further reduce the sex differential.

At the beginning of the 1970s, the low ratio of the overall average of women's to men's pay stood out among western industrial countries (combined, incidentally, with Britain's high women's participation rate). The overall ratio of about 50 per cent compares with ratios of 60–70 per cent (nearly 80 per cent for French manual workers) in Belgium, France, Germany, Italy and the Netherlands, and about 80–90 per cent in Sweden. The narrowing of the differential in Britain after the Equal Pay Act was essentially a catching-up with the other countries.

The overall dispersion of pay

The overall inequality of pay among individuals is in part the result of the differentials just described (and of others not separately discussed here, such as those between people of different ages or between regions), but it also results from differences in pay between people who appear identical in respect of the various statistical classifications. What changes have there been during the 1970s in this overall dis-

Table 9.4 The dispersion of total weekly pay,[a] 1970–9 (percentages)

	Men			Women		
	1970	1976	1979	1970	1976	1979
Manual						
Bottom decile	67.3	70.2	68.3	69.0	67.8	70.4
Median	100.0	100.0	100.0	100.0	100.0	100.0.
Top decile	147.2	144.9	148.5	144.8	140.6	140.6
Non-manual						
Bottom decile	61.8	62.5	63.4	64.2	65.1	69.5
Median	100.0	100.0	100.0	100.0	100.0	100.0
Top decile	175.1	167.5	163.0	173.7	172.9	160.7
Total						
Bottom decile	65.4	67.6	66.0	66.4	66.1	69.4
Median	100.0	100.0	100.0	100.0	100.0	100.0
Top decile	160.6	159.5	159.6	170.4	165.9	158.6

[a] Pay not affected by absence for full-time adults (men 21+, women 18+) in all industries and services.

Source: Department of Employment, *New Earnings Survey 1979*, Table 15.

persion of pay? Are there any signs of increasing or diminishing inequality?

The results are summarised in Table 9.4 in terms of the ratio of upper and lower deciles, in each 'labour market', to the corresponding median. By these measures, the changes in dispersion have been small – a modest improvement in the relative earnings of the lower paid in each of the four 'labour markets' and a more considerable compression at the top (except, taking the period as a whole, among manual men). From 1976 to 1979, however, there are signs of a reversal of the trend among manual men (possibly, at the top level, as a result of a slight increase in overtime working). But the famous log-normal curve, which has been found to hold – although not wholly without significant deviations – over all the wage censuses for manual workers since 1886, still provides the broad framework of the pay structure. The elongated upper tail hardly appears in the distribution for manual workers, but has been somewhat curtailed for non-manuals.

By this quantile measure, there are certain differences between countries. More or less comparable statistics are available only for 1972 and then only for broad industry groups. These data suggest that at that time Britain, with France and Italy, could be counted among the countries with relatively high degrees of inequality; Germany was, by several measures, the most egalitarian; Belgium and the Netherlands took intermediate positions (see Saunders and Marsden [5]). For subsequent years, we have data for France, up to 1977, indicating quite a marked narrowing of the overall dispersion and of the differentials of the cadres, and a small decline in the relative pay of skilled male manual workers compared with all manual men. Pay dispersions among manual workers in the Netherlands (1970–6), however, reveal no significant change.

Conclusion

The broad conclusion of this summary review is that the changes in the British pay structure during the 1970s have been:

(a) rather modest: the main exceptions are the rise in the miners' relative pay to the top of the list, the rise in women's relative pay and the decline in some higher pay differentials; the last two of these changes can hardly be attributed very directly to the operation of the collective bargaining process;
(b) to some extent – so far as historical data can reveal – a continuation of earlier trends (the narrowing of the women's differential and the rise in miners' pay being exceptions);
(c) not very different, in some respects, from the trends in some neighbouring countries.

Changes in Relative Pay Increases by Bargaining Groups

What follows is the report of one modest exercise to suggest, in more detail, in terms of what seems a particularly relevant grouping, the winners and the losers in Britain during the 1970s. The groups used for this purpose are the groups affected, directly or indirectly, by the major collective agreements for which earnings figures have been reported annually. The justification for using the negotiating group as the basis for this analysis is that the present study is concerned essentially with the results of the system of bargaining; the British bargaining system can cut across industries and occupations – in some cases bridging several statistical industries, in others being confined to a part of an industry or a part of the country, or to firms affiliated to a particular organisation.

The drawback of this grouping is that it cannot cover the whole employed population – for instance, where agreements cover very few people (say less than 12,000) or where individuals are not subject, or are not regarded by their employer as subject, to a listed collective agreement. Other cases are omitted because the coverage of the agreement has varied in the course of the years, or because for other reasons data about the agreement are not reported. Thus, for one reason and another the negotiating groups analysed here cover under 40 per cent of the total numbers sampled by the *New Earnings Survey*.

A second issue is the relevance of the *earnings* figures to the analysis. Changes in actual earnings, it is true, depend on a variety of circumstances besides the provisions of collective agreements; on the other hand changes in basic wage rates reflect only the changes in formal national agreements, ignoring the effects of collective bargaining at a lower level. Thus the earnings data classified by negotiating groups, seem to come closest (although not as close as might be desired) to expressing the results of the whole variegated, multi-level system of collective pay bargaining within each of the areas defined by the framework of union and management organisations.

Arguments about comparability can take at least two forms: (a) the job content argument: 'our job is as responsible, as skilful, as hard as that of job X and so should be equally paid'; (b) the historical argument: 'our job has normally, or traditionally, or at some date in the past, been paid as much as job X and so should be equally paid now'. This exercise is confined to the second type of argument. A winning group is one which has improved its relative earnings since a base period. The art of the negotiator, as all concerned with comparability negotiations recognise, is to choose a base period in the past which is advantageous for his particular case.

Three comparisons were made: 1970 to 1979; average 1970–2 to 1979; and 1970–2 to 1977–9. To define 'winners' and 'losers' in the inflationary race, any group whose earnings rose by 5 per cent or more in excess of the rise in average earnings in any of the three periods may be regarded as a winning group over that period; the losers are similarly defined, *mutatis mutandis*; the experience of the rest is described as 'neutral'. The rise in average earnings used is that for all workers in the sample in all industries and services, whether or not affected by the agreements listed, in the appropriate labour market. The criterion of a 5 per cent rise or fall is taken because a smaller change could well be due to the accident of the particular week or to the margin of error attributed to the sample (the standard error of the sample for small groups can be as much as 3 per cent).

Results of the bargaining tournament

The time period chosen did not in fact make much difference to the number of winning, losing and neutral groups. In total, whichever time period is used, just over a third of the groups gained 5 per cent or more in relative earnings, rather under a third were losers and rather under a third again remained within the ±5 per cent range.

Table 9.5 Average weekly earnings in 1977–9 compared with 1970–2 in negotiating groups analysed[a]

Labour market	Winners	Losers	Neutral	Earnings increase in: All groups analysed[b]	Earnings increase in: NES sample
	(no. of groups)			(percentages)	
Men					
Manual	11	6	14	179	175
Non-manual	5	5	3	162	155
Women					
Manual	2	1	2	227	223
Non-manual	6	6	1	199	199

[a] All groups for which data reported. Winners (Losers) are groups for which the rise in average earnings exceeded (fell short of) by at least 5 per cent the rise in average earnings for all industries and services in the NES sample in the same labour market. Neutral groups are those where the rise was within ±5 per cent of that in the whole NES sample.

[b] Unweighted averages.

Source: *New Earnings Surveys*, tables on 'Analyses by agreement'.

Secondly, there are marked differences between the labour markets. Among the *manual men's* groups, well over a third are classed as winners; but more than that come in the neutral class. The proportion of losers, however, is quite small – only about one in five. For *manual women* unfortunately rather few results could be analysed. For *non-manual men* and, even more so, for *non-manual women*, the divergences

Table 9.6 Winners among negotiating groups

	Relative gain[a]	Initial position[b]
MANUAL MEN		
Private Sector		
Food manufacturing	8[d]	96
Furniture	6[d]	99
Paper-making	6[d]	105
Building (Scotland)	6	94
Electrical contracting	11[c]	113
Agriculture	6	71
Public Sector		
Electricity supply	8[d]	100
Local authorities (Scotland)	15[d]	78
London Transport (drivers and conductors)	11[f]	111
Coal mining	32[d]	101
Iron and Steel	5	111
NON-MANUAL MEN		
Private Sector		
Engineering clerical	5[d]	78
Retail cooperatives	10[d]	65
Retail food (E & W)	20[d]	64
Retail furniture etc.	6[d]	67
Public sector		
NHS nurses	12	66
Police	21[d]	93
MANUAL WOMEN		
Private Sector		
Engineering	6[c]	111
Public Sector		
Local authorities (Scotland)	8[e]	86
NON-MANUAL WOMEN		
Private Sector		
Engineering clerical	15[c]	82
Retail cooperatives	7[d]	68
Retail drapery etc.	7[c]	74
Retail furniture etc.	13[c]	66
Public Sector		
NHS ancillary	9[d]	80
Post Office: clerical, exec.	5[d]	110

Sources and notes to Tables 9.6 and 9.7: as Table 9.5, except that all groups are listed which had a relative gain of 5 per cent or more in any of the periods 1970–9, 1970–2 to 1979, or 1970–2 to 1977–9. The period is chosen which shows the largest relative change. Groups which – over any one of those periods – showed a relative gain or loss of 10 per cent or more are shown in bold type.

Table 9.7 Losers among negotiating groups

	Relative loss[a]	Initial position[b]
MANUAL MEN		
Private Sector		
Engineering	5	107
General printing (ex-London)	17[d]	118
Dockworkers	6[c]	140
Public Sector		
National govt: industrial	5[c]	87
Post Office: engineering	13	113
Post Office: manipulative	11[d]	100
Railways: footplate	6[d]	106
NON-MANUAL MEN		
Private Sector		
None		
Public Sector		
Local authorities: admin, clerical (E & W)	5[c]	94
National govt: technical, scientific	9[c]	118
Post Office: manipulative	15[c]	87
Teaching: primary, secondary (E & W)	6[d]	96
Teaching: further education (E & W)	7[d]	122
Fire service	6	88
MANUAL WOMEN		
Private Sector		
Footwear	7[d]	114
Dressmaking etc. (E & W)	8	95
Public Sector		
None		
NON-MANUAL WOMEN		
Private Sector		
None		
Public Sector		
Local authorities: admin, clerical	7[c]	109
National govt: clerical	10[d]	104
NHS: admin, clerical	7[c]	103
Post Office: manipulative	10[c]	104
Teachers: primary, secondary (E & W)	14[d]	154
Teachers: primary, secondary (Scotland)	15[c]	156

[a] For definition see note to Table 9.5. The period is 1970–2 to 1977–9, except when otherwise indicated.

[b] Weekly earnings in 1970–2 as percentage of average for whole 'labour market'.

[c] 1970–2 to 1979.

[d] 1970 to 1979.

[e] Data not given in one year and estimated from reported change in earnings of matched sample from previous or subsequent year.

[f] 1979 data may not take full account of retrospective adjustments.

are greater: the proportions of both winners and losers are equal – each coming within reach of half the total – while the number of neutrals is very small. Is bargaining more competitive among non-manuals than among manuals? Incidentally, the average (unweighted) pay rise for the negotiating groups selected (although they cover in total less than 40 per cent of the total employed labour force) is very close to the average for all industries and services in each labour market.

The individual groups classed as winners *in any one* of the three time periods are set out in Tables 9.6 and 9.7 in which they are also divided between the private and public sectors (in the non-manual groups the public sector agreements account for the great majority of workers). The time period chosen significantly affected the classification of groups in only a few cases. There does appear to have been some slight convergence towards the mean, or reduction of inequality, for the totality of the bargaining groups (Table 9.8). But, in spite of the expected effect of pay restraint policies, the convergence has been modest, except for non-manual women.

For *manual men* the outstanding success is that of the coalminers with a relative pay increase of 20–30 per cent according to the comparison chosen; in 1970–1 earnings in the industry, even for underground workers, had hardly been above the average for all industries and services. The break came with the miners' strike of early 1972 and was reinforced by the settlement of the strike of early 1974 which brought coalmining pay by 1975 up to about 30 per cent above the manual men's average with 35 per cent for underground workers and 13 per cent for surface workers. (EEC data on *hourly* earnings in hard coalmining for underground workers show that relative hourly pay, compared with all index of production industries, had by 1977 reached about the same level in Britain as in Belgium and Germany, but was higher than in France; in Belgium the relative pay had not changed much since 1972 but in France and Germany it had increased, if rather less than in Britain.) Otherwise, the only notable winners are the electrical contracting industry with fairly consistent gains in relative pay, Scottish local authorities' manual workers (if 1979 is compared with 1970) and London Transport (but only if 1977–9 is compared with 1970–2).

Among the losers are the Post Office engineering and manipulative grades, and also general printing. The privileged position of the newspaper printing group is not separately recorded in all years; but the *New Earnings Survey* shows newspaper printing and publishing as the highest paid industry for manual men in 1970, 1972 and 1979. (In April 1979, newspaper printers' earnings were about on a par with those for underground coalminers.)

Otherwise, none of the manual groups shows consistent changes in relative pay significantly outside the ±5 per cent range. Nor, apart from coalmining, can any very systematic difference be noted between the public and the private sectors.

These changes confirm the modest amount of convergence – diminishing inequality – among manual men's negotiating groups. The eleven winning groups indeed were not on average particularly low paid in 1970–2. But of the seven losers five were more than 5 per cent above average in 1970–2 (including dock workers at 40 per cent above).

For *non-manual men*, more than for any of the other three labour markets, a clear distinction is apparent between the public and the private sectors. In the private sector, retail food (wages board) and to a lesser extent the retail cooperatives (a result of the rationalisation of retailing?) show marked gains in relative pay, and none of the rather limited (only four) other private groups are classed as losers. In the public sector, subject to special pressures from pay restraint policies, only two of the ten groups analysed are winners – male nurses and the police, both with quite marked gains. But six groups count as losers, the loss in relative pay being particularly marked for national government technical and scientific grades and Post Office manipulative grades.

Among *non-manual men*, the tendency towards convergence in pay levels between the bargaining groups is marked: all the winners in both private and public sectors earned well below average pay in 1970–2. The losers however include two rather low-paid groups as well as two high-paid groups (Tables 9.6 and 9.7).

For *manual women*, the few (7) groups that it was possible to analyse all show rather small changes in relative pay. There was a significant relative decline for the already low-paid dressmaking group, although subject to a wages board.

For *non-manual women* the winners are engineering clerical grades. retail furniture and, in the public sector, NHS ancillaries. No losers are found in the private sector. But of nine public sector groups analysed, six are classed as losers – roughly the same picture as for non-manual men. Further, all the public sector losers were earning in 1970–2 more than the general average for non-manual women, while all the winners except Post Office clerical and executive grades were below average. Hence the quite significant reduction in inequality between the groups which is shown in Table 9.8.

Table 9.8 Convergence of average earnings 1970–2 to 1977–9

	No. of groups analysed		Coefficient of variation[a]	
	1970–2	1977–9	1970–2	1977–9
Men				
Manual	*33*	*30*	13.7	12.7
Non-manual	*15*	*13*	23.2	20.9
Women				
Manual	*6*	*5*	11.1	11.6
Non-manual	*13*	*13*	28.3	22.6

[a] Standard deviation as percentage of mean (both unweighted).

Conclusion

In Tables 9.6 and 9.7 those groups which – over any one of those periods – showed a relative gain or loss of 10 per cent or more, are picked out in bold. The list of those groups which show such a relative gain or loss in all three periods is even more limited. On the male side there are three such gainers – coalmining, retail food (England and Wales), and male nurses – and one loser among the non-manual men – the Post Office manipulative group (though one of the three figures is not available for this group). On the female side, in the non-manual section, there are two such gainers – the engineering clerical group and retail furniture – and one loser – primary and secondary teachers in Scotland.

It is for the reader to assess (if he should be so rash) which of these various gains and losses can be justified – by market forces, by productivity, or by any rule of equity. (It will not, incidentally, escape notice that for the great majority of the conspicuous winning and losing groups, any measurement of productivity would present notorious problems). The reader may also like to judge whether an objective tribunal, sitting in the early 1970s, would have chosen these particular groups as the groups deserving better, or worse, relative pay over the next few years. What the analysis does demonstrate, however, is that the apparatus of competitive bargaining, even when constrained by incomes policies, has produced some limited changes in relative pay. How far has it corrected anomalies and how far created new ones? Finally, could not a less diffuse structure for collective bargaining – a more centralised structure with simultaneous agreements – have produced better results in real terms without the damaging consequences of a nearly fourfold increase in average nominal pay?

References

[1] Dean, A. J. H., 'Incomes policies and differentials', *National Institute Economic Review*, August 1978.

[2] Hankim, C., 'Occupational segregation'. Department of Employment Research Paper No. 9, 1979.

[3] Routh, G., *Occupation and Pay in Britain 1906–60*, Cambridge University Press, 1965.

[4] Royal Commission on the Distribution of Income and Wealth, *Report No. 8*. Cmnd 7679, London, HMSO, 1979.

[5] Saunders, C. T. and Marsden, D., 'A six-country comparison of the distribution of industrial earnings in the 1970s', Background paper No 8 for the Royal Commission on the Distribution of Income and Wealth, London, HMSO, 1979.

10 The Lessons of Wage Equations
T. D. Sheriff

The purpose of this paper is to consider what light econometric studies of wage determination – wage equations – throw on the questions which the other papers to this conference are considering: that is, whether there is a need for change in the pay bargaining system in this country, and, if so, what kinds of change might be desirable.

There are various ways in which evidence of wage equations could conceivably help in this matter. Here are three examples. If the equations strongly suggested, with a fair degree of precision, a specific level of unemployment at which the rise in earnings would start to decelerate, then a good deal of the debate would be about the acceptability, or otherwise, of that figure. If the equations strongly suggested a specific number for a 'target real wage', implying that the rise in money earnings had always accelerated in the past when that target was not reached, this would obviously have strong implications for policy. It might suggest combining tax cuts with any attempt to reduce the rate of increase in money earnings. Thirdly, if any equation, using economic variables alone, proved to be robust and well specified, with coefficients on the variables which altered little when the equation was fitted to different periods, then that might suggest that any political influences had been relatively unimportant in the past. These are the questions which it is the purpose of this paper to examine.

We shall consider first therefore the specifications for two basic types of wage equation – the expectations-augmented Phillips curve and the target real wage hypothesis. We shall then take recent examples of both these types of equation and consider the extent to which they were able to predict the period following the estimation period. This is in many ways a similar enquiry to that conducted by Artis in 1976, when he wrote a paper entitled 'Is there a wage equation?' [1]. This paper considers the same question four years on.

Table 10.1 Influences on wage settlements

	LA (1)	UB (2)	PO(T) (3)	INS (4)	T&G (5)	NUPE (6)	EETPU (7)	ASTMS (8)	POEU (9)
Past change in RPI	√	√	√	√	√	√	√	√	√
Expected inflation	X	√	X	√	√	√	√	√	X
Change in real post-tax earnings	√	X	X	X	X	X	X	√	X
Level of unemployment	√	X	X	X	X	√	X	X	X
Shortage/abundance of labour	√	√	√	√	X	X	√	X	√
Profitability of company	√	√	√	n.a.	√	n.a.	?	√	√
Post-productivity rises	X	X	√	X	√	√	X	√	√
Comparability	√	√	√	√	√	√	√	X	√
Is there a going rate for									
(i) the industry	n.a.	√	√	√	√	√	X	X	√
(ii) the economy	√	X	√	√	√	√	X	X	√
Is there a wage round	√	√	√	√	X	√	√	X	√
Is there a 'target' increase	√	√	√	√	X	√	X	X	√

Source: Interviewees (who were selected in an *ad hoc* fashion) were as follows: Mr Eddie Digman, Head of Personnel Services, Borough of Kingston-upon-Thames; Mr Alexander Scott, Director of Industrial Relations, United Biscuits Limited; Mr Noel Tappenden, Head of Division, Telecommunications Pay and Gradings, Post Office (Telecommunications); Messrs Frank Lee and Geoff Boutle of Provident Life Assurance Company Limited; Mr Regan Scott, Head of Research, Transport & General Workers' Union; Mr Ron Keating, Assistant General Secretary, National Union of Public Employees; Mr Frank Chapple, General Secretary, Electrical, Electronic, Telecommunications and Plumbing Union; Mr Barrie Sherman, Director of Research, Association of Scientific, Managerial Staffs; and Ms Vicky Kidd, Research Officer, Post Office Engineering Union. The author would like to thank them all.

Note: A number of qualifications were made to some of the replies. The ticks and crosses describe the broad situation.

One area which has caused problems to the economist who wishes to study wage equations concerns the data available. There are questions about whether earnings or wage rates are important; there are problems about the efficiency of proxies for inflationary expectations and excess demand in the labour market. There is also the question of incomes policy and whether there is a sufficiently long run of data unaffected by government intervention on which to estimate a wage equation. In considering these questions we draw upon qualitative evidence obtained by interviewing various trade unionists and employers' representatives who had experience of wage bargaining. Their views were considered when evaluating the relationships put forward in aggregate wage equations. Table 10.1 summarises the replies.

Finally we consider conceptual problems concerning wage equations. Specifically, it is asked whether the process of money wage determination in the UK lends itself to macroeconomic modelling.

Forms of Wage Equations

(a) *The expectations-augmented Phillips curve* (*EAP*)
EAP assumes that the rate of wage inflation is determined by the demand for and supply of labour plus expected future price inflation. In other words, the wage bargain is carried out in real terms.

EAP takes the form:

$$\dot{w} = f(u) + \dot{p}^e \qquad (1)$$

where w is the money wage rate, u is the level of unemployment and p^e are price expectations; dots over variables indicate rates of change. Some writers have argued that the rationale for (1) is found in Friedman [6]. However, Friedman argues that it is errors in inflationary expectations on the part of workers which cause movements in unemployment away from the so-called natural rate of unemployment, that is, it is a theory of unemployment. An alternative quoted authority for (1) is Phelps [15, 16] who argues that it is employers' errors in expectations which will shift unemployment – again a theory of unemployment. There is also a question concerning whose price expectations are relevant – employers' or employees'. Appreciating the lack of theoretical justification for an equation such as (1), Parkin, Sumner and Ward [14] derived an equation based on the assumptions that both the demand and supply of labour depended on the expected relevant real wage (for the employee net of income tax and social security contributions, for the employer including employers' social security contributions) and that wage bargaining takes place to maintain a cleared market in the current period. Their equation resembles (1) above:

$$\dot{w} = f(X) + a\dot{p}^{e}_{e} + b\dot{p}^{e}_{c} - aT^{e}_{1} - b(T^{e}_{2} + T^{e}_{3}) \qquad (2)$$

where X is the level of excess demand proxied by the level of unemployment, p^{e}_{e} is the expected wholesale price received by employers, p^{e}_{c} is the expected consumer price, T^{e}_{1} and T^{e}_{2} are the expected effective rates of social security contributions for employers and employees respectively, and T^{e}_{3} is the expected effective rate of income tax.

Equation (2) refers to a closed economy; extending it to an open economy means the addition of an extra inflationary expectations term, expected foreign market price changes. The sum of the coefficients on the three price expectations variables is equal to unity *a priori*.

(b) *The target real wage hypothesis (TRWH)*

TRWH has as its cornerstone a bargaining approach to wage determination. The reasoning behind the 'target' real wage hypothesis is that employees wish to increase their real wages by some target over time; if their aspirations are not fulfilled for whatever reason, attempts will be made to catch up what was not attained in previous periods. The target may be a simple trend rate of increase or it may be endogenous depending on economic variables such as unemployment or it may be hypothesised to change adaptively to past real wage increases. Thus the supply of and demand for labour are important to the extent that they affect the size of the 'target'. TRWH was originally put forward by Sargan [17]; his target was couched in pre-tax terms. Subsequently, others for example Henry *et al* [9] have considered the possibility of a post-tax real earnings target. An example of a target real wage equation is the following:

$$\frac{\dot{w}}{w_{-1}} = \log_e \left[\left(\frac{NE^*}{NE_{-1}} \right)^{\Lambda} \right] \qquad (3)$$

where, assuming it is post-tax earnings which are important, NE is real net earnings and NE* is desired real net earnings. That is, NE* = f(t, z) where t is time and z is a vector of economic variables, usually including the level of unemployment and inflationary expectations. Lagged real earnings enter the wage equation with a negative sign, *a priori*.

It can be argued that EAP and TRWH are not as different as they appear. Real wages may be hypothesised to be positively correlated with the level of unemployment – the higher the real wage, the less excess demand for labour and the greater unemployment. In this case, it is possible to interpret a TRWH with a time trend and price expectations as an EAP where the time trend is representing exogenous productivity growth. To assert that the EAP and the TRWH are equivalent requires the assumption that the demand and supply of labour depend only on the real wage.

A more intriguing argument in this vein comes from Parikh and Raj [13]. They estimate that the real wage term enters the wage equation with a positive sign which is contrary to the Sargan argument; however, this they argue is still equivalent to an EAP. Following Barro and Grossman [3], they argue that falling real wages will indicate excess supply in the goods market and, hence, more unemployment which will bring down the rate of money wage increases. There are, therefore, problems in disentangling the interpretations of the EAP and the TRWH. It may be noted that two of the union negotiators interviewed thought there was a 'target' real wage increase: one of them had a target in annual percentage terms and another aimed for two thirds average earnings.

How Well have Models Fared?

Artis *et al.* [2] present a discussion of the results obtained for various types of EAP and TRWH. This section does not repeat that discussion but simply looks at examples of each type of equation which were published in the mid-1970s. The choice of the examples was simply that it was felt that these particular papers were prominent.

Chart 10.1 is from Parkin, Sumner and Ward [14]. The equation is:

$$\log_e (W/W_{-1})*400 = 5.9108 - 1.9973u + 0.5027 \log_e (WPI/WPI_{-1})*400 + 0.2029 \log_e (EUVI/EUVI_{-1})*400 + 0.2944 \log_e (RPI/RPI_{-1})*400 \qquad (4)$$

where W is the basic weekly rate of wages (all workers); u is the number of wholly unemployed expressed as a percentage of the estimated total number of employees (Great Britain); WPI is wholesale price index for manufactures (home sales); EUVI is the export unit value index; RPI is the retail price index (all items). For purposes of plotting actual and predicted values of the rate of change of money wage rates, the actual rates of change of prices were used to proxy expected ones. This seemed unavoidable for the post-estimation period. In other words, rational expectations were assumed. It is hoped that actual and expected inflation did not diverge markedly and systematically post-1971 IV.

The equation presented excludes the Parkin *et al.* tax variables because their exclusion seemed to improve the fit of the equation over both the estimation and the forecast period. The equation begins to underestimate the rate of wage inflation towards the end of the estimation period, 1956 II–1971 IV, and underpredicts the rate of change of money wages until 1978 IV except for the incomes policy periods of 1973 and 1976–7. Sumner [18] has attempted to rescue the EAP by arguing that the unemployment variable is mis-specified. He argues that shifts in the replacement ratio (or benefits to earnings ratio) in favour of benefits has reduced the supply of labour at a given real wage. Thus, the rate of unemployment associated with any rate of change of money wages will be higher. An attempt was made to 'correct' the unemployment variable for this effect – the replacement ratio was held at its average level and 'corrected' unemployment was calculated using Sumner's coefficient on the benefits–earnings ratio in an unemployment equation.

Sumner has:

$$\log_e u = Z\hat{\gamma} + 1.1056 \log_e b_{-1} \qquad (5)$$

where γ is a vector of coefficients, Z is a data matrix of other variables and b is the benefits to earnings ratio. Sumner's 'adjusted unemployment' series was 'generated holding the benefits–earnings ratio constant at its average level'.

The benefits–earnings ratio used here was from Holden and Peel [10]. This adjustment did not seem to improve the predictive performance of the model. In any case, the argument that changes in the benefits to earnings ratio have no more than a small influence on unemployment has been supported by more recent work by Nickell [12] and by referring to the take-up and eligibility rates for earnings-related benefit.

The second equation considered is that of Henry and Ormerod [7] where the growth of desired real net earnings of 2.6 per cent per annum is imposed. This figure was chosen since it was close to the value discovered in previous empirical work; however, it is interesting that it should be so close to the trend rate of growth of output per head over the estimation period. It should be pointed out at this stage that the specification of the dependent variable chosen by Henry and Ormerod was the first difference of Δ_1 of $\log_e(W/W_{-1})$.

The equation is:

$$\Delta[\log_e(W/W_{-1})] = 0.0254 + 0.267\ \Delta[\log_e(RPI/RPI_{-1})] \\ - 0.391\ \Delta(\log NE) - 0.008D1 - 0.024D2 - 0.013D3 \qquad (6) \\ - 0.005D4 + 0.002D10 + 0.027D20 + 0.006D30 + 0.001D40$$

where NE is real net earnings, D1 to D4 are incomes policy dummies, D10 to D40 are 'catch-up' dummies and W and RPI are defined above.

Henry and Ormerod's equation, as expected, overpredicts the rate of increase of wage rates during the 1976/7 incomes policy and underpredicts generally thereafter. Because of the specification of the dependent variable, this equation will not go far off track when predicting the rate of change of money wage rates. However, it was possible to see what the 'dynamic' forecasts of this equation would be for the rate of change of wage rates; this is shown on Chart 10.1. Post-1975 II the rate of change of money wage rates would have been forecast to increase to over 40 per cent per annum. No incomes policy dummy variable could be claimed to bring the equation back on track. The reason for these high predicted values, of course, is the assumption of a 2.6 per cent target post-tax real wage. Real wages 1975–8 grew very slowly – the equation is exhibiting the assumption that workers attempt to make up for past real wage increases below the target. (It may be noted that seven out of the nine negotiators interviewed said that past movements in real post-tax earnings were not a factor which they considered; and targets did not seem to be set in terms of increases in real earnings.)

This exercise has not been a competition between the two types of equation. The point is simply that with the Parkin, Sumner and Ward equation predicting zero wage inflation in 1978 and the Henry

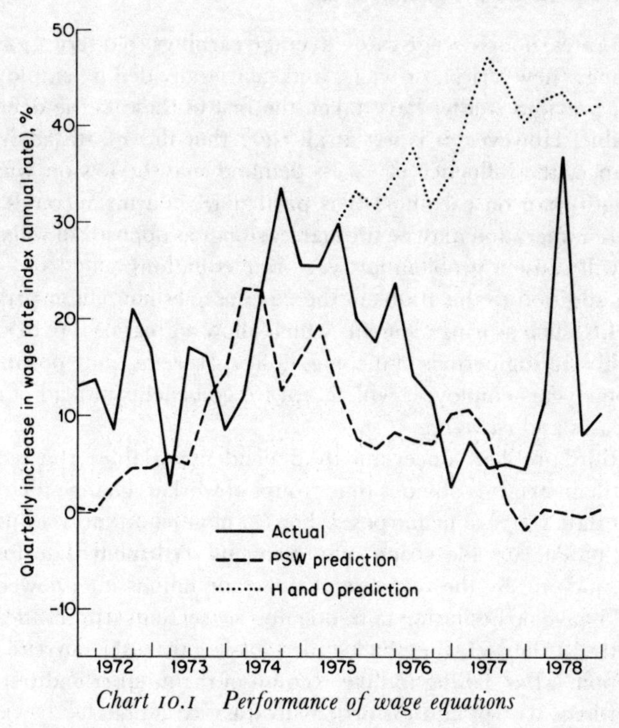

Chart 10.1 Performance of wage equations

and Ormerod equation predicting over 40 per cent, neither provides a satisfactory explanation of money wage behaviour outside its estimation period. It can be argued that other examples of wage equations (e.g. more recent ones) would have performed better. Alternatively, it could be said that all we can expect from wage equations is an ex-post examination of which economic variables appear to explain on average past wages behaviour. However, to have an anti-inflationary policy without intervention, it is necessary to be confident of what factors will determine money wage increases over the next few years. The performance of past wage equations, I suggest, should not lead us to be that confident.

Data Problems

(a) *The dependent variable*

The dependent variable in wage equations for the UK may be weekly wage rates, hourly wage rates, average earnings (old series), average earnings (new series), or wages and salaries divided by employment. Most previous studies have taken the first of these as the dependent variable. However, it is not at all clear that this is satisfactory. For instance, the influence of excess demand may be less on wage-rate changes than on earnings. It is particularly during incomes policy that remuneration may be through earnings as opposed to wage rates: this will cause a problem for wage-rate equations.

In addition to this problem there is the question of non-pecuniary benefits, such as fringe benefits which allow a great deal of flexibility, notably during periods of incomes policy. It seems quite possible that in some years employees will accept fringe benefits instead of money increases and *vice versa*.

A third problem concerning the dependent variable is the frequency of settlements. It is obvious that groups of workers change their settlement date for various purposes. For example, if an incomes policy is anticipated, a trade union may bring its settlement date forward. Also, judging by the response of the trade unions interviewed, they would have no hesitation in re-opening agreements within 'the twelve months' if they felt they had settled for less than the current rate of inflation. Thus, failing to take account of the number and frequency of settlements will add distortions to wage equations.

(b) *Inflationary expectations*

Inflationary expectations are postulated to enter EAP with a coefficient of unity or may be hypothesised to affect the size of the desired real wage in TRWH. In addition to the problem noted earlier regarding whose price expectations are important, the econometrician needs to proxy inflationary expectations. Early attempts assumed that past inflation was a good guide but this does not allow agents to learn. Others assumed that they were formed adaptively, that is to say inflationary expectations changed in the current period according to the extent to which there had been errors in the past. If these errors are for the last period only, then the adaptive scheme does not allow the anticipation of future *acceleration* in the rate of inflation. A second problem is that adaptive expectations do not allow for the fact that economic agents will consider economic factors when anticipating future inflation. More recently Minford and Brech [11] and Henry and Ormerod [8] have generated series for price expectations which are rational in the sense that agents do consider economic factors, so that,

$$E(p) = p_t + u_t \qquad (7)$$

where u_t is a random error. Thus, inflationary expectations are on average correct and errors are random.

The problem with the inclusion of inflationary expectations variables in wage equations is that it is joint hypothesis testing in the sense that both the hypothesis of what factors determine expectations and the hypothesis that the inflationary expectations affect wage rates are being tested; it is therefore difficult to interpret the resultant wage equation.

A more direct measure of price expectations has involved the use of qualitative survey data. Carlson and Parkin [4] presented a series for expected movements in the retail price index. Foster and Gregory [5] outline a number of problems with the Carlson and Parkin series. In addition, it has the unfortunate property that if all respondents believe that inflation will increase by a small amount the series will show a massive increase in expected inflation.

Thus there are problems about how to measure future expected inflation. The significance of price expectations terms in wage equations is as likely to reflect the success of the attempt to measure these expectations as it is their effect on wage inflation. In answer to the question concerning the effect of future expected inflation on wage settlements, two negotiators thought that it had little if any effect and two others said that the 1979–80 pay round was the first time that it had been important; this was due to the much publicised forecast of 17.5 per cent by the government. These respondents at least felt that it had been past inflation which was important and that any falling behind would be made good in the next pay round.

(c) *Excess demand*

Traditionally excess demand in the labour market has been proxied by either unemployment or movements in the relationship between the level of unemployment and vacancies. Artis *et al.* [2] discuss the shifts in the unemployed–vacancies relationship which have occurred in the last two decades. Indeed, the performance of the Parkin, Sumner and Ward equation indicated either that the level of unemployment was not a useful proxy for excess demand or that the influence of excess demand on wages had diminished. We do not feel that movements in the benefits–earnings ratio can explain the apparent breakdown of the EAP, which occurred in the mid-1970s, in the sense that the unemployment term was either insignificant or perversely signed (Artis *et al.* [2]); its re-emergence can probably be attributed to the period 1975–7 when there was an incomes policy and an increase in unemployment. An unemployment term appears in the most recent versions of the National Institute and Treasury models.

The general view of the respondents was that the level of unemployment in the economy had no effect on the level of wage settlements. The reason why this should be the case is that when demand slackens and the level of unemployment increases money wage settlements need not lead to greater unemployed *among those covered by wage bargains* – reduced employment levels can be achieved by 'natural wastage'. The annual turnover in manufacturing is in the 20–30 per cent range which gives a great deal of flexibility. Non-recruitment is also an option. To moderate wage claims and settlements because of increased unemployment implies a degree of altruism from those already in work to those not in work. Unemployment, which is also a function of demographic factors, is therefore unlikely to be a very good proxy for the pressure of demand on wage bargains. A more direct proxy might well be a variable which is some function of the level of redundancies.

(d) *Incomes policies*

In the last fifteen years there has been a greater proportion of time with incomes policies in operation than without. This poses problems for the modeller. One way round would be to estimate equations for periods with no pay policy; however, aside from the fact that more recently such periods are few and far between, policy-off periods could be affected by 'catch-ups' from the previous policy and anticipations of the next one. Another and more usual way round the problem is to insert intercept dummy variables into the wage equation; these variables will take the value of unity during pay policies and zero elsewhere.

Additionally, as noted earlier, Henry and Ormerod [7] insert catch-up dummy variables taking the value of unity for two quarters after an incomes policy on the grounds that workers catch up the real income lost during the pay policy. A difficulty with this latter approach is that it is difficult to define incomes policy – an incomes policy can range from a statutory wages freeze to vague exhortations by ministers about public sector pay. To insert dummy variables for all possible pay policies, and for catch-up periods – indeed possibly for periods when pay policies are anticipated – would make the equation very complicated and might well lead to spurious results. The point then is that the frequency of pay policy over the likely estimation period for any wage equation is likely to make interpretation very difficult.

Conceptual Problems and other Factors

One view is that for a variety of reasons, in addition to the paucity of data, and the problem of pay policies, one would not expect to get a stable long-run econometric relationship between the rate of change of money wages at the aggregate level and other aggregate economic variables. A good example of these sorts of views is provided by Wood [19]. He argues that, in addition to economic variables, wage increases for particular groups are set with reference to perceived 'norms' which are expressed in terms of relativities against other groups. Different groups have different perceived norms and each group thinks of itself more favourably than do other groups. He argues 'quite small changes in the supply and demand conditions in particular sectors, or in the availability of information, can . . . cause changes in the pace of wage inflation which are quite large and from a purely macro-economic point of view incomprehensible'. If Wood is at all correct, this would mean that an aggregate wage equation would not be able to forecast a proportion of money wage increases.

It is clear that comparability is very important in the determination of wage settlements in the UK. All the negotiators interviewed, with the exception of ASTMS, thought comparability was important. The EETPU respondent felt workers often compare their earnings with other groups without fully appreciating the basis for comparison; it very often is not relative productivity. In the long run, it is probably true that economic forces will determine relativities but this might indeed be a very long time and while economic forces are working some argue the system can be very inflationary. To change relativities which are accepted and long in the memory is very difficult.

Another mechanism by which money wages can seem to move in an inexplicable way with respect to aggregate macroeconomic variables is that of 'wage leadership'. Wage leadership is usually thought to occur in a pay bargaining framework where there exists a 'going rate'. The notion is that a key group of workers settles at a rate of money wage increase compatible with its companies' profitability and the demand and supply of workers in that industry. This settlement may be well publicised in the media. Other groups may feel they deserve the same sort of increase for the reasons of comparability outlined above. Certainly the settlement may fuel the inflationary expectations of groups of workers who may be in less profitable sectors or indeed the public sector. Most respondents interviewed felt that 'wage leadership did occur'. One felt that unless employees pushed for settlements similar in level to the high, well publicised, settlements there was the danger that other groups would, and that this particular group would lose out. The analogy was that of a potential commodity shortage; if an individual refused to 'panic buy' – the 'sensible' individual lost out. This view of the pay bargaining system would lead one to the conclusion that without intervention the rate of change of money wage increases could accelerate irrespective of the general macroeconomic conditions.

Another view of the pay bargaining system which emerged from a number of the respondents was that various economic factors are important in affecting expectations of wage settlements at certain particular times but not at others. For instance, ASTMS remarked that the rate of past and future expected inflation will have more of an influence on wage settlements when inflation is high. Most of the respondents felt that direct tax movements had no effect on wage settlements; however, one respondent felt that they might have an influence on claims if they occurred at the beginning of the pay round. The TGWU negotiator remarked that movements in economic variables were 'instruments' to be used in the pay bargain rather than determinants of money wage increase. The outcome of the bargain depended on the resolve of the negotiating team. This resolve was influenced by the level of company profitability and general economic conditions, as well as union policy. One respondent pointed out that trade union leaders could at certain times fuel expectations of higher settlements among members if it was felt that the popularity of the leaders in general could be improved by talking in the media of high money wage increases. Another respondent held the view that when the rate of inflation was high, union members were more likely to suffer from money illusion than when inflation was low.

The implication for the modeller of economic factors having varying effects on the rate of change of money wage rates depending on current political and other conditions is to raise the question of the stability of coefficients in wage equations. In the last two decades, successive governments have tried to make incomes policies work. The extent to which these policies have worked and the extent to which there has been catching-up subsequently has probably as much to do with social and political factors as economic ones. For instance, towards the end of 1978, the Labour government announced its 5 per cent wage guidelines. *Ex post*, with price inflation running at around 10 per cent, this turned out to be politically unacceptable to workers; the outcome of the pay round was a nearly 15 per cent increase on average earnings. Had a slightly higher figure been picked by the Labour government, it can be argued that the incomes policy would have been accepted and the outcome of the round would have been much lower than the outturn.

The purpose of this discussion has not been to argue that economic factors do not influence the movement of money wages; it has been to point out that there are sufficient data and conceptual problems to query the extent to which the macroeconomist should be relied upon to analyse wage determination.

Conclusions

This chapter has sought to cast doubt on those who believe there exists a known stable statistical relationship between the index of wage rates or earnings and macroeconomic variables. It has done so in three main ways. First, it assessed the performance of prominent wage equations of a few years ago; it was concluded that their performance would not lead us to have a great deal of confidence in current wage equations. Secondly, data problems were outlined. Thirdly, it was considered that under conditions of free bargaining, the existence of perceived differentials and comparability might well lead to earnings increases apparently unexplained by macroeconomic variables.

This is not to say that economic variables are unimportant in determining the growth of money wages. However, these variables are likely to have different effects at different times depending on political and social factors. For instance, the extent of success of a policy of wage restraint is likely to be a question of politics rather than economics. One view is that the rate of inflation can be brought under control by macroeconomic policy which excludes intervention in pay bargaining. To bring down the rate of growth of prices, it is necessary to bring down the rate of growth of wages. For policy-makers to be able to do this they must feel they are able to predict the effect on money wages of other economic variables. They must believe that they have an efficient wage equation. For instance, if one believed in an expectations-augmented Phillips curve, anti-inflationary policy would involve either a reduction in demand in the labour market or a reduction in inflationary expectations. On the other hand, if one believed in a target real post-tax earnings wage equation, an anti-inflationary policy would be cuts in income tax. Rather than deny that economic variables such as those mentioned above affect the rate of growth of money wages, it has been the intention here to show that there are good reasons for doubting the stability of parameters in wage equations; there are good reasons for believing there are social and political factors at work which could outweigh the economic factors.

The article by Artis [1] cited earlier concluded neither an EAP or a TRWH had been particularly successful in explaining money wage behaviour. Further, he said that the question of 'whether there are underlying economic forces determining the wage rate that are at least sufficiently important relative to social and political factors as to be capable in principle of being captured econometrically . . . needs to be entertained with some humility'. The conclusion of this paper is little different in 1980.

Note

For a survey of the literature on wage equations see Artis, M. J. and Miller, M. H., 'Inflation and real wages' in J. K. Bowers, ed., *Inflation, Development and Integration: Essays in honour of A. J. Brown*, Leeds University Press, 1979.

References

[1] Artis, M. J., 'Is there a wage equation?', University College of Swansea and University of Manchester mimeo, 1976.

[2] Artis, M. J., Temple, P. and Copeland, L., 'Wage equations', paper prepared for the seminar on UK Wage/Earnings Price Inflation, University of Manchester mimeo, 1977.

[3] Barro, R. J. and Grossman. H. I., 'A general disequilibrium model of income and employment', *American Economic Review*, March 1971.

[4] Carlson, J. A. and Parkin, M., 'Inflation expectations', *Economica*, May 1975.

[5] Foster, J. and Gregory, M., 'Inflation expectations; the use of qualitative survey data', *Applied Economics*, December 1977.

[6] Friedman, M., 'The role of monetary policy', *American Economic Review*, March 1968.

[7] Henry, S. G. B. and Ormerod, P. A., 'Incomes policy and wage inflation: empirical evidence for the UK, 1961–77', *National Institute Economic Review*, August 1978.

[8] Henry, S. G. B. and Ormerod, P. A., 'Rational expectations in a wage–price model of the UK 1972–9', paper presented to the Social Science Research Council Conference on Rational Expectations, University of Sussex, September 1979.

[9] Henry, S. G. B., Sawyer, M. C. and Smith, P., 'Models of inflation in the United Kingdom', *National Institute Economic Review*, August 1976.

[10] Holden, K. and Reel, D. A., 'The benefits/income ratio for unemployed workers in the United Kingdom', Discussion Paper in Economics No. 40, University of Liverpool, 1980.

[11] Minford, A. P. L. and Brech, M., 'The wage equation and rational expectations', SSRC-University of Liverpool Research Project on the International Transmission of Fluctuations in Economic Activity Secular Growth and Inflation Working Paper No. 7901, 1979.

[12] Nickell, S. J., 'The effect of unemployment and related benefits on the duration of unemployment', *Economic Journal*, March 1979.

[13] Parikh, A. and Raj, B., 'Variable co-efficients approach to wage–price behaviour in the United Kingdom', *Applied Economics*, December 1979.

[14] Parkin, J. M., Sumner, M. T. and Ward, R., 'The effects of excess demand, generalized expectations and wage–price controls on wage inflation in the UK: 1956–71' in K. Brunner and A. H. Meltzer, eds, *The Economics of Wage and Price Controls*, Carnegie Rochester Conference Series on Public Policy, Volume 2, Amsterdam, North-Holland, 1976.

[15] Phelps, E., 'Phillips curves, expectations of inflation and optimal unemployment over time', *Economica*, August 1967.

[16] Phelps, E. S., 'Money–wage dynamics and labour–market equilibrium', *Journal of Political Economy*, July/August 1968 amended and reprinted in Phelps *et al.*, *The Micro-economic Foundations of Employment and Inflation Theory*, 1970.

[17] Sargan, J. D., 'Wages and prices in the UK: a study in econometric methodology', Colston Paper, 1964.

[18] Sumner, M. T., 'Wage determination', in J. M. Parkin and M. T. Sumner, eds, *Inflation in the United Kingdom*, University of Manchester Press, University of Toronto Press, 1978.

[19] Wood, A., *A Theory of Pay*, Cambridge University Press, 1978.

Comment on Chapter 10

P. Warburton

There are four main questions on which I propose to concentrate. First of all, what are the key theoretical and policy issues at stake in attempting to explain the behaviour of wages? Secondly, granted that the data are deficient and that estimated wage equations have in the past been fraught with difficulties, can we still have any confidence in them? Thirdly, from looking at the empirical work available, can we reach any tentative conclusions? Lastly, should qualitative evidence concerning specific firms or industries lead us to modify those conclusions? (The inadequacies of the wage-rate variable are fully acknowledged. The term 'wage' is used for simplicity's sake and earnings are generally what is meant.)

Sheriff has rightly drawn attention to two pieces of economic information either of which it would be very useful to have at our disposal, the natural rate of unemployment and the target real wage. The first concept emanates from the Phillips curve analysis and represents the market approach; the latter idea comes from the Sargan-type equation and originates from a wage bargaining model. The expectations-augmented Phillips (EAP) curve, puts forward two propositions. First, there is no money illusion, so that on average, over a number of years, employees are exactly compensated for the price rises that occur. In practice, employees, or their unions, will make errors in their expectations of inflation, and will seek to correct these errors in subsequent years. How these expectations are formed is therefore highly significant. The second proposition is that there is a long-run trade-off between the rate of wage change, net of inflation expectations, and some measure of the slackness of the labour market; employees can expect to receive relatively smaller real wage increases during cyclical downturns than during upswings.

The target real wage hypothesis (TRWH) stands in marked contrast to the EAP curve. Here the rate of change of real wages is primarily determined by some independently fixed target increase of post-tax real earnings. Failure to achieve the target carries over into the next round of pay negotiations, and in general actual price increases from the previous period are compensated rather than the expectations about future price inflation. Sargan's policy conclusion from his 1964 paper is that 'it is impossible to restrain money wages indefinitely by maintaining unemployment at some appropriate level'. (He did, however, concede a relationship between changes in unemployment and changes in the real wage such that if unemployment doubled from 2 to 4 per cent, this would produce a 3 per cent fall in real wages.) The case for a permanent prices and incomes policy rests on the proposition that either it is impossible to restrain wages through a labour-market adjustment process (e.g. more unemployment) or that the size of the adjustment would be socially, economically, or politically unpalatable.

Two key issues are at stake in the analysis of the determination of wages. Does the state of the aggregate labour market affect the overall result of earnings negotiations and how is it possible to change widely held expectations of future price increases? If the imbalance between the effective supply (that is those who are willing to work at the existing wage) and demand for labour is important, then a policy of deflation and higher unemployment will choke off rapid wage inflation, even to the extent that current price inflation is not compensated. If it is possible for the government to alter people's perceptions of what future inflation will be by pursuing strict monetary and fiscal policies then this will confirm and strengthen the first effect. In the situation where the labour-market effect is weak or absent, then the government may only hope to change price expectations by using a permanent institutional framework to control incomes. Even in the latter case modifications to expectations would occur when the prices of internationally traded goods rose relative to domestic prices at the prevailing exchange rate.

The purpose of this elaboration is to stress the critical importance of any evidence which enables us to discriminate between the EAP and the TRWH. The two wage equations Sheriff uses as illustrations of these two hypotheses cannot be said to be directly comparable. Firstly, the estimation periods are different, Parkin, Sumner and Ward using 1956 II to 1971 IV and the Henry and Ormerod 1961 I to 1975 II. This has obvious implications for their likely predictive performance over the period 1975–8. (Nevertheless, Parkin, Sumner and Ward's equation displays much smaller average predictive errors than that of Henry and Ormerod). The statement that 'it is hoped that actual and expected inflation did not diverge markedly and systematically post-1971 IV' takes a lot of believing. Secondly, unemployment, however modified, is not the only measure of excess supply. It is widely believed that frictional unemployment increased during the 1970s; the female participation rate increased from 57 per cent to 63 per cent between 1970 and 1979; the average rate of productivity growth has slowed down. If we believe that the correct concept to use is effective excess labour supply, then we cannot continue to use measured unemployment as a reliable proxy variable. Various alternative approaches have been tried, in which variables are included to model the demand and supply effects separately. Holden and Peel [4] used industrial output to proxy demand and the working population to proxy supply. Rosen and Quandt [5] adopt a structural approach in their disequilibrium model of the labour market for the US and we (Beenstock and Warburton [1]) have developed a similar model for the UK in an equilibrium setting.

A further comment on Parkin, Sumner and Ward's representation of the EAP curve is that the starting-point of the equation is important. The equation contains no error correction mechanism which would allow for the possibility that, because of incomes policy for example, the UK labour market was in disequilibrium at the particular starting-point chosen. Quite possibly, if terms in lagged real wages and deviations of cumulative excess labour supply from a time trend were included, the equation would show greater stability, without diminishing the relationship between wage inflation and the level of excess labour supply.

Evaluation of the TRWH equation from Henry and Ormerod in Chapter 10 is made difficult by the lack of any equation diagnostics; reference to the source article reveals that the imposed value of 0.00254 for the constant is at odds with that in the freely estimated version. Taking the value −0.001 it was both insignificant and wrongly signed. The folly of imposing a data-rejected value is illustrated in Sheriff's Chart 10.1, where the equation continuously overpredicts wage inflation over the next three years. The specification of the equation in double differences (that is the acceleration of wages) with a real earnings stabiliser but no allowance for wage and price inflation adjustment is probably partly to blame. The TRWH, as Sheriff points out, is open to the criticism that the time trend represents the growth of productivity. The overprediction when a trend of 2–2½ per cent is assumed is explained by the negligible growth of productivity in recent years. Furthermore, because failures to achieve the target are cumulative, predicted wage inflation flies off into the great blue yonder. Productivity depends on employment and if employment is determined jointly with real wages, then productivity is far from an exogenous variable, able to be approximated by a trend, in a wage equation. If the employment term in the productivity variable is substituted out for its other reduced form determinants, (output, demographic factors, tax and national insurance contributions for example) then the TRWH collapses into an EAP curve equation. This point is acknowledged by Henry and Ormerod [2].

With regard to the second main question of the discussion, we cannot yet point to the perfectly specified wage equation. We do now have the techniques of estimation and specification testing, and a longer data sample on which to work, with which to test different hypotheses. Our confidence lies in the careful application of these testing procedures to wage equations over this longer data sample. Whether the development of rational expectations estimators will yield further benefits, through the replacement of the actual inflation term by expected inflation, remains to be seen.

It is in the nature of econometric analysis that hypotheses are easier to reject than to confirm. The weight of evidence leads us to reject the TRWH as a fruitful model for future research. The chief reason is that it is possible to construct a more general model, in which real wages and employment are jointly determined, and in which the TRWH appears as a special case. Testing the joint hypotheses that the coefficients on output and population in the more general wage equation are both zero we find the hypotheses rejected. In a similar way, the hypothesis of Hines [3] that trade union pushfulness is a direct cause of wage inflation has been largely rejected by the economics profession. The rejection again comes about because there is a wider explanation of both wage inflation and the rate of increase of trade union membership. Price inflation and the pressure of demand in the labour market are both correlated, positively and negatively respectively, with the growth of trade union membership. The effect of trade union membership can then be substituted out in terms of inflation and excess demand, as we did before for employment. This process of negative corroboration of hypotheses through the estimation of wage equations has greatly improved our understanding of the determination of wage inflation over the past fifteen years. There have been other tentative conclusions which can be summarised as follows. Temporary incomes policies produce only temporary reductions in wage inflation; the announcement of a 5 per cent wages norm by the government is not sufficient to alter price expectations when current inflation is closer to 10 per cent, and is rising; a £1 billion cut in income tax achieved by lowering the standard rate is not a perfect substitute for £1 billion added to wages. In other words, most people view nominal wage increases more favourably than equal cuts in the nation's tax burden which are likely, through the progressive tax structure to benefit them less.

Sheriff draws upon the qualitative data he has gathered at various stages of the paper. He observes that two respondents of the nine claimed to have a target real wage and one of these replied that the target was related to productivity. On the questions about the influence of unemployment and of the relative shortage/abundance of labour in the industry, while only two respondents (both in the public sector) agreed the first effect, six were prepared to accept some influence of the second. The results of such an exercise can tell us little about the determination of aggregate wage inflation. The pay bargaining procedure allocates a given increase in the nation's wage bill between the various groups. Relative labour shortages, local productivity and other factors are certain to be very important in the determination of an individual firm or industry's wage increase.

Only where some non-market criteria of comparability are introduced, as with the Clegg Commission, does the pay bargaining system itself stimulate wage inflation. Since the government is committed to pay the Clegg awards, it must accommodate the increase in the public sector borrowing requirement and thence the money supply that this entails.

If real national income is constant, real wages can rise only to the extent that real profits fall. By granting additional credit facilities to firms through the banking system the government can sanction a real wage increase without causing mass corporate sector bankruptcy only in the short run. However, as firms raise their prices to restore their liquidity the real increase in wages is wiped out. If monetary policy is not accommodating, then the consequence of excessive wage inflation is increasing unemployment as the national wage bill is divided between fewer people. It is quite possible to envisage a situation where the wage aspirations of certain groups of workers are satisfied, implying large real increases, while aggregate real wages remain constant.

Thus, aggregate analysis of the UK labour market in the context of a complete macroeconomic model is probably the best evidence we have of the determination of aggregate wages. So long as aggregate wage inflation reacts to demand pressure in the whole economy and to the changes in demographic variables then any attempt to institutionalise the wage bargaining process would impose added inefficiency on an already slowly clearing market.

In conclusion, the lack of success in finding a well-specified and stable wage equation is not a denial of the usefulness of the approach. What we have learned from wage equations has been largely by way of rejection of hypotheses rather than of acceptance. We believe that the balance of the evidence leads to the conclusion that there is an active aggregate labour market in the UK, in which both demand and supply factors matter, but in which the adjustment mechanism is inefficient. In our view, government measures to improve the efficiency of the labour market are more urgent than pay bargaining reform.

References

[1] Beenstock, M. C. and Warburton, P. J., 'An aggregative model of the UK labour market', Econometric Forecasting Unit Discussion Paper No. 75, London Business School, April 1980.

[2] Henry, S. G. B. and Ormerod, P. A., 'Rational expectations in a wage–price model of the UK 1972–9', paper presented to SSRC Conference, September 1979.

[3] Hines, A. G., 'Wage inflation in the United Kingdom 1948–62: a disaggregated study', *Economic Journal*, March 1969.

[4] Holden, K. and Peel, D. A., 'The internal/external labour market and the rate of wage inflation in UK manufacturing industry', *Manchester School*, April 1976.

[5] Rosen, H. S. and Quandt, R. E., 'Estimation of a disequilibrium aggregate labour market', *Review of Economics and Statistics*, 1978.

Index